The Making of
Modern Greece

The Making of Modern Greece

From Byzantium to Independence

D. A. ZAKYTHINOS

Translated with an Introduction by
K. R. JOHNSTONE

BASIL BLACKWELL · OXFORD

ISBN 0 631 15360 8

This edition has been based on a series of lectures
delivered by Professor Zakythinos to the School
of Political Sciences in the University of Athens,
published under the title ῾Η Τουρκοκρατία (Athens,
1957), and on relevant passages of ῾Η Πολιτικὴ
῾Ιστορία τῆς Νεωτέρας ῾Ελλάδος (Political History of
Modern Greece – Athens, 1965) together with
much hitherto unpublished material. This translation is published by arrangement with the author.

PRINTED AND BOUND IN GREAT BRITAIN BY
WILLIAM CLOWES & SONS, LIMITED
LONDON, BECCLES AND COLCHESTER

Contents

Author's Preface

The present book is an expansion of an older work entitled ʿΗ Τουρκοκρατία. Εἰσαγωγή εἰς τὴν Νεωτέραν ʿΙστορίαν τοῦ ʿΕλληνισμοῦ. (*The Period of Turkish Domination. An Introduction to the History of Modern Greece*), published at Athens in 1957. More than twice the length of the earlier book, this one still retains, basically, its structure and character, while introducing certain new elements—a more extended and more substantial exposition of its subject, a treatment of problems based on more recent research and a change in the general manner of presentation. Adapted to meet the needs of an international public, this English edition has a twofold aim—first, to provide the reader with a general picture of the fortunes of the Greek nation during the years of Turkish rule, and secondly, to make the relevant research and bibliographical material accessible to any who may wish to study the period in greater detail.

Whether in its previous or in its new form, the book is not offered as a systematic history of the Greek people and their culture. Generally, the political history of a nation has as its central theme that nation's independent sovereignty, which is given the leading role in any historical composition as expressing the native vigour of the national community concerned. But Greece during the Turkish period was deprived of its national sovereignty; it was thus non-political as it were, and is consequently hard to present in terms of historical narrative. Yet although, as the reader will see later, this view is not wholly true and admits of substantial reservations—since alongside the prime authority of the sovereign Ottoman Empire there stood the secondary autonomy of the Greek Church and community—it is clear nevertheless that the historian is obliged to concentrate his attention on the non-political forms of Greek life. The facts themselves confine him to a relatively static enquiry into the way of life of the Greek community and only exceptionally allow him contact with its more dynamic manifestations.

Another peculiar feature of the period under consideration is the lack of any physical frontier. The idea of a frontier as a geographical fact is bound up with the idea of the State. The historian of the Turkish period would find difficulty in restricting his enquiry to any definite geographical region. Certainly an easily recognizable and familiar picture of classical or Hellenistic or Roman Greece comes readily enough before the reader's eye, although we should be seriously mistaken if we were to take such a picture as a reliable reproduction of the reality. And in the Turkish period too the geographical term 'Greece' and the concept of 'Greek civilization' were no more synonyms for the same thing than they were in the Hellenistic or the Byzantine periods. It has often happened that the growing point of the historical energy of the Greek nation has transferred itself to regions totally alien to its original place of birth.

Given these assumptions, the present work might be described as an essay in the interpretation of Greek life and thought from the dissolution of the Byzantine Empire to the Greek Revolution—in other words, from the disintegration of a multinational empire to the foundation of a national state. When the first Greek text of it was written general surveys of the Turkish period were already numerous. The chapters which Constantine Paparrhegopoulos had devoted to it in his Ἱστορία τοῦ Ἑλληνικοῦ Ἔθνους (*History of the Greek Nation*), written between 1860 and 1874, were some of the best in the whole work. The book by Constantine Sathas, Τουρκοκρατουμένη Ἑλλάς (*Greece under Turkish Domination*), which appeared in 1869, was, as its title indicated, a 'historical essay on the revolutionary efforts of the Greek nation to shake off the Turkish yoke'. That expert on Greek, Eastern and Turkish affairs, Paul Karolides (1849–1930), devoted some masterly pages to the period of Turkish rule. Among foreign historians, George Finlay made an early attempt to produce a fuller account in his *Greece under Othoman and Venetian Domination* (1856) which later became the fifth volume of his *History of Greece from its Conquest by the Romans to the Present Time*, published in Tozer's edition in 1877. With the publication of the Ἱστορία τοῦ Νέου Ἑλληνισμοῦ (*History of Modern Greece*) by Apostolos Vakalopoulos, which appeared in three volumes (1961–8), the study of the Turkish period entered its definitive stage.

Before concluding this brief Preface, the writer feels bound to express his thanks to all who have afforded their valuable help in the revision and completion of his work; to Miss Vasiliki Papoulia, who was good enough to recast the first two chapters; to Mr. Leandros Vranousis, the Director of the Research Centre for Medieval and Modern Greek Studies in the Greek Academy, and Mr. Chr. Patrinelis, of the staff of that Centre, who went through the whole of the English text and contributed substantial corrections and additions. I should particularly like to express my gratitude to Mr. Kenneth Johnstone who devoted much care and patience to the preparation of the translation. Nor was his work only that of translator. He contributed suggestions of his own at a number of points in the text, and some of the footnotes, as also some of the Appendices, are from his hand.

Finally, it has been a great honour for the author that Messrs. Blackwell should have included this study among their publications.

Athens   D. A. Z.

Introduction

Except for the fifth volume of Finlay's great history and chapters in other general histories, little has been written in English for the non-specialist reader about Greece between the Turkish conquest and the War of Independence. The present work is intended to provide a brief account of this period and of the transition of the Greeks from a Byzantine Empire collapsing under eastern and western attack to the beginnings of modern Greece. It has been compiled from a number of writings on the period, some of them unpublished, by Professor D. A. Zakythinos of the University of Athens, its original basis being his series of lectures to the School of Political Sciences in that University, published under the title Ἡ Τουρκοκρατία (Athens, 1957), and relevant passages from his short work on the 'Political History of Modern Greece' (Ἡ Πολιτικὴ Ἱστορία τῆς Νεωτέρας Ἑλλάδος, Athens, 1965). The author has, however, revised and reworked all this material to form what is in fact a new and more complete survey of the subject.

Professor Zakythinos is most widely known outside his own country as a distinguished authority on Byzantine history but, besides a much wider range of interest in Greek history to which the titles listed under his name in the Bibliographical Appendix C bear witness, he has a keen sense of the unity and continuity of history from antiquity to the present day and of the central significance of the Turkish period as a link between ancient and medieval Greece and the independent nation-state of the nineteenth and twentieth centuries. The importance of his book, brief as it is, is not only that he gives us a general view of three and a half neglected centuries of Greek history but that he gives us an essentially Greek view, with its passionate feeling for the national past and a historical perspective strange to the west European or American student.

The period reviewed is one which is still in process of recovery, even by Greek historians. Much of the material for it is scattered in innumerable studies, articles and accounts of specialist research, mostly in Greek, and as Professor Zakythinos points out, there is still an enormous amount of work to be done on it in the sifting and publication of local and regional archives, as well as in the official Turkish archives of the time. This is all the more essential since what is loosely termed 'the Turkish period' was not only a time of gradual, though profound, change and development but a time when Greek history was more markedly than usual a composite of a number of widely diverse regional histories, each of which needs individual study, not to mention the history and development of the large and vital Greek communities outside the Ottoman Empire. This makes it even harder to give the kind of generalized impression which a short history of a long and complicated period requires.

Although this book is intended mainly as an introduction for the general reader, the author's references to his sources have been reproduced in full. They have been summarized in an Appendix which may serve as a short bibliography to the subject.

No attempt has been made to give a uniform transliteration of Greek place or personal names. Those with a familiar anglicized form (e.g. Athens, Constantine) are so rendered. In the case of places which appear under a different name in modern atlases the latter is, where necessary, given in brackets besides the Greek name for purposes of identification.

K. R. J.

I

The Establishment of Turkish Rule

Chronologically we may date the period of Turkish rule from the taking of Constantinople to the outbreak of the Greek Revolution (1453 to 1821). The fall of the Byzantine imperial capital marks a major turning-point in the history of the Greek people and indeed in world history. For the world at large, and for Europe especially, it set the seal on a long historical process in the course of which the Roman ideal of a single government of the civilized world gradually lost its hold. For the Greeks the fall of Constantinople drew the dividing line between the two main periods of their history. By creating the world monarchy of Alexander and its succession states, the Hellenistic kingdoms, the Greeks had prepared the way for the eventual rise of Imperial Rome and for the triumph of Christianity. Culturally, Greece had dominated Rome and had framed the moral standards of the new world government. When the walls of Byzantium were breached by the Turks this great construction of Greek political thought, which had governed the development of the ancient and medieval world, was finally shattered. Deprived of its political independence, the Greek nation entered on the most critical period of its history. It is significant that, while for western Europe 29 May 1453, was one of the dates which marked the ending of the Middle Ages and the emergence of state structures on a new basis, mainly national, for south-eastern Europe 1453 marked the beginning of a kind of retarded Middle Age which in turn ended, nearly three centuries later, in the creation of other nation-states, among them the Greek.[1]

A further significance of this date for western Europe lies in the fact that the fall of Constantinople was a main factor in upsetting the balance of power in the Mediterranean. So long as the Byzantine Empire still stood, however diminished, European activity was channelled towards the east; but once the eastern Mediterranean basin had passed under the control of the Ottoman Empire, the steadily mounting activity of the West was halted. Confined and stifled within narrow limits, it might have withered away. New outlets were sought, far from captive Constantinople, first in Africa, then in western waters. So, after many arduous attempts, a new continent was discovered and the life of Europe found a new axis, the Atlantic. It would perhaps be no exaggeration to say that the discovery of America and modern world history were directly linked with the upheaval caused by the downfall of the Greek Empire. Seen from this angle, it makes little difference whether we date the end of the Middle Ages from the fall of Byzantium in 1453 or, as others have done, from the discovery of America in 1492. The same is true of the choice of 1453 as the date of the establishment of Turkish rule in Greece since, as we shall see, some Greek districts were brought under Turkish occupation before that date, while others fell to the Turks within a shorter or longer space of time after Constantinople was taken. We have, therefore, first of all, to examine more closely the stages of the Conquest.

[1] The Turkish conquest of Constantinople has generally been accepted as a significant turning-point in European history, western as well as eastern. For an appraisal see the fourth and fifth essays by D. A. Zakythinos in his collection published under the title Ἡ ἅλωσις τῆς Κωνσταντινουπόλεως καί ἡ Τουρκοκρατία (*The Fall of Constantinople and the Period of Turkish Rule*) (Athens, 1954), entitled respectively *La prise de Constantinople et la fin du Moyen Age* (pp. 34–52) and *La prise de Constantinople, tournant dans la politique et l'économie européennes* (pp. 53–75). On the emergence of national states, including Greece, see L. S. Stavrianos, *The Balkans Since 1453*, New York, 1958, and George G. Arnakis, 'The Ottoman Empire and the Balkan States to 1900', *The Near East in Modern Times*, vol. I, Austin and New York, 1969.

The Turkish Conquest

The dissolution of the Byzantine Empire and of the minor Balkan kingdoms was not the only result of the Turkish Conquest. It also produced basic changes in regions in which the Greek element and the Greek political tradition had hitherto been predominant. It went through many stages but may mainly be divided into two—first, the descent of a number of Turkic tribes upon Asia Minor, which created the ethnic, political and economic conditions for the expansion of the Turkish element in the population and eventually for their organization into a state or states, and second, the specifically Ottoman phrase of the Conquest which ended by imposing political unity on the whole eastern Mediterranean region. It is with this latter phase that we shall be chiefly concerned.[2]

The descent of the Turks in force upon Asia Minor had been prepared by the Turkoman raids which began in the early decades of the eleventh century. Internal dissensions at this time had weakened the Byzantine defences and a decisive defeat of the imperial forces at Manzikert, near Lake Van, in 1071 by the Seljuk Turkish leader Alp Arslan led on to the permanent establishment of a Turkish power in Asia Minor which neither the efforts of later Byzantine Emperors nor those of Western Crusaders were able to dislodge.

The Seljuk state, with its capital at Iconium (Konya), remained the predominant power in Anatolia until its defeat, in its turn, by Mongol invaders in 1243. At its peak it was a well-organized, ably administered and highly cultured Islamic society which maintained its supremacy over the various

---

[2] For the early period of Ottoman history see Paul Wittek, 'The Rise of the Ottoman Empire', *Royal Asiatic Society Monographs*, vol. XXIII, London, 1958. Ernst Werner, 'Die Geburt einer Grossmacht-Die Osmanen (1300–1481). Ein Beitrag zur Genesis des türkischen Feudalismus', *Forschungen zur Mittelalterlichen Geschichte*, 13, Berlin, 1966. Claude Cahen, *Pre-Ottoman Turkey. A General Survey of the Material and Spiritual Culture and History c. 1071–1330*, Translation by J. Jones-Williams, London, 1968. Cf. *The Cambridge Medieval History*, vols. IV, 1; Chaps. XVIII and XIX, Cambridge, 1966.

Turkish principalities settled in the region not only by its superior force and civilization but by the time-honoured practice (which had the sanction of Islamic doctrine) of encouraging them to direct their energies against their non-Moslem neighbours and to expand outward at the latter's expense. Among the lesser of these Turkish communities were the Ottoman Turks, who were comparative latecomers into the area (probably early in the thirteenth century) and were allotted lands in the north-western part of Asia Minor, the part closest to Byzantine territory. It was their skilful exploitation of the possibilities of this seemingly modest assignment which laid the foundations of Ottoman greatness.

The crumbling and gradual disintegration of Seljuk power was followed by a period of rivalry between the larger Turkish principalities (Emirates) for mastery within Asia Minor, while the Ottomans concentrated on extending their own sphere of influence. Their first notable acquisition was that of the Greek cities near the south-eastern shore of the Sea of Marmara, Prusa (Bursa)—which became the Ottoman capital—Nicaea (Iznik) and Nicomedia (Izmit). These fell to the Ottomans between 1326 and 1337 and their capture presented the Ottoman leaders with fundamental problems of civil and military reorganization, involving the transformation of a chieftaincy, supported by enthusiastic Moslem warriors from other parts of Asia Minor, into a highly centralized Islamic state capable both of further military conquest and of the administration of a sophisticated urban population, only partly converted to Islam. It is a measure of the political ability of the earlier Ottoman rulers that, with the aid partly of Byzantine, partly of Seljuk precedents, they succeeded in making this adjustment. The civil administration, while conforming strictly to the requirements of Islamic law, came to resemble in many respects the Byzantine bureaucracy. The Ottoman army was divided into two main components, a standing force of infantry out of which there later developed its most famous component— the Corps of Janissaries—and a picked cavalry force, the

4

members of which received from the ruler estates in conquered territories, not as a hereditary possession but in virtue of personal military service. The whole expanding state was held together by the absolute supremacy of the ruler.

The second phase of Ottoman expansion was marked by advances both in Europe and in Asia.[3] It is with the former only that we are here concerned. Beginning with the capture of Kallipolis (Gallipoli) in 1354, the Turkish invasion pressed rapidly forward. Within a short space of time the more important cities of Thrace—Adrianople (the modern Edirne), probably first taken in 1362 and later used by the Ottomans as a European capital, Dhidhymotikhon and Philippopolis (Plovdiv)—were captured, the occupation of the towns being in all cases preceded by that of the surrounding countryside which was devastated for strategic reasons. The seizure of Thrace was followed by the definitive conquest of the interior of Macedonia and of a number of Macedonian towns, not including Salonica which, taken in 1387 but subsequently retaken by the Greeks, was ceded by the Byzantines to the Venetians in 1423 and finally became subject to the Ottomans in 1430, the year in which Ioannina also changed hands. With the crushing of Serbia on the battlefield of Kossovo (1389), the conquest of Thessaly (1393-4) and the defeat of the Burgundian and Hungarian crusaders and their allies at Nicopolis on the Danube in 1396—a defeat which sealed the fate of Bulgaria—the first phase of European conquest came to an end, leaving the Ottoman Sultan strong enough to turn to the reduction of the other Turkish Emirates in Asia Minor. It is noteworthy that

[3] Franz Babinger, *Beiträge zur Frühgeschichte der Türkenherrschaft in Rumelien* (*14-15 Jahrhundert*), Munich, 1944. Irène Beldiceanu-Steinherr, 'La conquête d'Andrinople par les Turcs: la pénétration turque en Thrace et la valeur des chroniques ottomanes', *Travaux et Mémoires*, Centre de recherche d'histoire et civilisation byzantine, vol. I, Paris, 1965, pp. 439-61. G. T. Dennis, 'The Second Turkish Capture of Thessalonica 1391, 1394 or 1430?', *Byzantinische Zeitschrift*, vol. 57 (1964), pp. 53-61. A. Vakalopoulos, 'Zur Frage der zweiten Einnahme Thessalonikis durch die Türken 1391-4', ibid. vol. 61 (1968), pp. 285-90.

this was only undertaken and accomplished after the establishment of Ottoman supremacy over the main bulk of the Balkan Peninsula. There remained in Greek hands only Constantinople with a few Thracian towns, the Despotate of the Peloponnese and the Empire of Trebizond. The sovereign rights of the Byzantine Empire were even further diminished, since the Emperor himself became tributary to the Sultan, with the obligation to take part in his military campaigns. A dramatic illustration of this vassalage is the fact that Sultan Bayezid I made the Emperor Manuel II accompany him to the siege of Philadelphia (1390–1), the last centre of Greek resistance in Asia Minor.[4]

During the first two decades of the fifteenth century the invasion of Asia Minor by Timur Lenk (Tamerlane), the defeat and capture of Sultan Bayezid in 1402 and the dynastic war of succession which followed Timur's withdrawal two years later gave Byzantium and the other opponents of the Turks a certain respite. They made, however, surprisingly little difference to Ottoman progress in Europe and after the accession of Murad II(1421) Ottoman power was swiftly reasserted. The last Western crusade on a serious scale was crushed at the battle of Varna in 1444 and the third major expansion of the Ottoman Empire began. Nine years later Constantinople itself fell. In 1460 quarrels within the Greek imperial family opened the way to the occupation of the Peloponnese and in 1461 Trebizond too was overrun. By the end of the sixteenth century most of the Greek lands had passed into Turkish possession except Crete, which was not taken from the Venetians until 1669, and the Ionian Islands which, apart from a brief occupation of Cephalonia and Zante and a longer occupation of Levkas, remained in Venetian hands.[5]

From what has been said it will be clear that the conquest of

---

[4] John W. Barker, *Manuel II Palaeologus (1391–1425). A Study in Late Byzantine Statesmanship*, New Brunswick—New Jersey, 1969, pp. 88 ff. Cf. Peter Schreiner, 'Zur Geschichte Philadelpheias im 14. Jahrhundert (1293–1390)', in *Orientalia Christiana Periodica*, vol. XXXV (1969), pp. 404 ff.

[5] The principal dates are as follows: Duchy of Athens 1456; Lesbos 1462; Euboea 1470; Samos 1475; Naupactos 1499; Rhodes 1522; Chios 1566;

the Greek lands was accomplished only over a considerable period of time and by stages. Many of these lands only passed to the Turks after having long been subject to other, equally foreign, masters. Looked at from this angle, the imposition of Ottoman power over practically the whole area peopled by Greeks contributed, in a way, to the eventual unification of all Greeks, which now found an ideological base in the unity of the Greek Church. At the same time the piecemeal character of the Conquest, the widely differing character of the various régimes which had preceded it in the various territories and other local peculiarities all combined to produce an equally wide variation in the conditions under which Greeks came to live in the Turkish period, so wide a variation indeed that one might rather speak of 'Turkish governments' than of a unitary 'Turkish Government'.

A further source of variety is to be found in the structure of the Ottoman state itself which rested, as we have seen, on two basic features: its theocratic character and the absolute nature of its dynastic government. From the religious angle, Islamic law provided for various degrees of dependence according to the circumstances in which a people had been brought under Turkish rule. Autocracy made the will, and at times the whim, of the monarch the law of the land. These two factors produced, on the one hand, a conservative attitude towards the revision of existing relationships and towards the creation of new cultural forms and, on the other hand, a variety and diversity in matters of marginal interest to the central government, including even the institutions which regulated relations between rulers and ruled.

The Administrative and Military Framework of the Conquest

This wide variety naturally had an influence on the administrative system which, as in all autocracies, was highly developed.

Cyprus 1571; Cyclades 1579. Of the Ionian Islands, Cephalonia and Zante underwent brief periods of Turkish occupation (1479–81, 1484 and 1485–1500) and Levkas a longer period (1479–1684 and again in 1699).

And yet, in spite of all its diversity of form, the administrative machine presents a certain unity of design, more particularly in the regions which had been organized at the time when Ottoman power was at its peak and the autocracy was reaching its full development, in European Turkey (Roumeli) and in Asia Minor during the fifteenth and sixteenth centuries. In these two main regions of the Empire the variations affected only the working of the system; they did not basically affect its shape, since its shape depended not on the legal relations (mainly financial and economic) between the subject populations and the central government, but on the relations between the Sultan and the military class from which the representatives of Government came.[6] This military class was originally made up of the holders of *timars* or non-hereditary military fiefs which were bestowed on Turkish and other warriors in return for military services. Later on, after the first phase of Ottoman expansion into Europe was ending and until the first signs of decline began to show (roughly, from the latter part of the fourteenth to the beginning of the seventeenth centuries), it also came to include slaves recruited through the forced levy of Christian children for military purposes, who received timars when they occupied administrative posts under the central or provincial governments. Such additions cannot have been numerous in the early years but with time and as the number of the forcibly enlisted grew, as well as the number of voluntary converts to Islam, and as both types of recruit rose to the highest posts—for two centuries the highest offices above the grade of *Sanjakbey* (District Governor within a province) were held by officers of Christian origin—it was expanded to meet

[6] General survey with bibliography: Halil Inalcik, 'L'Empire ottoman', *Actes du premier Congrès international des Études balkaniques et Sud-Est Européennes*, Sofia 26 août–1 septembre 1966, vol. III (Sofia, 1969), pp. 75–103; also *The Ottoman Empire*. London, 1973. Cf. Bistra Cvetkova, 'Quelques problèmes du Féodalisme ottoman à l'époque du XVIᵉ au XVIIIᵉ siècle', *ibid.*, pp. 709–20. On the taxation and the organization of the Ottoman Empire see the work of H. A. R. Gibb and Harold Bowen, *Islamic Society and the West. A Study of the Impact of Western Civilization on Moslem Culture in the Near East*, vol. I, pts. I–II: *Islamic Society in the Eighteenth Century*, London—New York—Toronto, 1950–7.

the administrative needs of the Empire. Even so, in relation to the size of the whole subject population of the Empire, these two types of newcomers to power made up a very small minority, a factor which in time had its effect on the whole development of the Ottoman state. Islamic law perpetuated the distinction between conquerors and conquered, rulers and ruled, and provided the appropriate framework for the expression of the Law's fundamental principles.

The chief characteristic of Ottoman regional organization was the concentration of the military and administrative authority over a given area in the hands of a single officer who was granted, at the same time, the financial and economic powers needed to cover both his military and his administrative requirements. These powers were secured by the allotment to such officers of the revenue from the taxes paid by the peasantry working on timar lands and by subordinates of every kind. The value of a military fief was determined by the tax-yield of the area in question, calculated in aspers (*akçe*).[7] On this basis, timars were rated in three categories—the *Timar proper*, bringing in from 2,000 or 3,000 to 19,999 aspers; the *Ziyamet*, bringing in from 20,000 to 99,999 aspers; and lastly the *Hâs*, bringing in over 100,000 aspers—these last being bestowed only on holders of the highest posts and on members of the imperial family. Both Timar and Ziyamet estates were made up of two components, the original fief, termed *Kilij* (Sword) and *Terakki* (Increase), the latter made up of occasional later additions to the timar; these, if need arose, might be taken away from one timariot (timar-holder) and given to another. All holders of timars belonged to the class of cavalrymen (*Sipahi*) who were bound to supply military aid. Thus, if their revenue exceeded twice the minimum value of a timar (i.e. if it exceeded 4,000 aspers), they were bound to bring with them to battle one additional horseman for every 3,000 aspers of revenue above

---

[7] The Greek *asper* proper was in fact a coin of higher value than the Turkish *akçe*, but the Turkish coin took over the name of the Greek one (both meaning 'white') and the two became identified.

this sum and to equip him themselves. This proportion was not always strictly observed and it varied according to the needs of each case and the type of equipment required, heavy or light.

The lowest stratum of the military class was formed by the *Askeri*, soldiery who had been granted a piece of land free of tax to be cultivated in return for military service in time of war. One section of these Askeri supplied only auxiliary services and certain Christian populations, e.g. the Bulgarian *voiniks*, belonged to this category. Other Christians also, the successors of landowners who had owned estates before the time of the Turkish conquest, were granted timars, usually small ones since if they remained Christians they were allowed to retain only a fraction of their original properties. This induced many powerful families to embrace Islam, more particularly in Bosnia and Albania. Christian timars were very readily declared to have lapsed if their holders failed to meet their military obligations or fell into disfavour since, as has been said, it was a typical feature of the timar system that such holdings were not by right hereditary. Even in cases where there was no question of the grant lapsing, the successor of the original holder might inherit only a portion of the timar, usually the original *Kilij*, unless he happened to enjoy the particular favour of the prevailing Government or some change took place in local conditions, which happened frequently enough during the period of Ottoman decline. But in spite of all restrictions and despite the fact that judicial authority was only enjoyed by representatives of Government acting in the Sultan's name and by the leading interpreters of the Sacred Law—the Cadis—many members of the landholding class in time acquired great power. This contributed to the decline of the entire system and had serious consequences for the development of the State as a whole. In the earlier centuries after the Conquest, however, and so long as the central authority remained vigorous and decisive, this system of land tenure was one of the fundamental factors underlying Ottoman military strength and provided both the structural framework and the base of the state organization.

The administrative system, wide as its ramifications were, was simple in its essentials. It was made up of the central administration, presided over by the Grand Vizir, and the provincial administration, the officers of which were chosen from among the more important timariots or from officers of the Sublime Porte. In earlier times the State was divided into two Governor-Generalships or *Eyalets*, Anatolia and Roumelia, the latter covering the Balkan Peninsula. These were administered by *Beylerbeys* or Governors-General and Commanders-in-Chief, who also exercised civil authority and usually bore the title of Vizir. Later on these higher commands were multiplied, both on account of the territorial expansion of the empire by conquest and also by subdivision of the original commands. Between the years 1590 and 1612, when the empire reached its greatest extent (barring the later acquisition of Crete), the number of Eyalets was thirty-two.[8] These high commands were subdivided into *Sanjaks*, administered by a *Sanjakbey*. Both the Beylerbeys and the Sanjakbeys, as representatives of Government, had the right to display horsetail standards (*Tuğ*), as well as the right of precedence in the Divan over all other Court officials, if they themselves enjoyed the title of Vizir. Immediately below them in the military administration and the military hierarchy came the *Alaybeys* who held the larger fiefs (*Ziyamet*) and were charged with the recruitment and administration of the cavalry (*Sipahı*) force in each Sanjak. In later times the Sanjakbey appointed a Deputy, the *Müteselim*, to whom he transferred a part of his civil jurisdiction. The Sanjaks were themselves subdivided into *Kazas*, corresponding to the number of Cadis' posts in each province. These worked with the subordinate officers known as *Subashıs*, and later with those known as *Voivodes*, in the preservation of order and the execution of judicial decisions, and with the *Muhtesibs* or the

[8] For an account of the growth of the Eyalet system see the *Encyclopaedia of Islam*, II (new ed.), Leiden, 1960, under *Eyalet*.

Ihtısâb Ağası responsible for a given town. These last controlled the economic and commercial life of the towns and the practitioners of the various trades.[9] The lowest administrative subdivision of the province was the *Nahiye* (urban or rural district) in which there was usually a representative of the Cadi known as the *Na'ib*. In areas with a Christian population a special jurisdiction, for those cases which did not fall under the ordinary criminal law, was exercised by the *Kodjabashis* (in Turkish, *Hocabaşı*) or Elders (in Greek, Δημογέροντες) who were selected from among the leading citizens of each community. Possibly in imitation of these appointments, there were later created in the seventeenth and eighteenth centuries, similar officials known as *Ayans*, who were local authorities, Moslem by faith, who represented the lower orders of the Moslem community. Both Kodjabashis and Ayans functioned as representatives of their respective communities of Raya in their relations with the government authorities and acted as their protectors and intercessors.

The officers mentioned above by no means exhaust the catalogue of the Ottoman military and bureaucratic hierarchy. Over and above these there were a number of other officials, this number varying in size according to the standing of each superior officer who as far as possible tried to equal in impressiveness and display the officer next in line above him. Thus the Sanjakbey reproduced in miniature the administrative apparatus of the Beylerbey and the Beylerbey that of the Grand Vizir. Basically, however, the office of each grade was composed of a Secretary for the despatch of the various types of business, an officer responsible for economic affairs and a Chavushbashi (*Çavuşbaşi*) or Chief of Police who saw to the execution of decisions by the administration or the courts of

---

[9] On the administrative organization of central Greece see the recent work of John Giannopoulos, ῾Η διοικητικὴ ὀργάνωσις τῆς Στερεᾶς ῾Ελλάδος κατὰ τὴν Τουρκοκρατίαν (1393–1821). Συμβολὴ εἰς τὴν μελέτην τῆς ᾿Επαρχιακῆς Διοικήσεως τοῦ κυριάρχου ᾿Οθωμανικοῦ Κράτους (*The Administrative Organisation of Central Greece under Turkish Domination, 1393–1821. Contribution to the Study of the Provincial Administration of the Ottoman Empire*), Athens, 1971.

law. In addition to the officials of the civil administration each senior officer also had a personal bodyguard of slaves modelled on that of the Sultan's Court.

An important body, connected with the civil administration and of major significance in the whole development of the Imperial Government, was the class of experts in Islamic law, the *Ulema*, who were organized as a Corporation. At the head of these were the *Cadis* of each province, the *Mullahs* who were senior judges in the more important cities of the Empire, the two Chief Justices of Roumelia and Anatolia and, at the head of all, the *Sheikh ul-Islam*, whose rank in the hierarchy was equal to that of the Grand Vizir and who could even declare the Sultan deposed insofar as he might be considered an enemy of the Faith. This power of his, however, was limited by the fact that the Sultan might himself proceed to depose him. Nevertheless, at some extremely critical moments the Sheikh ul-Islam did play a decisive part in the taking or rejecting of certain resolutions.

The same class of men learned in the Law also supplied those who performed religious duties in sacred foundations and educational duties in the various theological schools and colleges (*Medrese*). The body of legal experts was a single unit. A man might be transferred from one type of service to another, provided he had the relevant training, which in the case of the senior or top posts was long and arduous, extending even to forty years. The Cadis of the towns handled the property of the different religious and pious foundations known as *Vakıf* or *Evkav* which constituted the second great category of landed properties. Unlike timar lands these were not liable to confiscation by the central authority. This was one basic reason for the great increase in Vakıf lands as time went on, since a large number of officials consecrated a part of their property to sacred uses while keeping the right to the use of them in return for the payment of a fixed sum. Free farmers also, as in Byzantine times, dedicated their holdings to such institutions subject to certain terms, with a view to escaping the exactions of the powerful and of Government. The increase of sacred properties and the economic power derived from them helped to strengthen the influence of the Ulema, who were thus enabled to control important sectors of public life. This was all the easier because they did not form a closed ecclesiastical hierarchy of the Christian type but an open religious and political organization which pursued more secular and less pastoral ends.

The order of the Ulema and the military order formed, then, the two great buttresses of Ottoman power and embodied the political philosophy of the Ottoman State, that of a politico-military organization which was theocratic in conception and that of an absolute monarchy. Both bodies were based on the revenues derived indirectly from the exploitation of the land, that is to say they had the land as their common basis. This was natural since the land, as God's property in the first instance and, by extension, that of the Sultan as the Prophet's successor on earth, had no other function but that of providing the conditions necessary for the realization of the Islamic idea—the Kingdom of God on earth. It was precisely this which, according to the theorists of Islam, distinguished the Moslem from the Jewish and Christian religions. The Jewish religion, it was held, laid down definite commandments, but these were designed primarily for God's Chosen Race, the Jews. Christianity, on the other hand, was concerned with the universal spread of the true Faith among all peoples but its moral commandments were unrealizable by beings of such finite capacity as men. Only Islam supplied both the two basic needs by offering to all nations a single law for life and also the possibility of fulfilling that law in earthly conditions.

Systems of Land Tenure and Taxation

The military and economic system of Ottoman administration pre-supposed one other basic factor, namely the existence of subjects (*Raya*)[10] who provided the labour needed for the exploitation of the land. The theoretical principle that all conquered land belonged to the Sultan, who bestowed four-fifths of it on his warriors, was not of course capable of being uniformly applied. The conquerors were obliged to take into consideration the existing conditions of land tenure which had been shaped during the last centuries of Byzantine rule. The State lands, both imperial and timariot, as well as the lands held under Vakıf, did indeed occupy vast areas, but there was also a substantial amount of land belonging to proprietors enjoying full possession (*Mülk*). This was divided into tithe-lands (*Uşriye*), that is to say, lands subject to taxation under tithe, and lands which were subject to poll-tax (*Haraciye*), which were the property of non-Moslems. So far as the possession of timariot lands was concerned, their owners held these on life tenure or in usufruct, but those who actually worked them enjoyed the right to do so hereditarily, provided that they paid the prescribed dues to the current holder of the timar. This same provision also held good for those who worked imperial lands, but generally speaking the position of those who cultivated imperial lands was a good deal more favourable than that of other peasants who were dependent on timariots, since the oppressive exactions of tax-collectors fell less hardly and only to a limited extent on the labourers on imperial estates.

As already stated, the whole military and administrative system rested, from the economic point of view, on taxation. Taxes were divided into 'regular' or 'lawful' and 'extraordinary' or 'arbitrary', the latter being excessively burdensome. These were imposed to meet the needs of the administrative authorities, their transportation, and the cost of repairing fortifications, maintaining roads and bridges and equipping the army and the

---

[10] This term (literally 'cattle') is often thought of as applying only to Christian or other non-Moslem subjects, and as a term of contempt. In fact it was also applied to the lowest class of Moslem subjects. Originally, at least, it contained some conception of the Ruler as the shepherd of his people.

fleet, besides, in general, the extraordinary expenses of individual campaigns.

Of the 'regular' taxes some were personal, others were levied on property. The chief personal tax was the poll-tax (*Harac*), to which all non-Moslems were subject except the infirm, women, children, the aged and the crippled. The amount of this tax varied originally according to district, period and age, and later according to the economic capacity of the tax-payer. In the latter end of the Turkish period there were three scales of taxation under this head; upper, middle and lower. Besides the poll-tax, the cultivators of what were called 'inalienable' (ἄφθαρτοι) lands, that is to say lands under limited ownership, paid their landlords the *spendza* (*İspence*), a form of personal tax which was levied from the age of nine upwards.[11]

The land-tax (*Haraç-i-erazi*) was collected in accordance with the circumstances of each individual case, being based sometimes on yield and sometimes on a fixed rate, dependent on the size of the property. Cereals, tobacco, cotton, olive oil and figs were tithed in kind. On vineyards the tax was paid in cash per *stremma* (quarter of an acre). Other taxes were levied on sheep and cattle and on grazing, on domestic animals and bees. To these must be added the indirect taxes, customs duties and octrois, tolls and other taxes on circulation, taxes on consumption and so forth.

From the time of Mehmed II the taxes, apart from some special cases, were farmed out under the system known as *mukataa*. The farming out of a part or the whole of the privileges granted under *mukataa* was termed *İltizâm* and the tax-farmer

---

[11] Ap. E. Vakalopoulos, Ἱστορία τοῦ Νέου Ἑλληνισμοῦ, *History of Modern Greece* vol. II, Thessalonica, 1964, pp. 13 ff. Cf. on the *haraj* in the Byzantine Empire: Nicolas Oikonomides, 'Le Haradj dans l'Empire byzantin du XVᵉ siècle', *Actes du premier Congrès International des Études Balkaniques et Sud-Est Européennes*, op. cit., vol. III, (1966) pp. 681–8. The exact nature of the *Ispenje* has not yet been accurately determined. It has sometimes been considered to be a form of poll-tax, but in a *Kanunname* (Collection of Laws) of 1498 it is referred to as a property tax. See Paul Wittek, Devs̲h̲irme and S̲h̲arî'a, in the *Bulletin of the School of Oriental and African Studies* of the University of London, XVII (1855), pp. 271–8.

Mültezîm. The concession was usually for three years but might sometimes be granted for life, in which case it was called *Malikâne.* In the Greek lands ruled by the Turks there was also in force a distributive system of taxation under which the amount of tax demanded was fixed in advance and the local authorities were charged with the duty of sub-allotting it between the taxpayers. As will be shown later, these methods of taxation helped substantially towards the development of local communities.

II

The Condition of the Greek
Population

The dramatic changes of fortune which the Greek people had
experienced even before the Turkish conquest had reduced the
Greek lands to ruin and had greatly diminished their population. Ever since the establishment of the Latin supremacy in
1204 the plight of the country districts had been a hard one.
The incessant wars, the rivalries between Balkan states, Serb
expansion and the inroads of the Albanians, the great internal
crises of the Byzantine Empire during the fourteenth century,
banditry and piracy; all had contributed to further the destruction of the Greek population. Consequently, when the
Turks occupied the European provinces of the Empire from
the latter half of the fourteenth century onwards, the situation
which prevailed in them was already precarious from every
point of view.

The first centuries of Ottoman rule were no less critical for
the Greeks. The long wars which the Sultans waged with the
Venetians and with the powers of central Europe further prolonged the period of insecurity, while the mass emigrations and
forcible transfers of the Greek population, their deportation in
slave-raids and their conversions to Islam threatened their very
existence as a nation. As Finlay says:

> During the period of more than two centuries which elapsed
> from the conquest of Constantinople to the conquest of the
> Morea by the Venetians, the Greek nation declined both in
> civilization and in numbers. The Hellenic race had never

fallen so low in the social scale at any previous period of its history.[1]

Causes of Decline in the Greek Population. Conversions to Islam

One of the chief factors in the decay of the Greek population under Turkish rule was the number of conversions to Islam, both voluntary and enforced. Voluntary conversions were very widespread in Asia Minor, especially in the first years of the Ottoman occupation, while forcible conversion affected mainly those young Christian children who were trained to become members of the imperial Guard or officials of the administration. Conversion for either reason usually led to the complete transformation of the converts and their loss to the Greek national and cultural community. The causes of conversion, in both cases, were chiefly external. In the case of the children, whose re-education was proverbial for its thoroughness, it was force. Among the poorer classes the cause was economic; among the more powerful it was a desire to retain their position of leadership and their property, more particularly their landed property.[2]

It should be noted that in the specifically Greek areas the number of apostasies was smaller than in other Balkan countries. This may have been due to several causes but mainly to the stronger cultural tradition of the Greek regions which made the population more resistant to adversity and to hostile influences and pressures. Even so, the number of conversions to Islam in the initial period of the Conquest was fairly considerable in every region, although we cannot calculate the exact number,

---

[1] George Finlay, *History of Greece* (ed. H. F. Tozer), vol. V, London, 1877, p. 55.

[2] For an ample and comprehensive introduction to the major problems of this period see Speros Vryonis jr. 'The Byzantine Legacy and Ottoman Forms', *Dumbarton Oaks Papers*, no. 23–24 (1969–70), pp. 251–308 (with a rich bibliog.).

even approximately. Gennadius Scholarios (Patriarch, inter-mittently between 1454 and 1465) refers with deep distress to those who daily apostatize from the Faith on every side.[3] Among these converts there were many of the Byzantine ruling class, including representatives of the great Byzantine families and of the imperial family itself. Certainly there were some of the Palaeologi who achieved distinction in the Ottoman Empire after the Conquest, for example Hass Murad Pasha, Beylerbey of Roumelia—a close collaborator of Mehmed II, who met a tragic death in the waters of the Euphrates in 1475—and his brother, Mesih Ahmed Pasha, who attained the highest offices, becoming Grand Vizir in 1499–1500.[4] The greatest statesman of Mehmed's reign, the Grand Vizir Mahmud Pasha, was a connection of the imperial houses of the Angeli and Comneni. Other apostasies are found among the men of learning, as for instance the son of the scholar George Amoiroutzes of Trebizond, Mehmet Bey, who is mentioned as 'most learned in Greek and Arabic' and may have taken part in the capture of Trebizond by Mehmed II.[5] Three of the brothers of Theodore Zygomalas, the scholar and Protonotary of the Church of Constantinople, who flourished in the last quarter of the sixteenth century, abandoned their religion in their extreme youth. Even clergy gave up the beliefs of their

---

[3] L. Petit, X. A. Siderides and M. Jugie, *Oeuvres complètes de Georges (Gennade) Scholarios*, vol. III, Paris, 1930, p. 286, on conversions to Islam see Sp. Vryonis jr., *The Decline of Medieval Hellenism in Asia Minor and the Process of Islamizations from the Eleventh through the Fifteenth Century* (Berkeley, Los Angeles/London, 1971).

[4] Franz Babinger, 'Eine Verfügung des Paläologen Chass Murad-Pasa, von Mitte Regeb 876 h = Dez./Jan. 1471/2', *Documenta Islamica inedita*, Berlin, 1952, pp. 197–210.

[5] George Amoiroutzes was a high official in the service of the last Emperor of Trebizond. He was also a distant cousin of the Grand Vizir Mahmud mentioned above. It is not certain whether he did in fact assist the easy capture of the city by the Sultan, but he subsequently enjoyed great favour at court, especially in connection with Mehmed's geographical studies. Even if he did not himself change his religion, he encouraged his sons to become Moslems and put forward, though with little success, a scheme for a synthesis of Christianity and Islam.

fathers. A typical case is that of Meletius, metropolitan of Rhodes, who 'turned Turk' (ἐτούρκεψε) in 1647 and under the name of Aslan occupied a high post in the Court hierarchy. He was executed in 1661.[6]

But against these instances of infidelity in high places the Greek Church could set many martyrs from the humbler ranks of society, known in the calendar as Neo-Martyrs, among them men who had voluntarily or involuntarily accepted Islam, often in childhood, but who subsequently recanted at the cost of their lives and deliberately sought death by public confession.[7]

Mass conversions also occurred in later periods. The French antiquary, Michel Fourmont, in a letter of 1730, mentions the Turks of Leontarion in the Peloponnese who had lately become Moslems.[8] Similarly, it is known that at Easter, 1760, the inhabitants of thirty-six villages in the Karamouratades district of northern Epirus apostatized.[9] These later conversions were perhaps due, at least in part, to the unfavourable conditions created in the Balkans by the Russo-Turkish wars of the eighteenth century when the danger of Greek disaffection became more serious as foreign propaganda, and consequent hopes of foreign liberation, grew and Turkish policy was therefore more interested in conversion than it had been.

In the earlier periods, when this danger was less or was nonexistent, it was in some ways more profitable to keep the Christian Raya as a source of tax revenue and forced labour.

[6] F. H. Marshall, 'Two liturgical manuscripts recently acquired by the British Museum', *Byzantinisch—Neugriechische Jahrbücher*, vol. 6 (1927–8), p. 58.

[7] On these a general account for the English reader is in F. W. Hasluck, *Christianity and Islam under the Sultans*, Oxford, 1929, vol. II, pp. 452 ff. Cf. John Anastasiou, Σχεδίασμα περί τῶν Νεομαρτύρων, Ἐπιστημονικὴ Ἐπετηρὶς Θεολογικῆς Σχολῆς τοῦ Πανεπιστημίου Θεσσαλονίκης, Παράρτημα, Μνήμη 1821 (*Essay on the Neo-Martyrs*, Annual of the Theological Faculty of the University of Salonica, Annex dedicated to the Memory of 1821, Thessalonica, 1971, pp. 9–61).

[8] Henri Omont, *Missions archéologiques françaises en Orient aux XVIIe et XVIIIe siècles*, vol. I, Paris, 1902, p. 631.

[9] F. C. H. L. Pouqueville, *Voyage dans la Grèce*, vol. I, Paris, 1820, pp. 206 ff.

Even where mass conversions took place some of the converts kept their ties with their former religion. Hasluck quotes from Triandaphyllides' τὰ Ποντικά some curious details of crypto-Christians in the Trebizond area[10] and other instances occur commonly in Bosnia, Macedonia, the Morea, Crete and Cyprus. It would seem that the Church made things easy for these crypto-Christians, as may be gathered from the Instruction given in 1339–40 by the Patriarch of Constantinople to the Nicaeans. Christians who had abandoned their fathers' religion might be received back into the bosom of the Church; it was sufficient if they observed the Divine commandments. "As many as, for fear of punishment, wish to live to themselves and in secret, embracing and practising Christian ways, these too shall find salvation, provided only that, as far as possible, they study to keep the commandments of God."[11] This practice of crypto-Christianity is extremely important from the point of view of the history of religion and was one of the chief agents in

[10] F. W. Hasluck, op. cit., vol. II, pp. 469 ff.:

... They kept the Orthodox fasts strictly. Their children were baptized, and habitually bore a Christian and a Turkish name for secret and public use respectively: such Turkish names as 'Mehmet' and 'Ali' were, however, avoided. As to marriage, they never gave their daughters to Turks, but the men were not averse to taking wives from among their Turkish neighbours. In this case parties were married secretly according to the Christian rite in one of the monasteries before the consummation of the marriage. If pressure were necessary, the bridegroom threatened to leave his bride. When a crypto-Christian died, the burial service was read for him in a Christian church while he was being interred. Mollahs were sent to the crypto-Christian villages in Ramazan [the Moslem equivalent of Lent], but were got out of the way when services were held.

On crypto-Christians in the same area see also A. Bryer, 'The Tourkokratia in the Pontos. Some Problems and Preliminary Conclusions, in *Neo-Hellenica*', *Annual Publication of the Center for Neo-Hellenic Studies*, Austin, Texas, U.S.A., vol. I (Amsterdam, 1970), pp. 30 ff. Also, more generally, N. E. Milioris, Οἱ Κρυπτοχριστιανοί (*The Crypto-Christians*) Athens, 1962, and S. Skendi, 'Crypto-Christianity in the Balkan Area under the Ottomans', in *Slavic Review*, vol. XXVI (June 1967), pp. 227 ff. Cf. Sp. Vryonis jr., op. cit., pp. 300 f.

[11] Fr. Miklosich—Ios. Müller, *Acta et Diplomata graeca Medii Aevi*, vol. I, Vienna, 1860, pp. 183 ff., 197 ff.

promoting religious syncretism in Asia Minor, since with time those who had formally become Moslems ended by becoming assimilated under the influence of their environment.

The 'Tithe of Blood'. The Child-Levy

Of all the varieties of conversion to Islam the most oppressive was the Child-Levy. This practice (in Turkish *Devşirmé*) entailed the forcible recruitment of young Christians, who were given a Turkish education and then for the most part enrolled in the select corps of Janissaries (*Yeniçeri*, 'New Troops'). At regular intervals—every five years under Mehmed II, later every four or three years or even more frequently—this enlistment of Christian children was held on the basis of registers kept by the local or communal authorities. The recruits were usually between eight or ten and fifteen years of age. Greek sources use various terms to describe the institution—$\pi\iota\alpha\sigma\mu\grave{o}s$ $\pi\alpha\iota\delta\acute{\iota}\omega\nu$ (seizure of children) in 1430; $\gamma\epsilon\nu\iota\tau\zeta\alpha\rho o\mu\acute{\alpha}\zeta\omega\mu\alpha$ (Janissary-levy) in 1637); $\pi\alpha\iota\delta o\mu\acute{\alpha}\zeta\omega\mu\alpha$ (child-levy) in 1675. It was the last of these which eventually became the standard form.[12]

For the parents this seizure generally meant the total loss of the child, since they had little hope of seeing him again. Apart from the religious angle, the relatively low cultural level of the conquerors, or at least the low idea which the Byzantines had of 'barbarians' generally, caused the complete transformation of Greek children into Turks to be regarded as a great calamity. A typical, and natural, reaction is that expressed by Isidore, Metropolitan of Salonica, in a sermon preached in 1395 which constitutes the first direct evidence of the child-levy:

> What can I say, what can I think, with what eyes can I look on you, when I consider the measure of this disaster? I shudder as I hear the harsh decree against my dearest ones. I feel it as an unapproachable fire or as an irresistible sword.

[12] Basilike D. Papoulis, *Ursprung und Wesen der 'Knabenlese' im osmanischen Reich*, Südosteuropäische Arbeiten, 59, Munich, 1963.

... For what must a man not suffer, seeing his son whom he begot and reared and on whose behalf his eyes have often run with tears as he prayed that he might have happiness, suddenly and violently seized by the hands of foreigners, forced to change his ways for outlandish manners and for barbarian dress and speech and expected within a short time to become a vessel of impiety and uncleanness? ... And as the ultimate evil, he is to be pitifully cut off from God and most miserably knit to the devil and at the last committed to darkness and Hell with the demons. Whose bowels would not be rent at this, who would not be broken and bowed by such a calamity? If he were a beast, if he were stone or iron, he would feel like a man for this.[13]

It cannot be doubted that Isidore interprets here the affliction of many parents who lost their children for ever. In the Tübingen manuscript which was written by Andrew Argyrus and John Tholoïtis, and given in 1585 to Martin Crusius (Kraus), the same feelings are depicted with great realism ending with the cry, "Sooner you would have wished them dead!".[14]

That many parents uttered this tragic prayer is conveyed to us also by Stephen Gerlach, who relates the case of a woman of Panormus in Asia Minor who had two fine sons and daily besought "our Lord God that He would take them away because she would soon have to give up one of them".[15] The state of desperation to which mothers were reduced by the thought of their children becoming Moslems is illustrated by another incident which Gerlach also relates concerning a

[13] B. Laourdas, Ἰσιδώρου, ἀρχιεπισκόπου Θεσσαλονίκης, Ὁμιλία περὶ τῆς ἁρπαγῆς τῶν παίδων καί περὶ τῆς μελλούσης κρίσεως, ('Sermon of Isidore, Archbishop of Thessalonica on the abduction of boys and on the coming Judgement'), Ἑλληνικά, Suppl. 4: Προσφορά εἰς Στίλπωνα Π. Κυριακίδην (Tribute to S. P. Kyriakides), Salonica, 1953, pp. 390 ff.

[14] K. Dyovouniotes, Τό ὑπ' ἀριθμόν 21 χειρόγραφον τῆς Πανεπιστημιακῆς Βιβλιοθήκης τῆς Τυβίγγης, ('The Manuscript No. 21 in the Tübingen University Library'), in Πρακτικὰ τῆς Ἀκαδημίας Ἀθηνῶν pp. (Proceedings of the Academy of Athens), vol. 11 (1936), pp. 275 ff.

[15] Stephan Gerlach, Tagebuch, Frankfurt-am-Main, 1674, p. 257.

Christian woman, a captive from Cyprus, who had a child by her Turkish husband "which as soon as it was born she herself baptized and straightway threw it on the ground and killed it, so that it should not become a Turk".[16]

Clearly, however, the reactions of the population were not always the same. From certain evidence (such as that given by Trevisano, Crusius and elsewhere by Gerlach[17]) it appears that in times of extreme dearth some parents prayed for their children to be among those chosen, since it was customarily the best looking, healthiest and, so far as could be judged, the most intelligent children who were taken. Sometimes the parents themselves brought their children to those who were making the selection, both, it is clear, in order to be relieved of the burden of their upbringing and also in the hope of a better career for them. These cases of a favourable attitude towards the levy must, however, be regarded as exceptional since most of our evidence shows that parents made every effort to escape the levy and in many cases succeeded.

The most usual method was to bribe the Turkish officers and, from the fantastic amounts which came to light after the confiscation of the property of officers who had been in charge of the levy, it is clear that this line of approach was widespread. Many people cheated the Turks by buying uncircumcised infants from poor Moslems. The richer Christians certainly resorted to these methods, particularly in later times; the poor generally found other ways out. Many of them married off their children at a tender age since this made them, in principle, exempt from the levy; or they substituted Turkish children for their own, the Turks gratefully accepting this exchange in the hope of a brilliant career for their own children. Often the local Turkish notables themselves hid Christian children, because, as Christopher Angelus writes, the Turkish notables

[16] *Ibid.* p. 54.
[17] *Ibid.* p. 314. M. Crusius, *Turocograeciae Libri octo*, Basle, 1584, p. 193. Domenico Trevisano, *Relazioni dell' Impero Ottomano 1554*, ed. E. Alberi, Florence, 1840, p. 130.

"are friendly to the Greeks".[18] Many again fled to the towns where, owing to the privileged position of some of these, the levy was not carried out, or they completely forsook their homes and fled to the districts under Venetian rule. Voluntary exile of this kind seems to have assumed large proportions in Greece and Albania and many areas were depopulated, which displeased the Turkish timariots since it deprived them of labour. This motive, one may suppose, may also have inspired some of the Turkish protection of the Greeks mentioned above. The attitude of the Turkish landowning class, together with the discontent felt by those of Moslem origin at the exclusion of their children from the major posts in the State hierarchy, and also the gradual infiltration of Turkish elements into the different regiments of the imperial Guard contributed to the fading out of the levy over a period of time, more particularly from the first half of the seventeenth century, until it was completely abandoned at the beginning of the eighteenth. Christian resistance also contributed beyond doubt to the abandonment of this oppressive practice. Resistance was active as well as passive. In 1565 the inhabitants of Epirus and Albania rose and slaughtered the officers charged with carrying out the levy. The Sultan sent the local Sanjakbey a reinforcement of five hundred Janissaries and the revolt was put down.[19] In 1580 the people of Prijepolje in the Sanjak of Novi Pazar rose but the rebels were condemned to serve in the fleet and the galleys. Heavy as this penalty was at this time, sentences were usually even more severe. According to a document of 1601, ". . . if any infidel parent or other person should oppose the surrender of his son to be a Janissary, he shall be hanged forthwith at his own threshold, his blood being held of no account." We know also from other sources that the death penalty was in

---

[18] Christopher Angelus, Ἐγχειρίδιον περὶ τῆς καταστάσεως τῶν σήμερον εὑρισκομένων Ἑλλήνων (*A Short Treatise on the Condition of the Present-day Greeks*), Leipzig, 1666, p. 62.

[19] According to P. Aravantinos, Χρονογραφία τῆς Ἠπείρου (*Annals of Epirus*), vol. I, Athens, 1856, p. 218. It is to this period that the folksong translated in Appendix B, I (a) below is to be attributed.

fact imposed on parents who refused to give up their children.[20] A serious revolt against the officers of the levy took place at Naoussa in 1705, when the inhabitants refused to give up their children and killed the Government officers. Their punishment was harsh. The rebels were killed or strangled and part of the population was thrown into prison;[21] but this appears to have been the last attempt of the Turks to hold the levy in Greece, although in certain regions there may have been sporadic instances of it up to the mid-eighteenth century. It was more than a coincidence that the fighting spirit of the subject population began to manifest itself, timidly at first, more forcibly later on, just at the time when the 'tithe of blood' was beginning to disappear. Until that time the best and most vigorous section of the people had been filtered off into the Sultan's Chanceries and into the various corps of the imperial Guard, thus swelling the ranks of the conquerors.

The fate of these Christian children was not usually a very hard one. A part of those who had been selected, the handsomest and cleverest boys but also some of the youngest—from eight to fourteen years of age, since the training of these took longer— were sent to the four imperial palaces where they were educated and at the same time performed various Court duties. After the completion of their training they were ordinarily enrolled in the cavalry corps of the Porte, which was the *corps d'élite* of the imperial Guard. Those who were in personal attendance on the Sultan (the *Hass Oda*) and continued for a long term of years at the palace received a more rigorous and elaborate education. They were generally forty in number and supplied the great officers of state, though not exclusively, since others coming from the lower ranks of the Army might also rise to higher and even the highest posts if they showed the necessary bravery and devotion to their superiors.

[20] B. Papoulia, op. cit., p. 112, see also p. 109.
[21] J. Vasdravelles, Ἱστορικὰ Ἀρχεῖα Μακεδονίας, Ἀρχεῖον Βεροίας-Ναούσης (1598–1839), (*Historical Archives of Macedonia*), vol. II, Salonica, 1954, pp. 112 ff.

The majority—between the ages of fourteen and twenty—were destined for the Corps of Janissaries. These were sent initially to Turkish landowners to learn Turkish, to be brought up in the Turkish way of life and inured to hard labour and were later placed as cadets of the first rank in the Corps of Adjem Oglans (*Acemoglandar*) in which they received more specialized military instruction and learned the art of war. After some two years, depending on the needs of the service and the vacancies in it at any given time, they were drafted into the Janissaries, who were the most formidable body of infantry of their time and widely renowned both for their skill in warfare and their courage as well as for their iron discipline and their religious fanaticism. Their personal dedication to the Sultan was total and exclusive, so much so that ordinary Janissaries had no right even to contract family ties.

Those, on the other hand, who came from the palace training-centres, whether they assumed high office or were drafted to the cavalry Guard, were permitted to marry and to enjoy all the other privileges which their status as clients of the Sultan afforded them. Their position was governed by the Arab custom known as the *Wala*, a form of patronage under which slaves freed by their master were bound to show submission and devotion to him and to defend him at any time of danger but were regarded in return as members of his family, having the Sultan as their father. Their service, in short, was a kind of adoption which nevertheless left the exact terms of their dependence vague. This dependence was total in the case of those who entered the ranks of the Corps of Janissaries. These were dependent on the Sultan until their discharge at the age of forty. The organization of the imperial Guard on lines of such severity had been particularly essential in the early, transitional phase of the Empire, when a nomad people was adapting itself to the new conditions imposed by its permanent settlement in new territories and it provided the ruler with a firm basis for his authority during the first establishment of a closely organised state. Later on, young entrants who were neither Turks nor Moslems by origin had to undergo a stern and exacting training, ensuring their complete psychological transformation and a complete severance from all earlier connections.[22]

We have unfortunately too little detailed information which would throw light on this process but we do learn from certain sources that it was not rare for these young men to attempt to preserve their faith and some recollection of their homeland and their families. For instance, Gerlach writes:

> They gather together and one tells another of his native land and of what he heard in church or learned in school there, and they agree among themselves that Mahomet is no prophet and that the Turkish religion is false. If there is one among them who has some little book or can teach them in some other manner something of God's Word, they hear him as diligently as if he were their preacher.[23]

The Greek scholar Janus Lascaris, who visited Constantinople in 1491, found among the Janissaries many who not only remembered their former religion but also favoured their former fellow-believers. The renegade Hersek, the Sultan's relation by marriage, told him that he regretted having left the religion of his fathers and that he prayed at night before the Cross, which he kept carefully concealed.[24] But although there were undoubtedly cases of this kind, many, certainly most, of these converts were completely assimilated under the pressure of their environment and of the strictness of their way of life and lost all consciousness of their Christian or racial origins. In other cases the consciousness that they had been born of Christian parents not unnaturally bred in them feelings of guilt resulting in a strong aversion to their fellow-countrymen. It was this aspect which deeply pained the Christians, who felt

---

[22] B. Papoulia, op. cit., pp. 24 ff. and p. 115.

[23] Stephan Gerlach, op. cit., p. 314.

[24] Börje Knös, *Un ambassadeur de l'Hellénisme—Janus Lascaris—et la tradition gréco- byzantine dans l'Humanisme français*, Uppsala–Paris, 1945, pp. 54 ff.

that they had not only lost their children but had reared their own enemies.

The losses suffered by the subject populations through the levy were very considerable but it is impossible to calculate them at all exactly since it was not carried out on the same scale in all periods. Originally it was an extraordinary measure but from the time when it became systematized, under Murad II (1421-51), it took place every five years, or more often if need arose. It was not only the Greek populations of the Empire who were affected by it. Both the Serbs and the Albanians suffered particularly, whereas most Bulgarian villages, as suppliers of volunteer auxiliary services to the Army, were exempted from the levy. The greatest losses were sustained by the Christian population at the time of the Empire's height, since wars were more frequent then and the number of those serving in the imperial forces, auxiliary and other, was exceptionally large. It is reckoned that this number rose to about eighty thousand in the time of Süleyman I (1520–66). Certainly Greek losses were greatest during the fifteenth and sixteenth centuries since it was only with time that the Greeks devised various ways of evading the levy. That the greatest numbers of conscripts came from the Slavonic peoples is suggested by certain evidence that the common speech among the Janissaries was not Greek but a Slavonic dialect.

The Greek population was subjected not only to the child-levy but to an additional obligation to provide crews for the imperial fleet. Since naval recruitment, which took place annually from 26 April to 26 October, did not entail conversion to Islam and to the Turkish way of life, it did not have the same grievous effect on the Christians as the 'tithe of blood'. Even so, if one takes into account the casualties in the frequent encounters with pirates and enemy vessels, the general hardship of life at sea in those times and the diseases of every kind which took their toll of ship's crews, one must conclude that the losses due to this form of conscription were considerable. The number of conscripts varied both according to period and according to the needs of the State and it varied in different areas. The 'naval islands', Hydra, Spetsai, Psará and others, provided crews not in proportion to their populations but in proportion to the number of ships they owned. From the reports of the Venetian Ambassador at Constantinople in 1593 we learn that every twenty houses were obliged to supply one man. The same diplomatist writes in 1596 that a conscription of eight thousand men was being required. Of these, six thousand had commuted their service for a money payment but the rest had had to present themselves for duty as oarsmen in the galleys; but since even this number was in excess of requirement, others had also been allowed to buy themselves out.[25]

The number of sailors serving cannot have been very large since at the time of the greatest naval expeditions the total of the crews did not exceed twenty-five to thirty thousand, including many captives and slaves. In periods of relative peace the number of those serving cannot have gone above a thousand or so, while in winter only a few men were called upon, at most about one hundred and twenty, who were needed for the maintenance of the ships. The conscription did not operate in the same district each year but took place every fourth year; a sum of money, known as 'Αβαρίτς or 'Αβαρίτζι[26], being paid in each of the other three. The amount of this contribution varied, once again, in accordance with the needs of the time; the proceeds, which were often very considerable, were devoted by the Turkish Government to the provisioning and pay of crews and the hiring of sailors from other parts of the Empire. The recruitment of men from other districts, chiefly

---

[25] K. Mertzios, Μνημεῖα Μακεδονικῆς Ἱστορίας (*Monuments of Macedonian History*), Salonica, 1947, pp. 162 ff.

[26] See under '*Awarid*' in *Encyclopaedia of Islam* (New Ed.), vol. I, Leiden, 1960, pp. 760 ff., which describes the word as a generic term for "contributions of various types exacted by the central government in the Sultan's name" and gives as a typical example of the objects for which such special levies might be made the recruiting of "oarsmen supplementing the war captives and criminals likewise employed in the imperial galleys".

born Moslems, was more widely adopted in the last years of Turkish rule, that is to say from the end of the eighteenth century, when Sultan Selim III (1789–1807) was trying to bring the Ottoman fleet up to date. In these last years enforced recruitment, as opposed to the hiring of volunteers, was confined to the 'naval islands' and the number of Greeks serving in the Turkish fleet reached a total of some eight hundred. According to the witness of contemporary travellers and writers these islanders were the picked crews of the Turkish navy.[27]

It was at this time that there appeared the office of the *Bash Reis* who performed the duties of co-captain of the ship and was the commander of the Christian sailors. These Hydriote sea-captains—all those so far known came from Hydra—did much to improve the living conditions of the Greek crews and rendered many services to their mother-country. Greek sailors did not reach the higher grades of the naval hierarchy unless they embraced Islam. They were usually employed in a variety of duties on board, more especially those connected with the art of navigation. Their lives afloat must have been hard and laborious, to judge from the attempts of Christians to escape conscription and from the available evidence as to living conditions. The feeling, besides, that they were serving infidels who were fighting against the Christian powers from whom they expected their liberation, contributed to their frequent displays of indifference and insubordination which at times broke into open revolt against the Turks. Nevertheless, the Christian crews of Turkish ships did considerable service to the Turkish State. Their presence in the fleet and the use which the Turks made of them at moments of crisis, in spite of all the difficulties which their employment entailed, accounts in some measure for Turkish successes in naval warfare. But, to the Greeks too, their servitude in the Turkish navy was not without its balance of advantage. It helped in the development of that

---

[27] See in general, B. B. Sphyroeras, Τά ʽΕλληνικὰ πληρώματα τοῦ Τουρκικοῦ Στόλου (*The Greek Crews of the Turkish Fleet*), Athens, 1968.

Greek naval power which was to play a significant part in the struggle for independence.

Slavery and Piracy

There were further factors which contributed to the ruin of the Greek population under Turkish rule. Ever since Byzantine times the carrying off of captives into slavery had been the scourge of Greece.[28] The scenes of confusion and enslavement which took place at the time of the Turkish conquest were beyond description. The captives carried off from the Morea numbered thousands and the same tragedies were repeated at the fall of Euboea, Rhodes and Cyprus. This human material, the supply of which was daily increased by banditry and piracy, was used to repopulate ruined cities and to reinforce the population of rural areas; but the remainder was channelled through the international slave-markets or cast into the holds of Venetian, Turkish or pirate ships. The Church, Greek communities and private individuals were later to organize funds for ransoming those in captivity. Greeks were to be found as far afield as Germany endeavouring to collect ransom-money by begging.

Piracy flourished in Greek seas during the Turkish period.[29] The main bases of the pirate fleets in the Mediterranean were the coasts of North Africa and the islands of the Aegean Sea. The natives of Africa, Algeria and Tunis, had practised piracy throughout medieval times. Their power was still further consolidated after 1492, when the Moslems of Spain on their

[28] Ph. Koukoules, Βυζαντινῶν Βίος καί Πολιτισμός (*Life and Civilization of the Byzantines*), vol. III, Athens, 1949, pp. 148 ff.

[29] D. A. Zakythinos, *Corsaires et Pirates dans les mers grecques au temps de la domination turque*, Athens, 1939. Sp. Argyros, Ἡ πειρατεία ἀπὸ τοῦ 1500 π. X. ἕως τό 1860. Ἱστορία καί θρῦλος (*Piracy from 1500 B.C. to 1860. History and Legend*), Athens, 1956. Cf. St. D. Imellos (Στ. Δ. Ἤμελλος), Ἡ περί πειρατῶν λαϊκή παράδοσις (*Popular Traditions on Piracy*), Athens, 1968. J. Vasdravellis, *Piracy on the Macedonian Coast during the Rule of the Turks*, Salonica, 1970.

expulsion from that country settled beyond Gibraltar; but it reached its peak in the sixteenth century, in the age when the Ottoman Empire had attained naval supremacy and the African pirates had entered the service of the Sultans.

The most outstanding of these pirates was Kheireddin (Hayredin) Barbarossa.[30] In the years 1537–8 he besieged Corfu, ravaged Paxoi, Zante and Kythera and took and sacked Aegina, Mykonos and the Northern Sporades. Large numbers of prisoners were sent off to Constantinople. In the words of an anonymous chronicler, "Taking numbers of men and women, he brought them to the City by galley, since the plague had been so great among them in Constantinople that the living could not bury the dead. They therefore cast them into the sea and the sea-shores were to be seen filled with dead bodies."[31] Aegina alone yielded the pirate six thousand prisoners and was left bare of inhabitants. Until the French conquest of Algiers in 1830 the Barbary pirates continued to ravage the Greek coasts and islands. In their traditions and folksongs the people have preserved to this day the memory of the pirates and the 'slaves of Barbary'.

Sea-banditry was also practised on an extensive scale by Christian pirates. Among these a distinguished place is held by the Knights of the Order of St. John, whose unique state in Rhodes survived till 1522, and in Malta until their eviction by Napoleon in 1798. In both these phases of their history the Knights, who were simultaneously crusading enemies of Islam, soldiers of fortune and salt-water thieves, were the real masters of the eastern Mediterranean. Their activity reached its highest point in the seventeenth century and at the beginning of the eighteenth. Great leaders, mainly of French origin, like the brothers Théméricourt, Hughes Crevelier and the Chevalier de Hocquincourt, distinguished themselves by their daring and courage.

[30] For a recent biography of Barbarossa see Ernle Bradford, *The Sultan's Admiral*, London, 1968.

[31] Sp. Lambros, *Ecthesis Chronica and Chronicon Athenarum*, London, 1902, p. 81.

For the Greek population piracy remained a constant source of wastage. Whole islands were left deserted for periods of years and flourishing towns were left unpeopled. Both Greek and foreign sources, popular histories, the brief summaries of annalists and letters, all paint a gloomy picture of the state of desolation which the Greek lands had reached. Thus, to confine ourselves to a single piece of evidence, after Morosini's evacuation of Athens in 1688, Attica was left deserted for nearly three years. The Athenians fled to Salamis and in their petition to the Patriarch (written, it is thought, by Argyrus Bernardes) the following are given as the typical features of the local situation:

> . . . for the sea brings the pirate galleys of the barbarians who in their turn bring with them fearful captivity and fresh cause for lamentation. The seashore of Salamis resounded then with tumult and wailing. Wretched pregnant mothers endured the pangs of birth before their time and young babes calling for their mothers' help in quavering voices were done to death with stones. Young maids in their prime became the fearful victims of tyrannical lust and those who had reached an honoured old age closed their lives in slavery. Still more had their families scattered to the far extremes of foreign soil, the dearest possession of our nation became the spoils of barbarian violence and the wealth, which Athens once won by the spear, loaded to the water-line the ships of the infidels.[32]

In such conditions it is easy to understand why areas like the Morea had a very sparse population. According to Venetian statistics, in 1685 this large, rich country, omitting Corinthia and Mani, contained 85,468 inhabitants and in 1692 the whole of it contained about 116,000.[33]

[32] Quoted by P. Zerlentis, Ἀργυρὸς Βερναρδῆς ὁ Ἀθηναῖος (*Argyros Bernardes of Athens*), 1659–1720, Athens, 1921, p. 20.

[33] Sp. Lambros, Ἡ περὶ Πελοποννήσου Ἔκθεσις τοῦ Βενετοῦ προνοητοῦ Κορνέρ ('The Report on the Peloponnese by the Venetian Provveditore Corner'), in the Δελτίον τῆς Ἱστορικῆς καὶ Ἐθνολογικῆς Ἱστορίας τῆς Ἑλλάδος (*Bulletin of the Greek Historical and Ethnological Society*), vol. II, Athens, 1885, pp. 283, 301.

The Legal Position of the Subject Population and the Social Structure of the Greek Community

In respecting the lives and the religious liberty of the conquered peoples the Conqueror followed a long-standing Moslem tradition[34], granting tolerance to Jews and Christians, who received protection in return for money-payments (i.e. the poll-tax). This right of *aman* (literally, pardon or mercy) had been formulated from the first centuries of Islam and had prevailed in the relations between Arabs and Christians. The Ottomans had taken over this principle from the Seljuks and maintained this policy of toleration. The departures from it, which were recorded from time to time, were the result of passing out-bursts of fanaticism or the pressures of necessity and not of any settled intolerance.

Besides the poll-tax the Christian inhabitants of the Empire were liable to certain restrictions and obligations, some of which have been examined above. In addition, Greeks were forbidden to build or furnish churches, to carry arms and to dress like Moslems. This last restriction remained in force until the Greek Revolution; apart from the desire to emphasize Moslem superiority, it was thought that this outward distinction between the Moslem and non-Moslem elements made it easier to collect the poll-tax.

Under the pressure of internal or external events, the Sultans were repeatedly forced to take protective measures on behalf of the Christian population. Thus, on the recommenda-tion of the Grand Vizir Mustafa Köprülü, there were issued in 1691 the ordinances which bear the collective name of *Nizam Djedid* (the 'New System'). Under these regulations provincial Governors were called upon to act justly towards Christians and not to increase their burden of taxation. Much later, by the

---

[34] N. Moschovakis, *Τό ἐν Ἑλλάδι Δημόσιον Δίκαιον ἐπὶ Τουρκοκρατίας* (*Public Law in Greece under the Turks*), Athens, 1882. N. Iorga, *Byzance après Byzance*, Bucharest, 1935, M. Sakellariou, *Ἡ Πελοπόννησος κατὰ τὴν δευτέραν Τουρκοκρα-τίαν* (1715–1821) (*The Peloponnese during the Second Turkish Domination, 1715–1821*), Athens, 1939.

Hatti Sharif (Decree) of Gülhane of 3 September 1839, and above all by the later Decree (*Hatti Hümayun*) of February 1856, measures were introduced which aimed at enforcing equality before the law and equal civil rights between all subjects of the Ottoman Empire.[35] Generally speaking, it may be said that in the earlier period of Ottoman rule (roughly after the initial violence and confusion of the Conquest and until the end of the seventeenth century), when the central government at Constantinople was directed by strong Sultans or strong ministers, and again under the reforming Sultans of the first half of the nineteenth century, both political expediency and a genuine desire to rule justly prompted a certain tolerance towards the Christian population, insofar as Moslem religious principles allowed; but that in periods of weaker rule the bigotry, ambition and rapacity of local Governors and local Moslem populations (not all by any means Turkish by race) had free play, even at times when the oppression of Christians afforded opportunities for intervention (not always wholly disinterested) by external powers. As has already been noted, this intervention in turn often caused the central government to treat its Christian subjects with increased suspicion and severity.

The upheavals which resulted from the Conquest had an effect on the shaping of the Greek community under Turkish rule. The administrative and intellectual ruling class of Byzantium had been drastically reduced by voluntary exile, by destruction in war or simply by a decline into decadence or poverty. It would not be true to say that it had entirely disappeared. In the first years following the Conquest, and thereafter, we find at Constantinople representatives of the Byzantine houses of Palaeologus, Cantacuzene, Notaras, Mouzalon, Gavras, Chalkokondylis, Argyropoulos, Rhallis and others. Some of these Mehmed used as advisers and secretaries. Others attained power by devoting themselves to trade or by

---

[35] Bernard Lewis, *The Emergence of Modern Turkey*, London, 1961. Roderic H. Davison, *Reform in the Ottoman Empire 1856–1876*, Princeton, 1963.

renting from Turks concessions for the exploitation of salt deposits, fisheries or other public enterprises. Considerable power was obtained, for example, by Michael Cantacuzene who amassed great wealth as the *concessionnaire* of the salt industry and as a merchant on the grand scale; but he ended by attracting suspicion and was executed in 1578.

We have only very imperfect information about Greek rural communities in the years following the fall of Constantinople. The needs of the Conquest made a certain degree of toleration necessary towards the big estates which dominated the agricultural communities of the later Byzantine period. Thus we know that by an ordinance of 1430 Sinan Pasha confirmed the chief men of Ioannina in the possession of their landed properties:—"Those Archons (Notables) who hold estates, let them hold them still; let them keep, without further word, their families, their lands, and all their effects."[36]

In that same year Salonica was taken and delivered over to fearful pillage, but those of the inhabitants who returned kept their property. Similarly, Mehmed II, by letters dated December 1454, confirmed the possessions of the great Peloponnesian families—Sphrantzis, Lascaris, Frangopoulos, Rhallis, Philanthropinos, and others.[37] In Thessaly it seems that the old situation as regards land ownership was maintained for some time, in fact until the Turkish population was swollen by the settlement of thousands of Turks from Konya in Asia Minor.[38]

The extension and organization of the timariot system contributed to the absorption of the great estates which had at first been left in Christian hands, This in its turn helped towards a certain levelling off of the classes in the countryside, where the possession of land was almost the sole factor in social distinction.

[36] K. Amantos, Οἱ προνομιακοὶ ὁρισμοὶ τοῦ Μουσουλμανισμοῦ ὑπὲρ τῶν Χριστιανῶν ('The Charters of Privilege granted by the Mahommedan Religion to the Christians'), in Ἑλληνικά, vol. IX (1936), pp. 118 ff.

[37] Fr. Miklosich—Ios. Müller, *Acta et Diplomata graeca*, vol. III, p. 290.

[38] D. Tsopotos, Γῆ καί Γεωργοὶ τῆς Θεσσαλίας κατὰ τὴν Τουρκοκρατίαν (*Land and Farmers in Thessaly under the Turks*), Volos, 1912, pp. 30 ff.

With the exception of the great Christian landowners, who by enlisting in the Sultan's service preserved their estates during the first years of the Conquest (the 'Christian Spahis')[39], the bulk of the subject population formed the body of labourers who were used to farm the land. But the condition of these rural labourers varied. Some were serfs, others were tenants, others again were small freeholders. The landless labourers were divided into those who farmed the 'inalienable' and those who farmed the 'alienable' lands. Although the Sacred Law of the Turks forbade slavery—a prohibition not always strictly observed—those who had the right to cultivate 'inalienable' lands were in fact the equivalent of the serfs (*paroikoi*) of Byzantine times. While farming these lands and taking the produce, they paid the land-tax due to the Sultan and the other taxes due to the landlord. As in Byzantine times, so too under the Turks the *paroikos* was bound fast to the land he worked. If he ran away, the landlord had the right, for ten years, to return him by force to his holding.

The personal status of those who farmed the 'alienable' lands was different. These men were not indissolubly tied to the land they took to farm from a Turkish or Greek landlord. The relations between landlord and farmer were defined by agreements which eventually took, in the main, one of three forms: the *syntrophikon*, under which the two parties, after deducting tax payments and farming expenses, divided the proceeds equally; the *tritarikon*, under which three-tenths went to the landlord and seven-tenths to the farmer, who took on himself all charges and expenses; and finally the *geomoron* or *apokopi*, whereby the farmer paid down a fixed sum to the landlord and enjoyed the whole income from the farm but was liable for taxes and expenses.

Small freeholds were allowed by the Turks in mountainous districts where the local inhabitants had submitted voluntarily and without resistance. Holdings of this kind are met with in the Morea, in Epirus, in the mountainous parts of Thessaly and

[39] Ap. Vakalopoulos, Ἱστορία τοῦ Νέου Ἑλληνισμοῦ, vol. I, pp. 206 ff. Sp. Vryonis, op. cit., p. 293.

elsewhere. Whole villages in Christian possession were called *Kephalokhoria* (literally, head-villages). Small freeholdings, however, were liable to be encroached upon. Large landowners or high-ranking officials managed to incorporate these small farms into their own vast properties. The suppression of freeholdings in Epirus and Thessaly by Ali Pasha of Ioannina are a familiar instance of this. Small farmers were forced to cede their properties to officially constituted bodies and to individuals.

The most important factor in the social and economic life of the Greeks under Turkish rule proved to be the ownership of land by the Church and by monasteries. The conqueror recognized the Greek Church, granted it privileges and confirmed it in its landed property. The lands belonging to episcopal and metropolitan sees in each area were extensive, and so were those of the monastic foundations. Following the example of the Byzantine emperors, the Sultans hastened to ratify their ownership and to renew their privileges. Rescripts, firmans and other documents in this sense are to be found in most Greek monasteries to this day. For example, the following may be quoted among the oldest: three documents relating to the Monastery of St. John the Baptist near Serres in eastern Macedonia (order of Murad I, 27 December 1372–5 January 1373, conserved in Greek; note of Musa in Greek, one of the young sons of Bayezid I, January 1412; order of Mehmed I, January 1419, also in Greek)[40], a series of Firmans relating to the Monastery of Vlattades at Thessalonica, the oldest being one of Mehmed II, dated 1446;[41] a rescript of this Sultan to the Church of the Holy Wisdom (Hagia Sophia) at Salonica (1459)[42]; Firmans relating to the Monastery of St. John at

[40] Elizabeth A. Zachariadou—Oikonomides, 'Early Ottoman Documents of the Prodromos Monastery (Serres)', in *Südost—Forschungen*, vol. XXVIII (1969), pp. 1 ff.

[41] J. Vasdravelles, Ἱστορικὰ Ἀρχεῖα Μακεδονίας (*Historical Archives of Macedonia*), vol. III: Ἀρχεῖον Μονῆς Βλαττάδων, (1436–1839), (*Archives of the Monastery of Vlattades*), Salonica, 1955.

[42] Fr. Babinger, 'Ein Freibrief Mehmeds II., des Eroberers, für das Kloster Hagia Sophia zu Saloniki Eigentum der Sultanin Mara (1459)', in *Byzantinische Zeitschrift*, vol. XLIV (1951), pp. 11 ff.

Patmos (dated 1454–1522);[43] three Firmans relating to the Monastery of Kutlumus on Mount-Athos, the oldest being one of Bayezid II, issued in 1491[44], and many others.

Fortified by these official decrees and strengthened by the gifts of Orthodox rulers, particularly the Princes of Wallachia, and by the offerings of the faithful, Church and monastic property became, in spite of all encroachments, a very great economic force. It has been reckoned that by the end of the Turkish period it amounted to at least a quarter of the whole Greek territory.

Statistical information about landed properties in Greece under the Turks is of particular importance. Great value attaches therefore to the details collected by the Venetians for the compilation of their land register during their brief supremacy in the Morea from 1685 to 1715. But the main evidence on this subject derives from a memorandum drawn up by Capodistria[45] in 1828 at the request of the three Protecting Powers (Britain, France and Russia[46]). According to this, towards the end of the Turkish supremacy the ownership of land was in the ratio shown in the table overleaf.[47]

According to reckonings which have been made, the proportion of land owned by Greeks a little before the Revolution amounted, in the Morea, to 4.2 *stremmata* a head, and in the rest of Greece to about 10.6 *stremmata*. On the other hand, for every Turk resident in the Morea and Euboea the proportion was about 75 *stremmata*. These figures are highly typical.

[43] Elizabeth Zachariadou—Oikonomides, Συμβολή στὴν ἱστορία τοῦ Νοτιοανατολικοῦ Αἰγαίου (μέ ἀφορμή τά πατμιακά φιρμάνια τῶν ἐτῶν 1454–1522) (Contribution to the History of the South-East Aegean, in Σύμμεικτα, (Miscellany) based on the Firmans issued to the Monastery of Patmos 1454–1522) vol. I Athens, 1966, pp. 184 ff.

[44] Paul Lemerle, *Actes de Kutlumus*, *Archives de l'Athos*, II, Paris, 1946, pp. 234 ff.

[45] John, Count Capodistria (1776–1831), President of liberated Greece, 1827–31. See C. M. Woodhouse *Capodistria*, Oxford, 1973.

[46] See J. Capodistria, *Correspondance* (ed. Bétant), Suppl. to vol. IV Geneva, 1839, pp. 473 ff.

[47] The figures are given in *stremmata*, one *stremma* being approximately a quarter of an acre.

	In Greek Ownership	*In* Turkish Ownership
Western Greece	1,636,730	1,285,730
Eastern Greece[48]	5,178,440	2,082,990
Morea	1,500,000	3,000,000
Crete	1,520,000	2,280,000
Chios	200,000	1,600
TOTAL	10,035,170	8,650,320

[48] 'Eastern Greece' in this context does not include Thessaly (apart from Magnesia), on which there is at present no information. The whole of the land in the Cyclades belonged to the Greek inhabitants.

III

Liberties and Privileges

In following the Islamic doctrine which enjoined tolerance towards Christians and in recognizing the Greek Church, Mehmed II also acted in accordance with another dogma of the Sacred Law which equated religion with race. As a consequence of this, the religious Head of the Greek Church became also Ethnarch (*'Εθνάρχης*), that is to say, Head of the Greek Nation (Turkish *Millet*).[1]

The details of the recognition of the Church have not yet been fully clarified for lack of authentic documents, but according to the evidence of the existing sources Mehmed II filled the Patriarchal throne, which had been left vacant since 1450 owing to the dispute between Church and the Emperor over reunion between Constantinople and the Church of Rome, and confirmed the Patriarch's ancient privileges. George Scholarius, a writer and philosopher who had been an outstanding figure in the struggle against the Latins, was freed

---

[1] On the privileges of the Patriarchate see Steven Runciman, *The Great Church in Captivity*, Cambridge, 1968, pp. 165 ff. Cf. N. Eleutheriades, *Τὰ προνόμια τοῦ Οἰκουμενικοῦ Πατριαρχείου* (*The Privileges of the Oecumenical Patriarchate*), Smyrna, 1909. Th. Papadopoullos, *Studies and Documents Relating to the History of the Greek Church and People under Turkish Domination*, Brussels, 1952. N. J. Pantazopoulos, *Church and Law in the Balkan Peninsula during the Ottoman Rule*, Salonica, 1967. Josef Kabrda, *Le système fiscal de l'Église orthodoxe dans l'Empire ottoman (d'après les documents turcs)*, Opera Universitatis Purkynianae Brunensis, Facultas Philosophica, 135, Brno, 1969. Halil Inalcik, 'The Policy of Mehmed II toward the Greek Population of Istanbul and the Byzantine Buildings of the City', in *Dumbarton Oaks Papers*, nos. 23–24 (1969–70), pp. 229–49.

from the condition of slavery into which he was found to have fallen during the confusion which followed the conquest and was appointed Bishop and Patriarch as Gennadius II.

His accession took place on 6 January 1454. The Conqueror himself summoned Gennadius and, placing the pastoral staff in his hands, said to him: "Be Patriarch, and good fortune be with you. Count on Our friendship in whatever you will, possessing all those privileges which the Patriarchs enjoyed before you."[2]

According to the *Chronicon Majus* issued under the name of George Phrantzes or Sphrantzes, the Sultan gave written instructions to the Patriarch under the authority of the imperial signature that none should vex or oppose him but that he should be exempt from requisition and taxation and unshakable by any adversary and that he should be free of all duties and benevolences, both he and all Patriarchs after him for ever, as likewise should all the prelates under him[3]. Judging by this testimony, the privileges accorded to Gennadius were confirmed in writing. Unfortunately, the official texts have not been preserved. We may, nevertheless, with a good deal of reserve, accept what is written in the 'Chronicle of Pseudo-Phrantzes'. It is known today that this historical composition is a fabrication by Makarios Melissenas, Metropolitan of Monemvasia, forged in the years 1573–5. It follows that the text of 'Pseudo-Phrantzes' proves no more than that it was believed in the sixteenth century that Mehmed II had granted the Patriarchate of Constantinople its privileges by 'written instruction'.

On the other hand texts of greater authenticity, written at a date nearer the events in question, supply more accurate evidence on this subject. These texts are the *Apologia* of Patriarch

---

[2] *Historia Politica et Patriarchica Constantinopoleos*, ed. Imm. Bekker, *Corpus Scriptorum Historiae Byzantinae*, Bonn, 1849, pp. 27 ff.

[3] *Georgius Phrantzes, Ioannes Cananus, Ioannes Anagnostes*, ed. Imm. Bekker, *Corpus Scriptorum Historiae Byzantinae*, Bonn, 1838, p. 308. New ed. *Georgios Sphrantzes, Τά καθ᾽ ἑαυτὸν καί τινα γεγονότα ἐν τῷ χρόνῳ τῆς ζωῆς αὐτοῦ (1401–77) cum Pseudo-Phrantzes in appendice sive Macarii Melisseni Chronicon 1258–1481*, rec. B. Grecu, Bucarest, 1966, p. 456.

Gennadius himself to Theodore Branas (1463) and the recently published *Λόγος περὶ τῶν κατ᾽ αὐτόν* (*Discourse on his own times*) by Theodore Agallianos, also of 1463. In the first of these there is express mention of the privileges granted by the Sultan to the first Patriarch after the Conquest and to his direct successors.[4] The record speaks of the Conqueror's concessions and of their later consequences. Specifically, Agallianos writes:

> God, however, answering our indifference, not to say our dull insensibility, with His infinite goodness and forbearance, inspired the Sovereign to gather together once again the people of Christ, which indeed he has done as best he could, beyond all expectation, and has allowed us to live according to our own ancestral customs and laws and also to have churches and priests and prelates and every Christian institution. Furthermore, the Lord sent us a new Joseph to feed the starving people through Pharaoh or a new Moses to lead His people out of Egypt, for in His great mercy He, through the Sovereign, set a holy man, the venerable Patriarch Gennadius, at the head of the Church and of the Christian people by raising him to the office of Patriarch.[5]

In connection with the written ratification of these concessions, certain historians record that when, in 1521, Sultan Süleyman the Magnificent decided to embark on a persecution of the Christians in Constantinople and to turn their churches into mosques, Patriarch Theoleptus appealed to the privileges granted to his predecessor by Sultan Mehmed but, on being

[4] L. Petit, X. A. Siderides and M. Jugie, *Oeuvres complètes de Georges (Gennade) Scholarios*, vol. IV, Paris, 1935, pp. 265 ff.

[5] Chr. G. Patrinelis, *Ὁ Θεόδωρος Ἀγαλλιανὸς ταυτιζόμενος πρὸς τὸν Θεοφάνη Μηδείας καὶ οἱ ἀνέκδοτοι Λόγοι αὐτοῦ. Μία νέα ἱστορικὴ πηγὴ περὶ τοῦ Πατριαρχείου Κωνσταντινουπόλεως κατὰ τοὺς πρώτους μετὰ τὴν Ἅλωσιν χρόνους* (Theodore Agallianos identified with Theophanes of Medeia, and his unpublished 'Discourses'. 'A Fresh Historical Source on the Patriarchate of Constantinople in the First Years after the Conquest'), Athens, 1966, p. 98, Cf. pp. 62 ff. Also V. Laurent, 'Les premiers patriarches de Constantinople sous la domination turque (1454–76)', in *Revue des études byzantines*, vol. XXVI (1968), pp. 229–63.

called upon to produce the relevant papers, he asserted that they had been destroyed in a fire. He then resorted to the testimony of three aged Janissaries who confirmed that they had been present at the capture of the city and remembered that its nobles had submitted voluntarily to the Sultan. These nobles had come and had found Mehmed outside his tent and had brought him the keys of the city on a golden dish, asking him to accept certain articles of surrender to which the Sultan had agreed.[6] It is thought that this account of the surrender of Constantinople may in fact have been a story invented to explain the Conqueror's treatment of a city which had undoubtedly offered resistance and had been conquered by force of arms, but the incident is none the less relevant to any discussion of the written confirmation of the Patriarchal privileges.[7]

The oldest extant *Berat* (diploma or patent) issued to a Greek prelate is one of Mehmed II, granted some time after 1456 and preserved in the Bibliothèque Nationale at Paris (*Fonds Turc Ancien 39*). Unfortunately the name of the ecclesiastical district to which this Berat refers and that of the Metropolitan concerned are not specified in it, but it refers to an archbishopric in Macedonia. By virtue of this grant the Sultan, in return for a money payment, confers on a certain monk the title of Metropolitan. After enumerating the Metropolitan's administrative and financial rights and duties, the document goes on to declare him exempt from the obligation to provide couriers for the state service or to maintain military fortifications, as also from

[6] Steven Runciman, op. cit., pp. 189 ff. According to Chr. G. Patrinelis, "The exact time of the first attempt of the Turks to seize the Churches and convert the Christian People of Constantinople to Islam", in *Actes du Premier Congrès International des Études Balkaniques et Sud-Est Européennes*, Sofia, 26 août–1 septembre 1966, vol. III, Sofia, 1969, pp. 567 ff., the date of this incident was 1521 and the Sultan involved was Süleyman the Magnificent, and not, as had previously been thought, Selim I.

[7] Local annalists often liked to emphasize that the conquered had received the victors under treaty and to invoke lost privileges. See e.g., L. Vranousis, Ἰστορικὰ καί τοπογραφικὰ τοῦ μεσαιωνικοῦ κάστρου τῶν Ἰωαννίνων (*Historical and Topographical Notes on the Medieval Fortress of Ioannina*), Athens, 1968, p. 32.

the poll-tax and all extraordinary taxation.[8] It is no doubt a typical example of its date.

Among later examples mention may be made of the Berat of 1604 conferred upon the Metropolitan Leontius of Larissa.[9] The Berat granted in 1649 to Joachim, Metropolitan of Berrhoea (Veroia) and Naoussa, is also worth quoting for its additional details. This document, which was issued at the request of 'the Patriarch of the Romans (i.e. Greek Orthodox) of Constantinople' "in accordance with the prevailing custom, the ordinances [of Government] and their execution by the religious authority", sets out the privileges of the new Metropolitan after payment of the prescribed *peshkesh*.[10] It lays down that "the said Joachim shall be acknowledged as Metropolitan by the priests, monks and infidels (i.e. Christians) of Berrhoea Naoussa and their environs". All these are bound "to refer to him in matters coming within his jurisdiction and not to act contrary to his orders". The Metropolitan "is entitled to appoint and dismiss any priests or monks who merit appointment or dismissal, according to their own customs and ordinances, and no other person may interfere with his performance of his duties". In case of the death of a priest, monk or nun the Metropolitan is entitled to take over any objects bequeathed to the Patriarchate, and neither those who are making the inventory of the estate nor the officers of the State shall have the right to intervene. In cases where deceased priests, monks or infidels have bequeathed various objects to the church and to the Patriarchate, these legacies are to be

[8] N. Beldiceanu, *Les actes des premiers sultans conservés dans les manuscripts turcs de la Bibliothèque Nationale à Paris, I. Actes de Mehmed II et de Bayezid II du Ms Fonds Turc ancien 39*, École Pratique des Hautes Études, VIe Section: Documents et Recherches sur l'économie des pays byzantins, islamiques et slaves et leurs relations commerciales au Moyen Age sous la direction de Paul Lemerle, Paris—The Hague, 1960, p. 137 (no. 47).

[9] Dem. Ghinis, Περίγραμμα Ἱστορίας τοῦ Μεταβυζαντινοῦ Δικαίου ('Outline of the History of Post-Byzantine Law'), Πραγματεῖαι τῆς Ἀκαδημίας Ἀθηνῶν, (Dissertations of the Academy of Athens), vol. XXVI, Athens, 1966, pp. 112 ff. (No. 101).

[10] Literally, a gift; actually, a fee paid on appointment.

honoured and Roman (i.e. Greek) witnesses are to be admitted. Village priests are not to perform marriages of infidels if these have not been allowed, and permission given, by the Metropolitan. No one but he is to intervene in questions concerning the contraction and dissolution of marriages and, generally, in questions concerning relations between married couples. He is to control, as his predecessors did, all properties dedicated to the Church—vineyards, gardens, farms, pasturages, fields, consecrated wells or springs ('ἀγιάσματα), monasteries, mills and the like—and no third person shall hinder or intervene.[11]

The privileges of the Patriarchate, as finally formulated, were both ecclesiastical and political. The ecclesiastical privileges, exercised jointly by the Patriarch and the Holy Synod, consisted of the supreme control of all Metropolitans and Bishops in every place and of the clergy in general, as well as of churches and monasteries and their property; they included also the right to appoint, recall and transfer Metropolitans, Archbishops and Bishops, such appointments being subject to the State's ratification by Berat. Similarly, the Church exercised disciplinary and penal jurisdiction over the clergy. If the Patriarch or higher ranks of the clergy were being sued, the suit was heard in Constantinople in the presence of Commissioners of the Sublime Porte. The property of priests dying unmarried passed to the Patriarchate and every believer might give up one third of his estate to the Church and to its charitable and other works.

The political privileges of the Patriarchate concerned the administration of justice and the organization of education. Already, from late Byzantine times, especially after the reforms of Andronicus II (1296) and Andronicus III (1329–34), the Church, through its rulers, had a prominent place as a wielder of judicial authority.[12] Under Turkish rule this authority

[11] J. Vasdravelles, Ἱστορικὰ Ἀρχεῖα Μακεδονίας, (Historical Archives of Macedonia), vol. II, pp. 36 ff.

[12] Paul Lemerle, Documents et problèmes nouveaux concernant les Juges Généraux, Vol. III. In honour of S. Sotiriou (Bulletin of the Christian Archaeological Society) Athens, 1964, pp. 29–44; E. Schilbach, 'Die Hypotyposis der

related, first and foremost, to civil cases connected with religious life such as marriage, divorce, wardship of minors and so forth. But other kinds of civil case were also brought before the ecclesiastical courts whenever the litigants were Christians. In its administration of justice the Church based itself on canon and Byzantine law. The *Hexabiblos* of Harmenopulos[13], published in 1345 and translated into a simpler Greek, along with other manuals including the *Nomokanon*[14] of Manuel Malaxos which was compiled in 1561 in the learned tongue and subsequently translated 'into common speech', was used as a codified version of the law. Some very important legal literature and lawbooks on Civil Law were produced during the Turkish period.[15]

In addition to the religious reasons, political arguments also prompted the Sultans to grant and maintain the privileges of the Greek Church. First, by restoring the Patriarchate at Constantinople and by installing the Patriarch according to Byzantine practice the Conqueror secured, in a way, the recognition and, one might almost say, the assent of the subject

καθολικοὶ κριταὶ τῶν ʿΡωμαίων vom Juni 1398 (?)', in *Byzantinische Zeitschrift*, vol. 61 (1968), pp. 44–70.

[13] The *Hexabiblos* (Six Books) of Constantine Harmenopoulos, Guardian of Law (*Nomophylax*) and later (after 1359) General Judge, is a compendium of the laws written at Salonica in 1345: *Κωνσταντίνου ʾΑρμενοπούλου Πρόχειρον Νόμων ἢ ʿΕξάβιβλος* (*Constantine Harmenopoulos, Manual of Law or Hexabiblos a cura Constantine G. Pitsakis*), Athens, 1971.

[14] Dem. Ghinis, 'Ἡ εἰς 'φράσιν κοινὴν' παράφρασις τοῦ Νομοκάνονος τοῦ Μαλαξοῦ ("The Paraphrase of the Nomokanon of Malaxos into "Common Speech" "), ʿΕλληνικά, vol. 8 1935, pp. 29–47, and *Ὁ Νομοκάνων τοῦ Μαλαξοῦ ὡς πηγὴ Δικαίου τοῦ μετὰ τὴν ῞Αλωσιν ʿΕλληνισμοῦ* ('The Nomokanon of Malaxos as a Source of Greek Law after the Fall of Constantinople'), in *Πρακτικὰ τῆς ʾΑκαδημίας ʾΑθηνῶν* (*Proceedings of the Academy of Athens*), vol. 13 (1938), pp. 395–401. Cf. Sp. N. Troïanos, *Νομοκάνων 'πάνυ ὠφέλιμον καί πλουσιώτατον'. Ὁ ὑπ' ἀριθμόν 8 κῶδιξ τῆς Λίνδου* (Nomokanon, The 'richest and most serviceable'. The Codex No. 8 of Lindos), Athens, 1969. An ed. of the Text in the learned tongue is being prepared by the Centre for Research into the History of Greek Law (Academy of Athens).

[15] Dem. Ghinis, *Περίγραμμα ʿΙστορίας τοῦ Μεταβυζαντινοῦ Δικαίου*, op. cit., Athens, 1966. Cf. N. J. Pantazopoulos, *Church and Law in the Balkan Peninsula during the Ottoman Rule*, Salonica, 1967.

people to his rule. Secondly, by assigning a certain competence to the higher and lower organs of the Church he made the work of the Ottoman Government easier, utterly unprepared as it was for the administration of the huge empire. One may fairly add that the recognition of the privileges of the Patriarch of Constantinople was a political act since, by associating the Orthodox Church with himself and by encouraging internal schisms within Christendom, Mehmed II made united action by the Christian world difficult and thus frustrated the crusading policy pursued by certain European powers.

It is generally agreed that the Church was the preserver of the Greek race in the dark years of its slavery. Nevertheless, there are both older and recent Greek writers who do not accept this judgement in its entirety. Thus even Paparrhegopoulos, the greatest of nineteenth century Greek historians, qualifies this assertion by writing:—"The traditional religion never ceased to be one of the main moral forces behind the Greek people, but it does not solely and by itself represent Greek civilisation." Similarly, Alexander Diomedes terms this idea 'one-sided'.[16] Nevertheless, as Steven Runciman has pointed out, "it was Orthodoxy that preserved Hellenism throughout the dark centuries; but without the moral force of Hellenism orthodoxy itself might have withered".[17]

One may agree that the Church was the prime moral factor in the preservation of the Greek nation but such a judgement might indeed be shown to be one-sided if the ecclesiastical establishment were not studied in the context of its political situation. By the recognition of the privileges of the Constantinople Patriarchate there was created, within the framework of the Ottoman Empire, a para-statal body, the Orthodox Church-State of the Greek Nation. A whole network of Metropolitans, Archbishops, Bishops, Suffragans and monastic communities covered the territory under Turkish rule and this

---

[16] Alexander Diomedes, Βυζαντιναὶ Μελέται (*Byzantine Essays*), vol. I, 1st ed, Athens, 1942, pp. 402 ff.

[17] Steven Runciman, op. cit., p. 410.

network was both closer and more complete than that of the State, based as the latter was on the timariot system which helped towards the Empire's ultimate disintegration. Consequently, although one may pass an adverse judgement on this or that feature of clerical rule, one cannot ignore the massive influence of the Church system as a whole.

The first result of this form of organization was the achievement of Greek unity after the Greeks had been torn apart both by the dislocation of the Byzantine Empire ever since the twelfth century and by the domination of Latins and Serbs on Greek soil. Thus the Greek element was strengthened not only against its non-Christian rulers but also against the other peoples of the same religion as itself who were equally subjected, namely the non-Greek peoples of the Balkan Peninsula. In relation to these last, the Greeks were able to assume a certain leadership and to take certain initiatives which were on the whole beneficial to all.

Further, the Church, continuing the universalist tradition of the defunct Byzantine Empire, extended its activity to the outside world also. In this way it opened up to a Greek race which had lost its political status some possibility of conducting a foreign policy of its own by indirect means, namely by entering into diplomatic contact with foreign Churches and nations and with foreign rulers. The ecumenical role of the Patriarch of Constantinople was greatly enhanced during the years of Turkish rule. The Patriarchates of Akhris (Ohrid) and Ipek (Peć) in Macedonia and southern Serbia came virtually under the control of the Ecumenical Patriarch; indeed the two Archbishoprics were in time actually absorbed and became subject administratively to the Patriarch's direct jurisdiction (1766–7).[18] Finally by the creation of the Patriarchate of Moscow in 1589, in which a leading part was played by

[18] The publication of Turkish documents of the seventeenth and eighteenth centuries has thrown fresh light on the history of the Church in Ohrid and Peć; see D. A. Zakythinos, Συμβολαί εἰς τήν ἱστορίαν τῶν Ἐκκλησιῶν Ἀχρίδος καί Ἰπεκίου ('Contributions to the History of the Churches of Ohrid and Peć'), in Μακεδονικά vol. I (1940), pp. 429–58.

Patriarch Jeremias II, the Church of Constantinople gave up its rights over the Russian Church—which were in any case shadowy—but in doing so created far-reaching opportunities for ecclesiastical and political relations which later proved invaluable to the national cause. On the whole one can say that the Greek Patriarch practised, under the Sultan's rule, a policy of expansion which was inspired by the universalist idea of Byzantium.

In international relations we note that the Patriarchs of Constantinople came into direct contact with foreign rulers and with sovereign governments—with the Doges of Venice, for example, with the Kings of France, the Tsars of Russia, the rulers of Poland and Wallachia and others. Special mention should be made also of the relations developed during the sixteenth and seventeenth centuries, particularly under Jeremias II and Cyril I Loukaris, with Protestant princes, statesmen, court officials, theologians and scholars. Among these last may be cited Stephan Gerlach, who came to Constantinople in 1572 in the retinue of the Imperial Ambassador, and the learned Martin Crusius (Kraus), whose book *Turcograecia*, published in 1584, is our richest source for the history of the Church and the Greeks during those critical years.[19]

Besides the privileges granted to the Church others were also bestowed on certain classes of people and on the inhabitants of certain regions. As a prime example of this we may quote the commercial privileges granted to the Venetians and Genoese both before and after the fall of Constantinople.[20] These early grants prepared the ground for the capitulations which the French obtained in 1535 and 1604 and the English in 1580. In making these arrangements with Western powers the Sultans

---

[19] Gunnar Hering, *Ökumenisches Patriarchat und Europäische Politik, 1620–38*, Wiesbaden, 1968. Also Otto Kresten, *Das Patriarchat von Konstantinopel im ausgehenden 16. Jahrhundert*, Österreichische Akademie der Wissenschaften, Philosophisch—Historische Klasse, Sitzungsberichte, 266. Band, 5. Abhandl., Vienna, 1970. Cf. Steven Runciman, op. cit., pp. 238 ff.

[20] For the Greek Text of the treaty of 1446 between Mehmed II and Venice, see Franz Dölger, *Byzantinische Diplomatik*, Ettal, 1956, pp. 262 ff.

were following Byzantine practice for political and economic reasons, only to find in the end, as the Byzantine Emperors had found, that they brought the State dangerously near to the loss of political independence through foreign economic domination. The Greeks, however, profited greatly from this policy both because it contributed to the expansion of economic activity and also because there thus came into existence a class of Greek protected persons (in Turkish, *Beratli*). As interpreters, consular agents, commercial representatives and merchants, they enjoyed the protection of foreign powers—Venice, France, Russia, England, Austria—and on this ground received special fiscal and legal treatment.[21]

Again, special privileges were granted by the Sultan to the inhabitants of certain districts and islands. Mention has been made already of the order given by Sinan Pasha in 1430 in favour of the townsmen of Ioannina[22], who under its provisions were exempted from the child-levy and from slavery and maintained their churches intact. The Metropolitan continued to dispense justice and to enjoy all his ecclesiastical rights and the leading men of the town (Archons) secured the confirmation of their estates. These privileges were based on the older liberties which Andronicus II Palaeologus (1282–1328) had bestowed on the town in 1319 and 1321.[23]

Very extensive privileges were awarded to other cities and islands. Chios, for example, which was occupied in 1566, received special treatment under a charter from the Sultan —renewed and supplemented in 1578—and the island continued to receive imperial favour down to the time of the Greek Revolution, although its privileges had to be confirmed

[21] P. M. Kontoyiannis, Οἱ Προστατευόμενοι ('The "Protected Persons" '), off-print from the periodical 'Αθηνᾶ, vol. XXIX, Athens, 1917.

[22] K. Amantos, Οἱ προνομιακοί ὁρισμοί τοῦ Μουσουλμανισμοῦ ὑπέρ τῶν Χριστιανῶν, (*The privileges granted by Islam to Christians*) op. cit., pp. 119 ff. Cf. p. 38 above.

[23] Fr. Miklosich—Ios. Müller, *Acta et Diplomata graeca Medii aevi*, vol. V, pp. 77 ff. Franz Dölger, *Regesten der Kaiserurkunden des oströmischen Reiches*, IV, Munich, 1960, nos. 2412 and 2460. Cf. L. Vranousis, Χρονικὰ τῆς Μεσαιωνικῆς καί Τουρκοκρατουμένης 'Ηπείρου (*Chronicles of Epirus during the Byzantine and Ottoman periods*), Ioannina, 1962, pp. 54 ff.

at each Sultan's accession. The following account gives some idea of their extent:

> . . . They were given perfect freedom to build and consecrate churches (but without belfries); to carry the Cross and Icons in procession through the streets, and to celebrate all their religious services. There were to be no mosques except inside the fort. The Turks were forbidden to make converts, except when a man spontaneously came forward and expressed a wish to renounce his Christianity and did so in the presence of the Christian authorities. They were given permission to govern the island through five *deputati*, three Greeks and two Latins, whose decisions in respect of all Christian differences were not to be subject to appeal to the local Turkish courts. Their houses were to be free from taxes. They were only to pay the Capitation [Poll] Tax and 5,000 piastres Tree Tax. They were to dress as they pleased, and might wear spurs when on horseback. They further obtained the privilege of not paying any duty on goods arriving from Tchesmé [on the coast of Asia Minor opposite], if they could prove that duty had already been paid there; and the commerce of the island was to pass duty free through all the Custom Houses of the Black Sea.[24]

Similarly, the inhabitants of other Aegean islands received privileged treatment. Suleiman I granted certain liberties to Andros in 1539 and to the whole group of the Cyclades in 1565. Even more important for the future of these islands were the administrative and fiscal privileges accorded them by Murad III in 1579 and 1580. In 1522, when Rhodes fell to the Turks after a long resistance by the Knights of St. John, it and the neighbouring islands were given privileged status, which

---

[24] Taken from the English trans. of the Second Part of A. M. Vlasto's *History of Chios* (Χιακά), privately printed in London (Davy, Dryden Press) in 1913, pp. 68 ff. Prior to the Turkish conquest Chios had been, for over two hundred years, in the hands of the Genoese who had extensive trading interests in the Black Sea.

encouraged the concentration and increase of their population. They were declared to be Vakif or religious endowments and allotted to various Moslem foundations.

Athens, besides certain tax reliefs, enjoyed a special position, being placed under the *Kizlar Ağa*, the Chief Eunuch of the Palace. Particular privileges, again, were granted to Khimara in northern Epirus, to Malakasion on the Thessalian slope of Pindus, to Metsovon on the main westward pass across Pindus from Thessaly and the villages of the Zagorion district of Epirus, to the villages of Pelion, to Ambelakia in Thessaly, to the Mademokhoria in Chalcidice—the site of the famous iron-foundries—to Cydonia (Aivali) on the Aegean coast of Asia Minor and to other places. In some of the privileged regions and islands—Mani, Hydra, Spetsai, Psará—a kind of autonomy developed out of this situation.[25]

All these privileges made for a great diversity in the conditions of Greek subjection to Turkish rule. At the same time they also made it possible to organize an embryonic national existence and they brought into being the institutions by which alien rule was eventually broken.

[25] As will be seen in Chapter VI below (pp. 97–8), the Greek Dragomans of the Fleet had, at an even earlier date, acquired considerable authority in the Aegean Islands, which were also under the control of the *Kapudan Pasha*, the Turkish High Admiral.

IV

Self-governing Institutions

Under the general and local arrangements described in the previous chapter self-governing institutions gradually took shape.[1] "The first step to national liberty in modern Greece", Finlay wrote, "as in every country which has made any considerable advance in improving the condition of the mass of the inhabitants, was made in the municipalities."[2]

It is still premature to attempt a full description of the system of Greek self-government under the Turks, since the sources—or such of them as have survived—have not yet been adequately explored; but it is already clear that in this, as in most other respects, local development and practice varied from place to place. In some, self-governing institutions

---

[1] For works on the Greek commune see footnotes to the present chap. Also the following: N. Moschovakis, Τό ἐν Ἑλλάδι Δημόσιον Δίκαιον ἐπί Τουρκοκρατίας (*Public Law in Greece during the Period of Turkish Rule*), Athens, 1882. D. A. Zakythinos, 'La commune grecque. Les conditions historiques d'une décentralisation administrative', in *L'Hellénisme Contemporain*, 1948, pp. 295–310 reprinted in 'Η ἅλωσις τῆς Κωνσταντινουπόλεως καί ἡ Τουρκοκρατία (*The Capture of Constantinople and the Turkish Domination*), Athens, 1954, pp. 88–126. J. Visvizis, 'L'administration communale des Grecs pendant la domination turque', in *L'Hellénisme Contemporain*, 'Le cinq-centième anniversaire de la prise de Constantinople (29 Mai 1953)', pp. 217–38. N. Pantazopoulos, 'Öffentlich—rechtliche Institutionen der Griechen während der türkischen Herrschaft', in *Internationalrechtliche und Staatsrechtliche Abhandlungen, Festschrift W. Schätzel*, Düsseldorf, 1960, pp. 365 ff., and 'Community Laws and Customs of Western Macedonia under Ottoman Rule', in *Balkan Studies*, vol. II (1961), pp. 1–22. Ap. Vakalopoulos, Ἱστορία τοῦ Νέου Ἑλληνισμοῦ (*History of the Modern Greeks*), vol. II, Salonica, 1964, pp. 279–314.

[2] George Finlay, *History of Greece*, op. cit., vol. V, p. 287.

remained in an undeveloped state; in others, they attained a complete and settled shape. although only within narrow territorial limits; in others again, they developed widely and formed a complete system of federal organization. A comparative study is needed with similar developments among other nationalities formerly under Ottoman rule.

The chief self-governing institution was the Commune (κοινότης).[3] This constituted a legal entity, independent of the administration of the ruling power, but nevertheless enjoying its toleration. Every town or village, other than those which belonged to feudal estates, might combine to form a commune. In very rare instances a single town formed part of two communes, as in Naxos where we have 'the Castle Commune' (κοινὸν τοῦ Κάστρου) and 'the Town Commune' (κοινὸν τοῦ Μπούργου); conversely, a number of villages might form a single commune, their inhabitants all being members of the commune insofar as they all paid poll-tax. In certain circumstances only the native-born enjoyed the right of membership and immigrants were excluded, that is to say, all inhabitants who for any reason had come as casual settlers to the village concerned.

The institution of the Commune flourished in the Cyclades from the seventeenth century onwards. In the case of the Commune of Mykonos the actual deed establishing the Commune in 1615 has been preserved, but substantial evidence also survives with regard to the other islands. In these the commune as a legal unit was administered by officers termed variously Commissioners ('Επίτροποι), Elders (Δημογέροντες), Archons ("Αρχοντες) or Notables (Πρωεστῶτες) or by a Turkish Kocabaşı (Kodjabashi or Headman). The number of these varied but their term of office was mostly for one year. They were elected, or in rare cases appointed, by the agents of the Ottoman authority. They were chosen by the local population, gathered with the clergy in general assembly (termed in the

[3] Cf. 'La ville balkanique. XVe–XIXe siècles', *Studia Balcanica* 3, Sofia, 1970.

documents κοινὴ μαζωξις).[4] Sometimes this assembly was more limited in its composition. In the islands of Hydra and Spetsai, from the year 1803 and most probably from an earlier date, only the shipowners and ships' captains had the right of election. Elsewhere, as on the island of Psará, the 'elders' were indirectly chosen by a body of 'electors'. Originally all inhabitants of the commune were eligible for election, but in some communes, as in Athens and Andros, the right to stand was confined to members of the highest class of society.

The powers of communal officers were very wide. They covered the whole management of communal affairs, the collection and sub-allocation of taxes, the education and health services and so on. 'Commissioners' had also the duty of market inspection as well as a limited judicial authority. In discharging these duties the communal authorities were assisted by other officers, the Clerk to the Commune (Καγκελλάριος or Καντζιλλιέρης), the Overseer ('Επιστάτης), the Accountants (Λογαριαστάδες) and others. From the eighteenth century onwards we meet with communal envoys to the Ottoman Government bearing such titles as 'Επιτροπικοί, Προκουρατόροι or, in Turkish, Kapukehaya.[5]

This general pattern of organization prevailed, with some exceptions, throughout all the communes of Turkish-occupied

[4] P. Zerlentis, Σύστασις τοῦ κοινοῦ τῶν Μυκονίων (Constitution of the Commune of Myconos), Hermoupolis, 1924. A. Sigalas, 'Η πατέντα τῶν Κοτζαμπάσηδων ('The Patent of the Kodjabashis'), in 'Ημερολόγιον Μεγάλης 'Ελλάδος (Almanac of Great Greece), 1930, pp. 403–21, and 'Ανέκδοτα ἔγγραφα ἀφορῶντα εἰς τὴν ἐκλογὴν τῶν Κοτζαμπάσηδων (Unedited Documents relating to the Election of the Kodjabashis'), in 'Ελληνικά, vol. III (1930), pp. 69–88. J. Visvizis, Δικαστικαὶ ἀποφάσεις τοῦ 17ου αἰῶνος ἐκ τῆς νήσου Μυκόνου (Judgments of the seventeenth Century from the Island of Naxos), in 'Επετηρὶς τοῦ 'Αρχείου τῆς 'Ιστορίας τοῦ 'Ελληνικοῦ Δικαίου τῆς 'Ακαδημίας 'Αθηνῶν (Annual of the Archives of the History of Greek Law, Academy of Athens), vol. VII (1956), pp. 21–154.

[5] A. Sigalas, 'Επιστολαὶ τῶν ἐν Κωνσταντινουπόλει Καπουκεχαγιάδων τῆς Σύρου ἐπί Τουρκοκρατίας ('Letters of the Kapukehaya of Syros in Constantinople under Turkish Domination'), in 'Ελληνικά, vol. II (1929), pp. 11–96. The term Kapukehaya was generally used for the political and diplomatic agents at Constantinople of high provincial dignitaries, e.g. Provincial Governors (Valis) and the Princes of Wallachia and Moldavia.

Greece. In the Morea self-government reached a particularly advanced stage under the second Turkish occupation (1715–1821); it was in fact in this region that the trend towards autonomy had found its earliest expression. Owing to the privileges accorded it by the Byzantine Emperors and the Despots of the Peloponnese[6], Monemvasia enjoyed administrative liberties during the fourteenth and fifteenth centuries. The people of Mani may even have possessed their own chief appointed by the Byzantine Governor of the Peloponnese since as far back as the tenth century, and paid taxes (known as Πάκτα) which were sub-allocated by him.[7] Frankish and Venetian rule had further strengthened the movement towards emancipation. The composers of the Chronicle of the Morea[8] know the term Προεστοί (i.e. Notables). In 1495 we find a 'Πρωτόγερος (Chief Elder) of the Morea' representing the Commune of Patras, in 1509 a Πρωτόγερος τῆς ἐκλαμπροτάτης αὐθεντίας ('Chief Elder of the Most Illustrious Signory', i.e. Venice) at Nauplia[9], and in a document dated 1572 there is mention of Archons of the district of Diakopton ("Αρχοντες τῶν μαχαλάδων) and of a commune (Κοινότης) there.[10]

Under the second Turkish occupation the Morea obtained a complete system of self-administration functioning parallel

[6] The Despotate of the Peloponnese (1348–1460) was established as a Byzantine imperial principality for the government of Byzantine possessions in the Morea reconquered from the Latins. It fell to the Turks seven years later than Byzantium itself.

[7] Cf. D. A. Zakythinos, Le Despotat grec de Morée, vol. II, Athens, 1953, pp. 7 ff., 116 ff.

[8] The Chronicle of Morea is a history of the Latin occupation of the Peloponnese and other Greek lands, written in popular Greek and in verse early in the fourteenth century. Versions also exist in medieval French, Aragonese and Italian. On this and other problems see the edition and trans. by the American scholar J. Schmitt, The Chronicle of Morea. Τό Χρονικὸν τοῦ Μορέως, London, 1904. An English trans. has been made by Harold E. Lurier, Crusaders as Conquerors: the Chronicle of Morea, New York—London, 1964. Cf. H.-G. Beck, Geschichte der byzantinischen Volksliteratur, Byzantinisches Handbuch, Pt. III, vol. III, Munich, 1971, pp. 157 ff.

[9] D. A. Zakythinos, Le Despotat grec de Morée, vol II, p. 122.

[10] N. A. Bees, Χαρτία τοῦ Κλαβαζοῦ ('Documents of Klavazos'), in Πελοποννησιακά, vol. I (1956), pp. 446, 452.

with the Turkish ruling authority and distinguished in three successive grades—the lowest grade dealing with autonomous towns and villages, a middle grade corresponding to the provincial organization and the highest grade covering the region as a whole. The elders and notables, one or more from each village, designated the representatives at provincial level (μωραγιὰν βιλαετλῆδες) and these, coming together in a General Assembly, elected the two representatives (μωραγιαννῆδες) who resided at the headquarters of the Turkish Governor of the Morea. Their election was ratified by imperial Firman. The Morea had the right to communicate direct with the Porte through its own representatives who were called *Vekils* (in Greek Βεκιλῆδες). These institutions formed the germ of the Messenian, later the Peloponnesian, Senate (Γερουσία) of the first years of the Revolution.[11]

The system of self-government was also highly developed in Epirus, Thessaly and Macedonia. Besides the flourishing town of Ioannina the mountain districts of Pindus and its offshoots—of cardinal importance as passages through the main range and as highways for nomadic populations—developed communal institutions. The region known as Zagori or Zagorokhoria, the mountain country of the Agrapha and the villages of Malakasi and the important village of Metsovon, on the way from Thessaly to Epirus, kept their institutions intact right up to the last years of Turkish rule. Tradition and later documents based on it take this autonomy back to the fifteenth century; we can speak of it with full assurance in the seventeenth century. From this period up to the year 1868 the Commune of Zagorokhoria formed a federation of forty-six villages (κοινὸν τῶν Ζαγορησίων). Documents of 1828 and 1832 bear witness to an attempt to codify local custom and to the existence of an ordinance, peculiar to the region, regulating dowries.[12]

[11] For further particulars of self-government in the Morea see M. Sakellariou, Ἡ Πελοπόννησος κατὰ τὴν δευτέραν Τουρκοκρατίαν (*The Peloponnese under the Second Turkish Occupation*), Athens, 1939, pp. 87 ff.

[12] Zagori, Zagoria or Zagorokhoria is a district in the north of the Greek province of Epirus, between Konitsa and Metsovon, north of Ioannina. Cf.

In eastern Thessaly we have the communes of Pelion. Their most flourishing period begins in the seventeenth century, but in general their shape shows to a greater extent the influence of the Turkish system of land-tenure and of local economic development. From the mid-eighteenth century Pelion was already emerging as a centre of educational and intellectual revival.[13] Among the communes of eastern Thessaly a distinctive place is held by Ambelakia, on the slopes of Ossa above the Vale of Tempe. According to Beaujour's *Tableau du Commerce de la Grèce (1800)*, "Ambelakia, by its activity, appears rather a borough of Holland than a village of Turkey. This village spreads, by its industry, movement and life, over the surrounding country, and gives birth to an immense commerce, which unites Germany to Greece by a thousand threads . . .".[14] Settled in the seventeenth century, it reached its peak in the eighteenth and presented a complete model of a federative commune. Shortly before 1780, its inhabitants formed a large textile and dyeing company on a co-operative basis. As David Urquhart writes:

> . . . by the simplicity and honesty, not the science of its system, it reads a lesson to commercial associations and holds up an example unparalleled in the commercial history of Europe of a joint stock company, ably and economically and successfully administered, in which the interests of industry and capital were long equally represented.[15]

And again:

> To give a just idea of the prosperity of Ambelakia, it would be

---

P. Vizoukides, 'Ηπειρωτικῶν θεσμίων ἔρευνα (Enquiry into Epirote Institutions), in 'Ηπειρωτικὰ Χρονικά, vol. II (1927), pp. 5 ff.

[13] N. Pantazopoulos, Κοινοτικὸς Βίος εἰς τὴν Θετταλομαγνησίαν ἐπὶ Τουρκοκρατίας ('Communal Life in Thessalomagnesia under Turkish Rule'), in 'Επιστημονικὴ 'Επετηρὶς τῆς Σχολῆς Νομικῶν καί Οἰκονομικῶν 'Επιστημῶν τοῦ Πανεπιστημίου Θεσσαλονίκης (*Scientific Yearbook of the School of Legal and Economic Studies of the University of Thessalonica*), Salonica, 1967.

[14] Félix Beaujour, *Tableau du commerce de la Grèce, formé d'après une année moyenne, depuis 1787 jusqu'en 1797*, vol I, Paris, 1800, p. 272.

[15] David Urquhart, *Turkey and its Resources*, London, 1833, p. 53.

necessary to describe the poverty and depression of the surrounding country, because it is by the contrast alone of the state from which it had emerged, and the evils it had escaped, that the energies and institutions which had caused its prosperity can be duly appreciated. Here were to be seen springing again [Urquhart quotes once more from Beaujour] "grand and liberal ideas, on a soil devoted for twenty centuries to slavery; here the ancient Greek character arose, in its early energy, amidst the torrents and caverns of Pelion [actually, Ossa] and, to sum up the whole, here one might see the talents and virtues of ancient Greece born again in a corner of modern Turkey".[16]

In the shaping of self-governing institutions under Turkish rule Salonica was a special case. This great city had enjoyed extensive privileges for centuries and these had been further strengthened by the conditions prevailing during the disturbed times of the Palaeologi. Under the brief first Turkish occupation (1387 and 1394–1402/3) the 'Curators of the Commune' (τῶν κοινῶν φροντίσται) or Heads of the Commune (προϊστάμενοι τῶν κοινῶν), that is, the local notables, played a certain leading part. The Venetians during their own tenure of the city, which was likewise brief (1423–30), promised to respect its ancient rights. The central organ of self-government was the Senate (Γερουσία or Σύγκλητος), an aristocratic body with a membership of twelve. When, in 1430, Salonica finally returned to Ottoman rule, Murad II appears to have granted it a certain degree of liberty. At any rate, from a document of 1502 it is clear that a corporation of twelve, comprising clergy and laity, continued to exist.[17] A council of twelve is also to be found

[16] Ibid., p. 52. On Ambelakia cf. also Elias Gheorgiou, Ἱστορία καὶ Συνεταιρισμὸς τῶν Ἀμπελακίων (The History and the Co-operative of Ambelakia), Athens, 1951.

[17] O. Tafrali, Thessalonique au XIVᵉ siècle, Paris, 1913, pp. 66 ff. Ap. Vakalopoulos, Συμβολὴ στὴν Ἱστορίαν τῆς Θεσσαλονίκης ἐπὶ Βενετοκρατίας (1423–1430) ('Contribution to the History of Thessalonica under Venetian Domination 1423–30'), in Τόμος Κωνσταντίνου Ἀρμενοπούλου ἐπὶ τῇ ἑξακοσιετηρίδι τῆς Ἑξαβίβλου αὐτοῦ (1345–1945), (Volume in honour of Constantine Harmenopoulos

in another Macedonian town, namely Serres, elected (in 1613) by a 'Grand Assembly' (μεγίστη σύνοδος) of the people and responsible for the management of 'the common expenditure of the Castle and the Town'.[18] Further north, the town of Melenikon (now Melnik, in Bulgaria, in the hills east of the Strymon valley) had an aristocratic system of communal government: its constitution was printed in Vienna in 1813 and is a most valuable text for the study of local government.[19]

Others of the larger towns in Macedonia—Veroia, Kozani, Siatista, Kastoria, Monastir (Bitola)—all had flourishing communes. In Khalkidiki a special type of government grew up in the Mademokhoria, a group of villages which developed into the iron-mining centre of Siderokapsa (the Byzantine Siderokausia). A Turkish document, written between the years 1451 and 1478/9, already refers to their organization[20] and Pierre Belon du Mans, in the middle of the sixteenth century, gives an important account of them.[21] In the years of Ottoman decline the industry was organized on a co-operative basis out of which there subsequently grew and flourished communal institutions. According to Urquhart:

A central committee was formed of deputies from the twelve 'boroughs'. Each subject of discussion was debated by the different municipalities separately; if the whole committee did not agree, the members returned again to the municipal

---

on the 600th Anniversary of his Hexabiblos) Salonica, 1952, pp. 127–49. Also by the same A History of Thessaloniki, trans. by T. F. Carney, Salonica, 1963.

[18] Dem. Ghinis, Περίγραμμα τοῦ Μεταβυζαντινοῦ Δικαίου, op. cit., p. 117 (nos. 108 and 109).

[19] P. Pennas, Τό κοινὸν Μελενίκου καὶ τὸ Σύστημα διοικήσεώς του (The Commune of Melenikon and its Constitution), Athens, 1946. Th. N. Vlachos, Die Geschichte der byzantinischen Stadt Melenikon, Ἑταιρεία Μακεδονικῶν Σπουδῶν. Ἵδρυμα Μελετῶν Χερσονήσου τοῦ Αἵμου 112, Salonica, 1969.

[20] N. Beldiceanu, Les actes des premiers sultans conservés dans les manuscrits turcs de la Bibliothèque Nationale à Paris, vol. II, Paris—The Hague, 1964, pp. 183 ff.

[21] Pierre Belon du Mans, Les observations de plusieurs singularitez et choses memorables, trouvées en Grèce, Asie, Iudée, Egypte, Arabie, et autres pays estranges, Paris, 1588, Bk. I, Chaps. XLIX et seq., pp. 99ff.

bodies, to re-argue the question, as it was necessary for them to be unanimous upon every measure. To secure this unanimity, no decision was considered valid without the seal of the committee; and that seal was formed of twelve compartments, one of which was entrusted to each municipality. These portions had to be united before the seal could be used. . . .[22]

Alexis de Tocqueville said that "it is man who makes kingdoms and creates republics; the commune seems to come directly from the hands of God". It seems to come directly from the hands of God because it is the most spontaneous creation of man. But, in the last resort, "it was the spirit of resistance to oppression, of mutual aid, of brotherhood, which had created the communes".[23] The Greek commune came to birth under the Conquest on the fringe, as it were, of the Turkish administration, in a supreme effort by the people to ensure their religious and national survival. It developed and deepened as the struggle to mitigate their slavery gained ground. For the Greeks of the Turkish period the commune was not simply an embryonic social and political organism, it was also a means of self-preservation.

The origin of Greek communal institutions is a subject of scholarly dispute. In a study published in 1846 Paparrhegopoulos asserted that the origin of the communes goes back "to the autonomy or self-administration of the Greek cities in Roman imperial times" and that "the intervening thousand years necessarily brought many changes, but the traditions and practices of self-government were preserved and strengthened in particular by the special circumstances of Byzantine and Ottoman rule".[24] A less extreme view was advanced by the

[22] D. Urquhart, op. cit., pp. 64 ff.

[23] Ch. Petit—Dutaillis, *Les communes françaises. Caractères et évolution des origines au XVIIIᵉ siècle*, Paris, 1947.

[24] Constantine Paparrhegopoulos, Ῥωμαίων πολίτευμα πρὸς τὴν Ἑλλάδα (*The Roman form of government in Greece*), first published, 1846, reproduced in Ἱστορικαὶ Πραγματεῖαι (*Historical Studies*), Athens, 1858, pp. 188–225. Passage quoted p. 223.

same historian in his *History of the Greek Nation*[25], and in recent times a Greek jurist, Aristides Vrekosses, has rallied to the older historian's theory and supported it with new arguments.[26]

According to others the commune was of Byzantine origin. Moschovakis, however, maintains that "the origin of the communes of Turkish times is not to be sought either in the city-states of antiquity or in the institutions of the Roman imperial age or at a later period when all independence had vanished and there remained only a certain degree of internal autonomy, since we find neither any external resemblance nor any inner link between ourselves and any of these". This scholar concludes that the communes are "of purely Byzantine origin", that they were the result of the weakening of the central government, that they were not the fruit of formal legislative action and, finally, that those organs of self-government which did come into existence in Byzantine times were nothing more or less than these same communes of the Turkish period "which were either fully formed already or were continually adapted to meet new needs but which always bore the same character, so that it is no longer possible to ignore their external and internal continuity and their identity from, certainly, the ninth century down to our own great Revolution". For Moschovakis, the Greek commune has its roots in Byzantine practice, to be exact in that of the Macedonian dynasty (867–1057) who, in their struggle against the great landowners, allowed the communes a corporate existence in the eyes of the law. The Turkish fiscal system subsequently made use of these regional liberties for the better collection and allocation of taxes.[27]

Yet a third theory distinguishes the Greek commune of Turkish times from its classical or Byzantine predecessors.

[25] Constantine Paparrhegopoulos, Ἰστορία τοῦ Ἑλληνικοῦ Ἔθνους (*History of the Greek Nation*), vol. V, 2; new ed., Athens, 1930, pp. 114 ff.

[26] A. Vrekosses, Τά Ἑλληνικὰ κοινὰ τῶν Ῥωμαϊκῶν χρόνων ('The Greek Communes of Roman Times'), in the Ἐπιστημονικὴ Ἐπετηρὶς τῆς Ἑταιρείας Διοικητικῶν Μελετῶν (*Scientific Yearbook of the Society for Administrative Studies*), Athens, 1934.

[27] N. Moschovakis, op. cit., pp. 71 ff.

According to this interpretation the regional decentralization of the Turkish period owed its birth and development to the special conditions of foreign rule. Urquhart, the British diplomatist who was among the first to study the question, observes: "The rayas owe these [municipal] institutions to the Turkish dominion." It was above all the requirements of financial administration which encouraged decentralization. "The collection of tribute was the origin, and has ever continued to be the bond and end, of the municipal bodies and led to their uniform establishment throughout the country, wherever it submitted unconditionally."[28] This view has since been taken up by Greek scholars and jurists, by S. Antoniades in 1842 and by P. Argyropoulos in 1843.[29]

This debate, then, seems to lead to the conclusion that in its origins the commune probably goes back to the Byzantine era, but I have tried to show that it is a mistake to look for an exact prototype of the commune of Turkish times in any Byzantine institution, since we have in fact to deal not with a single form of commune but with a number of different forms and it follows that these must derive from different sources of historical tradition.

The simpler forms of commune under Turkish rule—those which never reached maturity and those of which no details are known, since there is no written or traditional record of their recognition by the Turkish conquerors—must however be referred back to a definite Byzantine model, namely the 'village commune' (κοινότης χωρίου) and the 'village group' (ὁμὰς τοῦ χωρίου) which existed for the purpose of tax collection. The small freehold farmers who belonged to these bodies were

[28] D. Urquhart, op. cit., pp. 19, 23.

[29] Spyridon Antoniades, Τά Δημοτικά, ἤτοι βιβλίον περιέχον τὸν δημοτικὸν νόμον ἐξηγημένον, μετάφρασιν τῆς θεωρίας τοῦ Δημοτικοῦ Δικαίου, τὰς ἐπὶ Τουρκοκρατίας, Δημοκρατίας καί ἐπί Κυβερνήτου δημοτικὰς θεσμοθεσίας (Communal Administration: comprising an exposition of Communal Law, a translation of the Theory of Public Law, and a description of Communal Legislation under Turkish Rule, under the Republic, and under the Presidency [of Capodistria]), Athens, 1842. Pericles Argyropoulos Δημοτικὴ διοίκησις ἐν Ἑλλάδι (Communal Administration in Greece), Athens, 1843.

jointly responsible to the State for the payment of taxes.[30] Within these rural groups and because of these fiscal obligations there appeared very early on men of probity or power who took the initiative in communal affairs. In a hagiological text dating from the end of the eighth century there is mention of the 'headmen of the village' ($\pi\rho\hat{\omega}\tau o\iota \tau o\hat{\upsilon} \chi\omega\rho\dot{\iota}o\upsilon$).[31] In more recent documents of 1338, 1341, 1355 and 1404, there occurs the title, also familiar later, of 'chief elder' ($\pi\rho\omega\tau\dot{o}\gamma\epsilon\rho o\varsigma$).[32] There can be no doubt that the Turkish conqueror, having taken over his Byzantine predecessor's methods of government and having introduced the system of land apportionment, was forced to tolerate these rural communes.

Elsewhere the communes of the Turkish period had a different origin. Byzantium had been obliged to accept various degrees of limited autonomy both for districts and for individual towns and it was in these that the institutions of self-government proper were forged. It was in this way that the independent administration of Venice had originally come into being, to develop later into a sovereign state; so also did those of the cities of the Dalmatian seaboard. In the ninth century the Byzantine colony of Cherson in the Crimea was governed by a Chief Citizen ($\pi\rho\omega\tau o\pi o\lambda\dot{\iota}\tau\eta\varsigma$ or $\Pi\rho\omega\tau\epsilon\dot{\upsilon}\omega\nu$), assisted by a local Council, the City Fathers ($\pi\alpha\tau\dot{\epsilon}\rho\epsilon\varsigma \tau\hat{\eta}\varsigma \pi\dot{o}\lambda\epsilon\omega\varsigma$).[33] Later on, from the twelfth century, after the central government had weakened there ensued a general relaxation of provincial government and as a result certain districts and towns came to

[30] G. Ostrogorsky, 'Die ländliche Steuergemeinde des byzantinischen Reiches im X. Jahrhundert', in *Vierteljahrschrift für Sozial-und Wirtschaftsgeschichte*, vol. XX (1927, pp. 1–108 and 'La commune rurale byzantine', in *Byzantion*, vol. XXXII (1962), pp. 139–66. Paul Lemerle, 'Esquisse pour une histoire agraire de Byzance: les sources et les problèmes', in *Revue Historique*, Janvier—Mars 1958, pp. 49 ff.

[31] M. H. Fourmy and M. Leroy, 'La Vie de S. Philarète', in *Byzantion*, vol. IX (1934), p. 137.

[32] N. Oikonomides, Actes de Dionysiou, édition diplomatique, *Archives de l'Athos*, IV, Paris, 1968, pp. 169, 188.

[33] Georges Bratianu, *Privilèges et franchises municipales dans l'Empire byzantin*, Paris—Bucarest, 1936, pp. 66ff., 73 ff.

acquire *de jure* or *de facto* liberties. Thus, Salonica, as we have seen, enjoyed a wide liberty of self-government from the earliest times, and Athens was the subject of a petition against interference by the provincial authorities. Indeed, the provincial governor (Πραίτωρ) was actually forbidden to enter the city. Equally extensive privileges were granted to Monemvasia and to Ioannina. By a charter of the year 1319 the emperor Andronicus II recognized the rights of the Church and of the citizens of Ioannina to their landed properties and laid down that officials known as 'Goodmen' (᾽Ανθρωποι καλοί), elected by the citizens, should try certain civil offences. As has been noted earlier, it is established that this decree served as a basis for Sinan Pasha's later ruling.[34] Other flourishing communes of the Turkish period no doubt owed their beginnings to similar causes.

The Greek communes of Turkish times did not derive from classical models either. They were the product of necessity and the natural consequence of the conqueror's easygoing ways and administrative deficiencies; but while the commune, being Byzantine in origin, has no direct connection with classical models, the whole shape of its subsequent development follows from a purely Greek line of thought and shows a Greek spirit. In a period of national suppression the Greek people, taking as their basis the tax-collecting machinery of their medieval empire, fashioned on their own, without any outside intervention, without even any initiative on the part of their own intellectual or spiritual leaders, democratic institutions the conception and spirit of which brings them nearer than their medieval models to the sources of classical tradition.

The self-governing institutions of Turkish times had a very great influence on the fortunes of modern Greece, which through its communal organisations contrived to mitigate its sufferings under foreign rule. Further, it created the elementary preconditions of political life, developed welfare and educational services, afforded practice in the art of politics, promoted the

[34] See above, pp. 38 ff.

growth of political awareness and in many different ways led on towards freedom and national independence. In the years of the Revolution, and in those immediately following, the machinery and the personnel of government were used by the leaders of the struggle. On this point it has been well said that "the Revolution of 1821 presents us with a political system and political institutions. Some of these, certainly, are modelled on the institutions of local self-government. The Directorate of Achaea, the Messenian Senate, the provincial Inspectorates (ἐφορίαι) and the local sub-inspectorates in each commune, these formed the hierarchy of three grades in Peloponnesian self-government. The contribution of these political institutions was considerable; and they were entirely the fruit of local self-government."[35]

[35] Cf. M. Sakellariou, op. cit., p. 98.

V

Fighting Formations of the Resistance

In the towns, islands and villages the Greek people laid the foundations of a new political life. In the mountains and the by-ways they prepared the military instruments of resistance and liberation. The fighting formations in which the subject people were organized were those of the Armatoles and Klephts.[1]

The *Armatoles* were originally bodies of local Christian irregulars whom the conquerors used for the suppression of banditry, for local security and for guarding the passes. Some derive the word from the Italian *armato* or *armatore* and from its diminutive *armatulo*. A more likely derivation is from the Greek

[1] Constantine Sathas, Ἕλληνες Στρατιῶται ἐν τῇ Δύσει καί ἡ ἀναγέννησις τῆς Ἑλληνικῆς τακτικῆς ('Greek Stradioti in the West and the Rebirth of Greek Military Science'), reprinted from 'Εστία, XIX, Athens, 1885. D. G. Kambouroglou, 'Αρματολοί καὶ κλέφτες (*Armatoles and Klephts*), Athens, 1916. T. Kandilores, Ὁ 'Αρματολισμός τῆς Πελοποννήσου (*The Armatoles of the Peloponnese*), Athens, 1924. G. Vlachoyiannis, Οἱ κλέφτες τοῦ Μοριᾶ. Μελέτη ἱστορικὴ ἀπὸ νέες πηγὲς βγαλμένη, 1715–1820 (*The Klephts of the Morea. A Historical Study from new Sources, 1715–1820*), Athens, 1935. J. Vasdravelles, Αρματολοί καὶ κλέφτες εἰς τήν Μακεδονίαν (*Armatoles and Klephts in Macedonia*), 2nd ed. Salonica, 1970. Cf. Ap. Vakalopoulos, 'Ιστορία τοῦ Νέου Ἑλληνισμοῦ, vol. II, pp. 314 ff. Milan Vasić, 'Die Martolosen im osmanischen Reich', in *Zeitschrift für Balkanologie*, vol. II (1964), pp. 172–89.

Mention should be made of certain Turkish publications: Robert Anhegger, *Martoloslar Hakkında*, Istanbul, 1940–42 (Cf. J. Vasdravelles, op. cit. pp. 9 ff.). Cengiz Orhonlu, *Osmanli Imparatorlugunda Derbend Teşkilati* (*The Organisation of the Defence of the Passes under the Ottoman Empire*), Istanbul, 1967. An abr. in Greek of this has been pub. by the Ἵδρυμα Μελετῶν Χερσονήσου τοῦ Αἵμου (Institute for Balkan Studies) in their Δελτίον Τουρκικῆς Βιβλιογραφίας (*Bulletin of Turkish Bibliography*), Year 10, Fasc. 10, Salonica, 1970.

word ἀρματολό(γ)ος (man-at-arms): there is evidence in Byzantine times of the use of the word ἀρμᾶτος in this sense. In Turkish the armatole is called *martolos* or *martoloz* and the officer commanding armatoles is called *martolozbaşı*. Earlier terms found in Venetian sources are *martalosi*, *martelosi* and *martolosi*. Johannes Leunclavius (Löwenklau) in the sixteenth century, and later Von Hammer, regard these as being of Turkish or Hungarian origin, but it seems more likely that the Turkish or Hungarian word was derived from the Greek than vice versa.[2]

The practice of employing armatole forces flourished from the fifteenth to the eighteenth century and was widespread throughout the European provinces of the Ottoman Empire. Its origin has even been sought in Asia Minor under the earliest Ottoman Sultans in the fourteenth century. In Europe the earliest mentions of it are found between 1421 and 1438. Christian armatoles were employed at a very early date to guard mountain passes and frontiers. By the sixteenth century their presence is recorded on the Danube at Belgrade, Smederevo and Vidin as well as in Albania, Epirus, Macedonia and Bosnia. Venetian documents from 1503 onwards speak of bandits who were ravaging the countryside and storming guard-posts and were regarded as independent princelings. Bodies of Greek *stradiotti* were employed by the authorities against these freebooters.[3] The sources clearly distinguish between these latter and the Greek regular troops in Venetian service whose leaders came from well-known Peloponnesian and other families and who served Venice not only against the Turks but also against marauding elements in Dalamatia, Illyria and Epirus. It seems clear that out of these early protective frontier forces there later developed the fully formed armatole bodies of later times.

While the exact date and place of the earliest appearance of armatoles cannot be fixed, their military purpose from the first

[2] See Ernst Weber, 'Die Geburt einer Grossmacht—Die Osmanen . . .', op. cit., p. 104. M. Vasić, op. cit., accepts the Greek derivation of the word.
[3] Constantine Sathas, *Documents inédits relatifs à l'histoire de la Grèce au Moyen Âge*, vols. VII, pp. 73, 83 ff. and VIII, p. 407 ff.

is clear. It was the defence of strategically sensitive or important points and the suppression of banditry by the use of local man-power. The force was certainly on a well-established basis by at latest the sixteenth century[4] and in the Turkish records of Macedonia in the seventeenth century we find interesting material on its working in its mature form. Thus the following entry occurs in the archives of Veroia under the date 1 May 1627. On that day "the Veroia (Berrhoea) armatoles Kokkinos, George Doukas and others, when bringing in the taxpayer Prodromos, a native of the village of Grammatikon in the Kaza of Ostrovo, deposed as follows: The said Prodromos had for some time past been going round the villages with other like delinquents and had committed a great many robberies and murders and had pillaged various properties. We have now effected his arrest in Naoussa and request that the case be examined and justice done. . . .[5] It is clear from the above that the armatoles of Macedonia were recognized by the Government and that their task was the pursuit of bandits, whom they then handed over to the Turkish authorities. The other aspect of their work is illustrated by the action of the Cadi of Veroia in the year 1628 by which Greek armatoles, under Dimos and Nikos, were appointed to guard the pass of Veroia near the village of Megalos Ayiannis.[6]

Other documents provide information which gives us a still clearer and fuller view of the armatole forces. More particularly, we may note here an imperial Firman of 1699 to the officer administering the Sanjak of Salonica. It contains *inter alia* the following:

> . . . for the guarding and defence of the hazardous and dangerous parts of the passes and bridges leading from

---

[4] Constantine Paparrhegopoulos, op. cit., vol. V, 2, pp. 134 ff., cites the names of armatoles in western Greece as the first individual mentions known to him. These are from the end of the sixteenth century. At the same time he agrees that the armatole service must have been formally established earlier, although he places it as late as the reign of Süleyman I (1520–66).

[5] J. Vasdravelles, Ἀρματολοὶ καὶ Κλέφτες pp. 32, and 85 ff.

[6] Ibid., pp. 33ff., 87.

Salonica to Larisa, Ioannina, Servia [i.e. the Macedonian town of that name], Grevena, Yiannitsa, Edessa (formerly Vodena), Doiran, Stromnitsa (Strumitsa), Monastir (Bitola), Perlepen (Prilep), Velessa [now Titov Veles] and for the safety and peace of mind of merchants passing through, there were employed, from among picked men of the Vilayet, armatoles whose pay was charged to the inhabitants and Raya of the Vilayet; and for the collection of their pay an allocation was made to each of the villages and the list which was made of these allocations was given into their hands. When, however, these men went round from village to village in numerous bands collecting their dues, they were not content with this collection but exacted by force and contrary to all right—two, three, five or six *grosia* as a transit tax on the baggage and waggons of the merchants, poor folk and Raya which came through the passes and over the bridges under their guard. It is impossible to describe these extortions and excesses. . . .[7]

It is worth noting that the armatoles who were charged with the guarding of bridges and passes are defined as 'local notables'; that the local population paid their wages and that transit dues were exacted. The system of letting, as it were, the mountain passes and charging tolls was very widespread in the Morea also.[8]

In the course of time the armatole districts were organized regionally. Pouqueville records that mainland and northern Greece contained originally fourteen armatole districts (ἀρματολίκια) or Captaincies (καπετανᾶτα).[9] His table seems

---

[7] Ibid., pp. 37ff., 99ff.

[8] M. Sakellariou, Ἡ Πελοπόννησος κατὰ τὴν δευτέραν Τουρκοκρατίαν, op. cit., Chap. IV, pp. 143 ff.

[9] F. C. H. L. Pouqueville, *Histoire de la Régénération de la Grèce*, vol. I, Paris, 1824, p. 53. A list drawn up in 1835 gives a detailed description of "the most notable Captaincies" of northern Greece with the names of the Captains at their head and the number of men in each. See Kosmas Thesprotos and Athanasios Psalidas, Γεωγραφία ᾿Αλβανίας καί ῾Ηπείρου (*Geography of Albania and Epirus*), Ioannina, 1964, p. 88.

incomplete, but the number of regions was altered from time to time. The very extensive development of the armatole system in western Macedonia was due to the great highway, mainly following the line of the Roman Via Egnatia, which passed through this part of the country to the Adriatic coast. The armatole districts were divided into smaller areas called *kolia* (κόλια). Originally, the commanders or Captains (καπετάνιοι) were appointed for a definite term, but in time the service became virtually hereditary and there thus developed a peculiar form of military aristocracy. Violent disputes arose between the various armatole bodies and obedience to the ruling power was lax.

Folksongs have preserved the names of some famous armatoles of Turkish times and described their perilous and active lives. Very important material for the history of the armatoles is also supplied by the *Military Recollections* (Στρατιωτικὰ Ἐνθυμήματα) of Nicholas Kasomoules who was born about 1797 and died in 1871. He recalls as the 'oldest' and 'most famous' of the armatoles Megdanis. This man flourished about the middle of the seventeenth century and:

> drove the Ottomans from all the mountain districts of western Thessaly and Macedonia (round Kastoria, Vodena, Veroia, Servia and the Thessalian Trikala) as far as the Pindus range and routed them in a number of battles. Then the Turks, having failed to overcome him after fighting him for a long time, turned to crafty promises, which perhaps flattered his vanity, and, either for the peace and quiet of the local Christian population or urged by greater hopes of a more prosperous life (since the Turks promised to share their authority with him in the mountain districts), he started to parley with them. Finally, as a result of negotiations between the Vizir of Trikala and himself and his recognition by all the local Turkish dignitaries as the authority over the mountain region, he agreed:
>
> *1.* that the Turks should not enter the districts under his charge;

2. that the population of those districts should send their taxes, when collected, and the poll-tax through the notables of each village to the appropriate Turkish authorities;

3. that the armatoles under his command should remain exempt from all tax and poll-tax.

After making a ceremonial entry into Trikala, the seat of the Vizir, to make his submission and having been thus formally received, he was handed by the Cadi his commission for the different districts and the robe of honour which confirmed his appointment. He then left with ceremony and returned to his territories as a man highly honoured.

Megdanis, however, met with a tragic end, being killed by the Turks in 1700[10]. From every point of view the history of this armatole is most instructive.[11]

By a Firman of 1721 the armatole force was officially disbanded, but in practice it continued in being. After the Peace of Belgrade in 1739 the Porte employed Moslems of Albanian origin to guard the mountain districts and passes. Experiences, such as that with Megdanis, had convinced them that Greek armatoles were becoming unreliable and Russian influence was spreading. Süleyman of Argyrokastron (Gjinokastër) was therefore appointed Pasha of Ioannina and *Dervendji Pasha* (Warden of the Passes). He was succeeded by Kurd Pasha and by the famous Ali Pasha of Tebelen. This dealt a fatal blow to the armatole service. The institution nevertheless continued to exist until 1829, when it was finally disbanded.

Comparable bodies to the armatoles were those of the

---

[10] N. Kasomoules, Στρατιωτικὰ 'Ενθυμήματα (*Military Recollections*), ed. by G. Vlachoyiannis, vol. I, Athens, 1940, pp. 4 ff. See also Sp. Lambros, 'Ενθυμήσεων ἤτοι χρονικῶν σημειωμάτων συλλογὴ πρώτη ('Recollections or Chronological Notes', Pt. I), in Νέος 'Ελληνομνήμων, vol. VII (1910), pp. 205 ff. Ap. Vakalopoulos, 'Ο ἀρματολὸς Μεϊντάνης ('The armatole Meidanes') in 'Ελληνικά, vol. XIII, 1954, pp. 160 ff.

[11] For an illustration of the dangers of submission, see the Ballad of Captain Malamos in Appendix B II (a) below.

Meydanides (Μεϊντάνηδες) and the *Kapoi* (Κάποι) in the Peloponnese. The first were former bandits whom the Venetians employed in the Morea to guard the passes and to maintain order. The *Kapoi* also reached their fullest development in the same region. Organized into units and paid by the Greek communal authorities, they performed police duties in the towns and countryside and were used as bodyguards for Greek notables.[12]

The *Klephts* formed the other armed body of Greeks in Turkish times. It was made up of the more active elements of the population who had taken to the hills after lapsing into crime, or because they were on the run from the Turkish authorities for some other reason. The number of these fugitives was increasingly reinforced as, with the passage of time, communities of free fighting men were formed in the Greek mountains. Similar bodies also sprang up in the Slav countries of the Balkans—the Uskoks (Slav pirates along the Croat and Dalmatian coasts), the Haiduks among the Serbs, the Haiduts among the Bulgars.

Banditry was an old institution in the Balkan Peninsula—it had existed before the Turkish conquest and even before and during the Byzantine era—nor did it entirely vanish from Greece after the establishment of the free Kingdom. Confining our attention to the Turkish period, we note that the term Klepht (in Greek κλέπτης or κλέφτης, meaning robber) occurs very early. The treaty concluded by Mehmed II with Venice in July 1480, and drawn up in Greek reads as follows:

> Regarding Pastia they have reported to My Puissant Majesty that it is a place of thieves (κλεπτῶν) and an abode of robbers and that all the fugitives who go to dwell there are Albanians. . . .[13]

[12] On these last see B. P. Panayiotopoulos, *Νέα στοιχεῖα περὶ τοῦ θεσμοῦ τῶν κάπων ἐν Πελοποννήσῳ* ('New Evidence on the Institution of the *Kapoi* in the Peloponnese'), in *Δελτίον τῆς Ἱστορικῆς καί Ἐθνολογικῆς Ἑταιρείας τῆς Ἑλλάδος* (*Bul. of the Historical and Ethnological Society of Greece*), vol. XI (1956), pp. 78 ff.

[13] Miklosich & Müller, *Acta et Diplomata graeca*, vol. III, p. 304. See also Franz Babinger, *Johannes Darius (1414–94), Sachwalter Venedigs im Morgenland*,

This latter term is probably used in its geographical rather than in a purely racial sense.

We have in this text perhaps the first known mention of the word 'Klepht' in its double significance, i.e. that of a common bandit and that of a resistance fighter against alien rule. The term 'Klephts' is used to denote both land and water thieves in a letter to the Doge of Venice from Bayezid II, written in Greek and dated 7 April 1503. This refers to bandits operating in the pass of Platamon, in Thessaly, and to acts of piracy in the northern Aegean.[14] Both of these, however, may have been cases of robbery with violence rather than of political resistance. It is, at this early stage at any rate—when national resistance was not yet fully organized—hard, if not impossible, to distinguish the two senses, especially in official Turkish documents, since the Turkish authorities, both genuinely and for propaganda purposes, classed both types of Klepht together. The word has certainly overtones of its dual meaning in the following extract from a Greek source, a brief chronicle of the year 1534 written by the scholar Likinios of Monemvasia:

> In the year 1534 the Franks all left Koroni and then there came a Turkish Standard-bearer [*Bairaktar* in Turkish: φλαμπουριάρης in Greek] and took post in the Morea and seized [or according to another reading, reduced to order] the Klephts (κλέπταις) of the Morea.[15]

Like the armatoles, the bodies of Klephts flourished more particularly in mainland Greece, in Epirus, Thessaly and

---

und sein griechischer Umkreis, Bayerische Akademie der Wissenschaften, Philosophisch-Historische Klasse, Sitzungsberichte, Jahrgang 1961, Heft 5, Munich, 1961, pp. 86 ff. The place-name Παστία (Pastia, Bastia) is likely to be identified with Μπαστία, mentioned in a Greek Portolan of the first post-Byzantine period and situated on the coast of Northern Epirus (the ancient Θύαμις ἄκρα, observes a reader in a marginal note), Armand Delatte, *Les portulans grecs*, Liège, 1947, p. 204.

[14] Hélène Ahrweiler, 'Une lettre en grec du Sultan Bayezid II (1481–1512)', in *Turcica. Revue des Études Turques*, vol. I, Paris, 1969, pp. 150–60.

[15] Sp. Lambros, Βραχέα Χρονικά ('Brief Chronicles'), ed. by C. Amantos, Μνημεῖα τῆς Ἑλληνικῆς Ἱστορίας Ἀκαδημία Ἀθηνῶν (*Academy of Athens. Monuments of Hellenic History*), vol. I, Athens, 1932, p. 26.

Macedonia. This is as one might expect since, as we have seen, the mountainous parts of these regions were ideal country for bandits and the chief functions of the armatoles were precisely to suppress banditry and to keep clear the more vulnerable roads and passes. But the distinction between the two became increasingly blurred as the national resistance movement gathered strength and the guardians of the peace joined it in growing numbers. In the Morea, under the second Turkish occupation, armed resistance to Government was limited. Information about the Klephts of the Morea, more especially about the celebrated Zacharias Varvitsiotes, are contained in the *Memoirs* ('Υπομνήματα) of Anagnostes Kontakes of Ayios Petros in Kynouria.[16]

This transformation of robber bands into national resistance bodies is an exceptional historical feature.[17] Normally in such

[16] Anagnostes Kontakes, 'Απομνημονεύματα (*Memoirs*), ed. by Emm. Protopsaltes, Athens, 1957.

[17] Claude Fauriel in the 'Discours Préliminaire' to his *Chansons populaires de la Grèce moderne* (see below), p. lii, well describes the situation:

"... their transition from the state of Armatole to that of Klepht, and *vice versa*, was so often and so rapidly made, that the titles of Armatole and Klepht might be used almost interchangeably for either, and either might serve to describe two ways of life which were no doubt very different but each of which perpetually verged on or merged with the other. There were districts in which the word Armatole was, or might be, used for both. In others, as in Thessaly, it was the word Klepht which was customarily used to denote both the armatole as a peaceful militiaman and the rebel Klepht in the mountains. If need arose, the two opposed ways of life were merely distinguished by two different adjectives. One spoke of the peaceable armatole, armed for the security of his area, as a 'subject' or 'tame' Klepht (κλέφτης ἥμερος), but of the rebellious Klepht proper as a 'wild' Klepht (κλέφτης ἄγριος). . . .

If a Captain of Armatoles were uneasy in his post or if he got wind of some plot being hatched against him by a Pasha or the Dervendjibaşi, he at once took to the nearest mountain with his braves, who either followed him straightway or came to join him there; and the armatole company which had been responsible for policing an area saw itself transformed in a flash into a band of Klephts at open war with the Turkish authorities."

Thus one Klephtic ballad speaks of "... Nicholas Tsouvaras, who was Armatole and Klepht at Karpenisi". See also the ballad in Appendix B II (c) below.

cases the armed resistance is of course directed against established native authority but in the case of Greece and the other Balkan countries that authority was in the hands of a ruler of alien race and religion. In addition, the transformation was assisted by the long series of wars between Turkey and Christian powers which had as their main theatre, or as an objective, the Greek lands and seas—the first Turco-Venetian war of 1463–79, the naval campaign of Lepanto (1571), the Cretan War of 1645–69, the Turco-Venetian wars with the ensuing Venetian occupation of the Peloponnese (1684–1715), the Russo-Turkish wars of 1768–74 and 1787–92, to name only the major instances. These upheavals greatly encouraged the development of Greek resistance as well as deciding the Turks to employ Albanians as police rather than Greeks, and it was in these conditions that the typical figure of the Greek Klepht of pre-revolutionary times took shape.

The scanty records, whether written or oral and traditional, especially the brilliant epic of the Klephtic ballads, help the scholar to reconstruct the portrait gallery of the brave men who, whether as armatoles or Klephts, took up arms against the foreign overlord. Since we are dealing here with organizations and institutions, it is not possible to dwell on the remarkable exploits of individual fighters for freedom. At a time when the Greeks were engaged in their supreme struggle in 1824, Claude Fauriel was collecting and translating the folksongs of Greece which evoked the admiration of the intellectual world of Europe.[18] In the long preface to his work the writer describes the moral character of the Klephts. Later research has corrected a detail here and there, but in the main the picture Fauriel drew remains clear and accurate.

"In modern as in ancient Greece", says the French writer, "the word Klepht signifies thief; and if one goes no further than the first associations which the word immediately suggests, the

[18] On the life and the work of Fauriel see Miodrag Ibrovac, *Claude Fauriel et la fortune européenne des poésies populaires grecque et serbe. Étude d'histoire romantique suivie du Cours de Fauriel professé en Sorbonne (1831-2)*, Paris, 1966.

exploits and adventures of the Klephts must appear to have been, in Greece as everywhere else, merely those of bandits—a theme little treated in poetry and song and with little variety. But in this case one would be wrong to judge the actuality by the name; and nothing in fact bears less resemblance to the common bandits of the highways of Europe than the Klephts of Greece. . . ."[19] On the contrary, the Greek Klephts had a higher notion of life and freedom. Moving in the mountains, living in the midst of dangers and hardships, they formed the ideal model of courage and physical strength. When quartered in their 'lairs' (λημέρια), they exercised themselves in trials of strength which recall the gymnastics of the ancient Greeks. The Klephts had an amazing ability to disregard hunger and thirst and to hold out against torture and pain. Their attitude towards death was full of a calm pride. Their rugged living conditions toughened them, but these unsophisticated, rough-mannered men showed themselves magnanimous and capable of noble feeling and action. They respected the women they captured, Turkish as well as Greek, even when these were the wives or daughters of men who had violated their own womenfolk. Indeed one instance is quoted of a Klephtic leader who was killed by his own men for having insulted a Turkish woman whom he was holding captive pending her ransom. Deepest of all, and wholly natural, was their reverence for God; their friendships were pure; their love for their country without limit; and the lure of danger irresistible. "Closely confined to the wildest parts of the country," Fauriel concludes, "these armed bands formed there a people apart, sharply distinguished from that of the lands under cultivation. Thus there grew up by degrees in the midst of a Greece conquered and oppressed a new Greece which was warlike, independent and reduced to living off the oppressors and the subject part of the oppressed. In short, for all Greeks who were poor, discontented and brave there

[19] *Chants populaires de la Grèce moderne, recueillis et publiés, avec une traduction française, des éclaircissements et des notes,* par C. Fauriel, tome Ier, *Chants historiques,* Paris, 1824, p. xliii.

existed in the mountains a homeland of their own—a state of affairs probably much like that which the first conquerors found when they were compelled to come to terms with the conquered".[20]

One might even compare the Greece of pre-revolutionary times with the picture painted by Thucydides of Greece in the archaic age of its history. The whole country was full of armed bands. Men heedless of danger "turned to banditry, led by others, not the least capable of their fellows". These men took to violence and "made most of their livelihood from it, since this occupation was not yet considered disgraceful but even carried a certain glamour with it".[21] The only point in which the ancients differed from the moderns was that the former were fighting for gain and personal power, the latter for the greatest of all prizes, liberty.

We return to the problem of the less remote but still ancient origins of the resistance bodies. Already in the first half of the last century Kasomoulis wrote: "When we survey the past from our present, there is no lack of evidence—even if we cannot get at the whole truth and some doubt remains with us —that the origin of these lies very far back and derives from the age of the [Byzantine] Empire."[22] Finlay's view is similar, namely that, "The armatoli were a Christian local militia which had existed in the Byzantine Empire, and which had in some degree protected the Greek population against the Franks, the Servians, and the Albanians, during the anarchy that reigned in Greece and Macedonia, while the worthless race of the Palaeologi reigned at Constantinople."[23] This raises from one aspect the formidable problem of the various ways in which Byzantine example influenced the political, military, administrative, social and economic arrangements of the Ottoman Empire—a problem which has been the subject

[20] Ibid., p. lxxv.
[21] *Thucydides*, I, 5.
[22] Kasomoules, op. cit., vol. I, pp. 2 ff.
[23] George Finlay, op. cit., vol. VI, p. 19.

of passionate debate among historians but cannot be examined here.[24] It is certain, however, that the Sultans of the time of the Conquest, in their urgent need to meet outside pressures and to stabilise their new dominions, adopted many of the institutions they found in existence and, as we have seen, the particular need to make use of local manpower forbade the taking of any substantial measures against the non-Moslem population. It was in these circumstances that Christian timariots, Greek armatoles and Bulgarian Voiniks came into being.[25]

The earliest models of both the Klepht and the Armatole bodies are to be sought in the military arrangements which prevailed in Asia Minor in Byzantine times. The needs of regional defence, the needs of local security and the limited military strength of the State combined to create military forces of an unusual kind, especially in the remote districts of the Taurus and Cappadocia. The *Apelatai* (whose name derived from the verb ἀπελαύνειν, to drive off—those who drive off the cattle, the stock-thieves) were in fact robbers living in outlawry and subsisting in the mountains. Their life was rough and perilous. Legends and traditions grew up about these reckless men. The epic of the *Akritai* (frontiersmen) sang the deeds of these heroes, much as the Border ballads did those of the cattle-raiders and freebooters of the Anglo-Scottish frontier. Renowned among them were the 'first' of the Apelatai— Philopappos, Kinnamos, Ioannikios and Digenis Akritas himself, the most famous of all, who had joined the Apelatai before he took service with the State.[26]

[24] See the study, mentioned above, of Speros Vryonis jr., 'The Byzantine Legacy and Ottoman Forms', in *Dumbarton Oaks Papers*, Nos. XXIII–XXIV (1969–70), pp. 251–308.

[25] Eugen Stanescu, Les 'Stratiotès'. Diffusion et survivance d'une institution byzantine dans le Sud-Est de l'Europe, *Actes du Premier Congrès International des Études Balkaniques et Sud-Est Européennes*, vol. III, Sofia, 1969, pp. 227–47.

[26] See the new ed. of the Acritic Epos. Erich Trapp, *Digenes Akrites. Synoptische Ausgabe der ältesten Versionen*, Österreichische Akademie der Wissenschaften, Kommission für Byzantinistik, Institut für Byzantinistik der Universität Wien, *Wiener Byzantinische Studien*, vol. VIII, Vienna, 1971.

Byzantium, whenever it was in no position to destroy these dangerous robbers, 'hired' (ἐρρόγευεν) them and enrolled their bands in the irregular forces of the Empire. The Apelatai were thus transformed into Akritai and proved the merciless persecutors of their former comrades. The Akritai had the custody of the 'limits' (ἄκρα), the frontiers and the frontier provinces. In the definition of the Byzantine text their duty was "by every device and ruse and by unsleeping vigilance to study and strive to keep the lands of the Romans unscathed and unvexed by enemy attack". In this way there were created in the outer provinces, and particularly in the mountain passes, bodies of Akritai who had often been recruited from the Apelatai. Later on, the State entrusted the guardianship of the passes to soldiers of fortune, mostly Armenians. Such a one was Melias, a man of quick intelligence and "fit for barbarous thievery", whom Leo the Wise (886–912) appointed Turmarch (Τουρμάρχης) of the Euphrates region and later Warden (Κλεισουράρχης) of the Lykandos. After Leo's death this particular pass was upgraded to a Provincial Governor's command.[27]

In the Balkans banditry was more or less endemic from ancient times. Medieval sources, mostly lives of the Saints, afford us information enough about robbers who infested the mountain defiles and the fords of rivers. The gorges of the Strymon were much to be dreaded. St. Gregory the Decapolite, journeying to Salonica between 815 and 820, fell into the hands of Slav robbers who were river-borne and given to pillage. Much later, in 1325/6, the historian Nicephorus Gregoras describes fearfully the passage of the river, the wildness of the spot, the threats of these men. No less hazardous were the

---

English trans. J. Mavrogordato, *Digenis Akritas*, Oxford, 1956 (reprinted 1963). Cf. H.-G. Beck, *Geschichte der byzantinischen Volkliteratur, op. cit.*, pp. 48 ff., 63 ff.

[27] For a new study of the Akrites and the Apelates see Agostino Pertusi, 'Tra Storia e Leggenda: Akritai e Ghâzi sulla frontiera orientale di Bisanzio', in *XIVe Congrès International des Études Byzantines*, Bucharest 6–12 September 1971, *Rapports* II, pp. 27–72.

crossings of the Axios (Vardar). And besides these, western and north-western Macedonia and mountain Thessaly were the lurking-places of robbers. These belonged mainly to the nomadic and semi-nomadic tribes who lived in the mountain districts—Vlachs, Cumans, Vardariote Turks, Slavs. In the eleventh and twelfth centuries, the Vlachs controlled the Pindus range and, from this base, overran the whole of lowland Thessaly. This state of affairs became still more critical after the Byzantine Empire was broken up by the Latins and the country was subjected to the rule of weak and warring princes.

To sum up, Byzantines and Franks alike had made use of irregular bodies of freebooters for the defence and guarding of strategic points. Certain foreign or local elements were enlisted under the supervision of the State or of local landowners to whom the State granted lands in return for military services. These methods of recruitment were brought to their highest development in the territories governed by Venice after the fall of Constantinople. Venice made the most extensive use of Greek formations in her struggle against the Turks. Her Greek fighting men, whether they came from local sources or had fled to Venetian territory and had formed bands of irregulars, were conscious that, in fighting under the banner of St. Mark, they were making war for their own country. Hence the tremendous military activity which the Greek nation developed after the loss of its national independence. The Ottoman Empire was forced to adopt these same methods and thus out of banditry there arose the outline structure of resistance. By the adaptability, which is a feature of everything Greek, the rough and reckless men of the mountains were transformed into champions of freedom.

The Resistance by Sea

By way of supplement and comparison some comment may be added on the forces of resistance by sea. Just as banditry provided the framework of these forces on land, so piracy helped indirectly to increase the fighting potential of the nation.

Something has already been said on the subject of piracy but · mainly from the angle of its harmful effect on the population. But Greeks too took part in piracy and distinguished themselves by their skill as seamen. The Aegean islands were the refuge of sea-robbers. Ios was called by the Turks 'Little Malta' on account of the islanders' activity in this profession. Nameless privateers attacked passing ships but the pirate Antonios Kapsis achieved a personal reputation and made his name as a daring sailor. Having won the goodwill of the Melians, he was proclaimed Prince of their island, but his reign lasted only three years, since the Turks managed to lay hands on the bold adventurer and he was hanged at Constantinople in 1680.

Following an older tradition, the inhabitants of Mani also showed themselves adventurous pirates. Established on the sheer cliffs of their inhospitable coast, they followed the movements of ships rounding the Peloponnese, ready to fall on any prize that offered. In the second half of the eighteenth century the Maniotes possessed a substantial fleet with which they made descents on the islands. In 1794 they attacked Pholegandros and Antiparos. In 1797 they ravaged Amorgos. A folk poet has described in 'political'[28] verse the disaster which struck this last island.

In the eighteenth century the Greek fleets grew in strength. The islands of Hydra, Spetsai and Psará had begun to assemble their navies and the rivalry of the Great Powers in the eastern Mediterranean gave them opportunities for action. In the Anglo-French war of 1756–64 Greek pirates—'Anglo-Greeks', as the consular sources termed them—were enrolled in the

[28] The metre called 'political' in Greek has been characteristic of Greek national and popular verse ever since the early Middle Ages. It is a fifteen-syllable line with a caesura between the eight and ninth syllables. It may be rhymed or unrhymed. A similar metre may be found in some old English ballads, e.g.:

In Scarlet town where I was born / there was a fair maid dwelling.
Made every youth cry Wellaway / Her name was Barbara Allen.

service of Britain, the most eminent among them being the corsair Panayiotis, a Greek from the Greek community in Minorca, who inflicted severe losses on French shipping under the British flag. "The well-known English corsair, Captain Panayiotis, a Greek from Maone [Port Mahon]", the Venetian Consul at Salonica wrote in 1757, "fought for twenty hours on end off the island of Tinos with an armed French pirate ship until he had spent all his ammunition. He then embarked in two boats with his crew and taking with him the best of what there was on board, he withdrew to the island. Meanwhile, his ship had burst into flames from a trail which he had lighted before leaving."[29] This pirate continued his career off Chios, Skopelos and Psará.

The activity of these miniature Greek fleets was of importance during the Russo-Turkish war of 1768–74. In the first descent of the Russian fleet into the Mediterranean the Greeks gave assistance. Greek pirate vessels scoured the sea, some of them flying the Russian flag. A Turkish document of 1772 speaks of the small craft "of the infidel islanders of Psará, who go about as pirates with the flag of the accursed Muscovites".[30] The Venetian Consul at Salonica writes in 1770: "Innumerable corsairs are to be found in the Archipelago. The greater part of them are Sphakiotes [from south-western Crete] and men of Hydra and Spetsai who have ventured to enter the waters of Cassandra armed in Caïques. . . . If the Russian fleet does not put a stop to the piratical exploits of the Greeks, I am afraid that there will be some very serious incidents to report, since these fugitives from justice have no idea of the flags of the different sovereign States. It is asserted here that there is not a single Russian officer to be found in these pirate ships."[31] The Turks sought to reinforce the garrison of Salonica. During his brief occupation of the Cyclades the Russian administrator,

---

[29] C. Mertzios, Μνημεῖα Μακεδονικῆς Ἱστορίας (*Documents of Macedonian History*), Salonica, 1947, p. 380.

[30] J. Vasdravelles, Ἱστορικὰ Ἀρχεῖα Μακεδονίας, *op. cit.*, vol. I, p. 277.

[31] C. Mertzios, *op. cit.*, p. 415.

Paul Nestorov, was obliged to take action against the "sea-bandits".[32]

The familiarity of the Greeks with the sea, renewing ancient traditions, was the basis of their later development of a powerful fleet, of which more is said below.

[32] Klon Stephanos, Ἀνέκδοτα ἔγγραφα ἀποσταλέντα πρὸς τοὺς κατοίκους τῶν Κυκλάδων κατὰ τὴν ὑπό τῶν Ῥώσων κατοχὴν αὐτῶν ('Unpublished Documents addressed to the Inhabitants of the Cyclades during their Occupation by the Russians'), in Ἀθήναιον, vol. VI (1877), pp. 203–43.

VI

The Rebirth of the Greek Nation:
I. The Restructuring of Greek Society

From the second half of the seventeenth century the Greeks show clear signs of a revival which becomes a solid reality in the eighteenth century. This and the following chapter present briefly the different aspects of this revival, its causes, its progress and its achievements.

The first feature requiring notice is the improvement from the demographic point of view. In spite of the loss of blood which the Greeks had suffered towards the end of the seventeenth and during the eighteenth century—in the Turco-Venetian wars (1645–99, 1714–18), in the Russo-Turkish wars (1768–74, 1787–92), the operations of Orlov and the revolt of the Greeks in 1770 and its savage repression in the Morea by Athenian troops, and in other periods of violence—the population figures showed an unmistakable and steady increase, even allowing for a wide margin of uncertainty and error. Recent advances in statistical and demographic science have greatly reinforced historical research but, in dealing with periods for which the necessary data are sadly incomplete, the conclusions of research can only be applied with caution and their application has sometimes led to hasty conclusions. This is particularly true of the study of the non-Turkish and non-Moslem populations under Ottoman rule. Nevertheless, the existing evidence—information supplied by writers and travellers and still more the evidence from Venetian archives—deserves consideration and the interpretation of it opens up new prospects for research. We owe to Professor Apostolos Vakalopoulos the first broad survey of the movements of the Greek population both inside and outside the territories of the Turkish Empire.[1]

Professor Vakalopoulos terms the drift of the Greek population back towards the lowlands and the towns, 'the movement of return' ($\pi\alpha\lambda\iota\nu\delta\rho o\mu\iota\kappa\grave{\eta}$ $\kappa\acute{\iota}\nu\eta\sigma\iota\varsigma$). After the stabilization and consolidation of the Turkish conquests from the sixteenth century onwards there is a noticeable increase and a consequent shift of the Greek population, a deliberate trend towards the country towns and other centres, where economic activity offered chances of a livelihood. But there was also some forcible transplantation in which the Ottoman State itself took a hand, repeating the policy employed earlier by the Byzantine Empire.[2] This early resettlement was not confined to the Balkan Peninsula but extended to the islands and to the coastlands of Asia Minor. The figures given below, though not completely reliable, are instructive. According to Turkish statistics, in the years 1520 to 1530 European Turkey south of the Danube, together with the islands of Lemnos, Mytilene, Imbros, Thasos, Rhodes and Cos, but excluding Constantinople, contained a population of 5,202,285. The city of Athens, which during the same period contained 12,633 inhabitants, in the years 1571 to 1580 contained 17,616. The demographic pattern presented by Salonica is quite unique. In 1478 the Macedonian capital contained 1,884 Christian and Moslem households. The settlement of the Spanish Jews after 1492 helped to swell its population, so that by 1529 the number of households established in Salonica had risen to 4,863, of whom 2,645 were Jewish. In 1723 the population had gone up to 50,000. In spite of repeated and disastrous epidemics it went on increasing steadily, to 80,000 in 1741, with a drop to 70,000 in 1777 and a return to 80,000 in 1788.

[1] Ap. Vakalopoulos, Ἱστορία τοῦ Νέου Ἑλληνισμοῦ, *op. cit.*, vol. II, p. 62 ff., 337 ff.

[2] Ö. L. Barkan, 'Les déportations comme méthode de peuplement et de colonisation dans l'Empire ottoman', *Revue de la Faculté des sciences économiques de l'Université d'Istanbul*, 11th Year, Nos. 1–4, 1953.

In eastern Macedonia the town of Serres numbered 1093 households in 1521 to 1530 and 1204 in 1571 to 1580.

In the Peloponnese, towards the end of the fifteenth century, we find a number of flourishing towns: Karytaina (3,387 inhabitants); Mistrá (3,287); Kalavryta (2,360); Corinth (3,589); Aigion (3,108). But when, as noted in Chapter II above, the Venetians occupied the Morea in 1685, the population had reached its lowest point. Thereafter recovery began, the figures rising to 116,000 by 1692 and 250,000 by 1707.[3]

The increase in population was due to a number of causes, general and particular. The earlier centuries of the Turkish conquest had been harsh, partly because of the long and ruinous wars which the Ottoman Empire undertook in Europe and Asia, and the consequent heavy drafts made on the Greek population by the child-levy. The decline and eventual abolition of the levy in later years was one of the chief factors in the rise of the population figures, to which the development of local self-government also made a substantial contribution, entailing as it did the improvement of living conditions in a more tolerable social environment. But one of the most important factors in the changed situation was the trade revival which took place in the eastern Mediterranean during the eighteenth century and had a decisive effect on the economic and social life of the Greeks.

The New Social Structure of the Greek Community and the Origins of the Administrative Aristocracy

The common experience of disaster under the Conquest had ironed out the class structure of the Greek people. The rarity of

[3] Ö. L. Barkan, 'Essai sur les données statistiques des régistres de recensement dans l'Empire ottoman aux XVᵉ et XVIᵉ siècles', in *Journal of Economic and Social History of the Orient*, vol. I,1, Aug. 1957, pp. 9–36. N. Todorov, 'La situation démographique de la péninsule balkanique au cours des XVᵉ et XVIᵉ siècles', in *Annuaire de l'Université de Sofia. Faculté de Philosophie et d'Histoire*, vol. 53, 2 1959, pp. 193–232 (in Bulgarian with short French summary). See also by the same author, La Ville Balcanique XVᵉ–XIXᵉ Siècle. (Institute of Balkan Studies. Studia Balcanica, 3.) Sofia, 1970.

the exceptions emphasized all the more the huge scale of the catastrophe. The last representatives of the old Byzantine imperial dynasties gradually vanished or suffered a change of station, although some of their members distinguished themselves in the economic field.

In spite of this the Constantinople of the Sultans—what Nicholas Iorga called 'Greater Constantinople'[4]—emerged as the centre of a reviving Greek nation. One of the first preoccupations of Mehmed II was the repeopling of the capital. Greeks from Thrace, Asia Minor, the Morea and the islands reinforced the sadly reduced population.[5] Within the Greek element in Constantinople thus revived there took place in the course of time a process of social differentiation and a new social hierarchy grew up. New men began to make their mark both in the Palace and in the Patriarchate, as well as in economic life. From the earliest years of the Conquest, Greeks bearing the general designation of Archons had exercised considerable influence with the Sultans. Many of them were the agents or lessees of public services, whether for the collection of taxes or for the exploitation of mineral resources or salt mines. Under Mehmed II, for instance, Thomas Katavolinos and Demetrius Apokaukos were powerful figures at Court, as others became later, among them such men as Tsernotas or 'Tsernota Bey', a notable from Corinth. It was he who contributed to the recognition of the Patriarchate of Alexandria by Selim I in 1517, on the Sultan's conquest of Egypt. He also rebuilt the Monastery of the Archangels ($T\alpha\xi\iota\acute{\alpha}\rho\chi\hat{\omega}\nu$) near Aigion on the

---

[4] N. Iorga, *Byzance après Byzance*, Bucharest, 1935. Reprinted, Bucharest, 1971.

[5] N. B. Tomadakis, Ὁ μετὰ τὴν ἅλωσιν τῆς Κωνσταντινουπόλεως (1453) ἀποικισμὸς αὐτῆς κατὰ τὰς Ἑλληνικὰς πηγάς ('The Repopulation of Constantinople after its Fall in 1453, according to Greek Sources'), in Πεπραγμένα τοῦ Θ' Διεθνοῦς Βυζαντινολογικοῦ Συνεδρίου Θεσσαλονίκη 12–19 Ἀπριλίου 1953. (*Proc. of the Ninth International Congress of Byzantine Studies*, Salonica 12–19 April 1953), vol. II (Athens, 1956), pp. 611–29. Cf. Halil Inalcik, 'The Policy of Mehmed II towards the Greek population of Istanbul and the Byzantine Buildings of the City', in *Dumbarton Oaks Papers*, nos. XXIII–XXIV (1969–70), pp. 228–249.

Gulf of Corinth and was buried there on his death in 1531.[6] The Archon Xenakis was another who exercised great influence with the Turks and was of service to the Church on many occasions during the first half of the sixteenth century. He was in fact the resourceful lawyer who produced the three aged Janissaries whose testimony so effectually swayed Sultan Süleyman at a critical moment of the Church's fortunes.[7]

The Church hierarchy offered a career for members of the upper class or others who had entered the ranks of the clergy, particularly those who had taken monastic vows; but in addition there sprang up, very early on, beside the Patriarchal throne a class of lay officials, also known as Archons, who played an important part in Church and national affairs. In the first rank of these stood the Grand Logothete (ὁ μέγας Λογοθέτης) who, besides his other duties, acted as liaison officer between the Patriarch and the Porte. Next to him came the Grand Warden of the Treasury (ὁ μέγας Σκευοφύλαξ), the Grand Keeper of the Records (ὁ μέγας Χαρτοφύλαξ), the Grand Orator (ὁ μέγας Ῥήτωρ), the Grand Ecclesiarch (ὁ μέγας Ἐκκλησιάρχης) and the Chief Justice (ὁ Πρωτέκδικος). These high officers of the Patriarch's Court and the general influence which the leading men of Constantinople commanded, both within the Church itself and under its protection, contributed to the rise of "the first lay intellectual aristocracy since the Conquest".[8] The

---

[6] L. N. Politis, Ἡ Μονὴ τῶν Ταξιαρχῶν Αἰγίου ('The Monastery of the Archangels at Aigion'), in Ἑλληνικά, vol. XI 1939, p. 77.

[7] Steven Runciman, *The Great Church in Captivity*, p. 189; and see Chap. II, p. 46, above.

[8] P. Karolides, Ἱστορία τῆς Ἑλλάδος ἀπὸ τῆς ὑπὸ τῶν Ὀθωμανῶν ἁλώσεως τῆς Κωνσταντινουπόλεως (1453) μέχρι τῆς βασιλείας Γεωργίου τοῦ Α΄ (*History of Greece from the Capture of Constantinople by the Turks in 1453 to the Reign of George I*), Athens, 1925, pp. 233 ff. For a more detailed account of the Patriarchal administration see Runciman, *op. cit.*, pp. 173 ff., and Th. H. Papadopoullos, *Studies and Documents relating to the History of the Greek Church and People*, Bibliotheca Graeca Aevi Posterioris, I, Brussels, 1952. Chr. G. Patrinelis, Συμβολαί εἰς τήν ἱστορίαν τοῦ Οἰκουμενικοῦ Πατριαρχείου. Α΄. Πρωτοψάλται, Λαμπαρδάριοι καὶ Δομέστικοι τῆς Μεγάλης Ἐκκλησίας (1453–1821), ('Contributions to the History of the Oecumenical Patriarchate. I. Protopsaltai,

Patriarchate of Constantinople was installed in the Monastery of the Pammakaristos from 1455 until 1586, when the church was transformed into a Moslem shrine.[9] In the year 1601 the Patriarchate was more permanently established in the Monastery of St. George of the Phanar (Lighthouse), where it remains today. It was from this suburb of the Phanar, on the Golden Horn, that there came the name 'Phanariot' by which the leading families of the Greek community in Constantinople were collectively known.

But whether as individuals or as a social group, the influence of the Greeks of the capital was not confined to the Sultan's Court or to purely administrative posts, nor were they restricted to the offices for which they were eligible within the Church bureaucracy. From the seventeenth century onwards certain new careers became open to them in which they proved themselves outstandingly successful. These were, first and foremost, the posts of Grand Dragoman (Interpreter) to the Court and Grand Dragoman of the Fleet and the Princedoms of Wallachia and Moldavia.

We find the office of Interpreter (ἑρμηνεύς) mentioned in Byzantium from the fifth century and from the twelfth century that of Grand Interpreter (μέγας ἑρμηνευτής). In the time of the Paleologi (1259–1453) there appear the titles of Dragoman (δραγο(υ)μάνος) and Grand Dragoman, taken from the Arabic *terguman*, employed in Western Europe in the form Drogman.[10]

One of the first Greek Secretaries in Turkish service (about 1422, in the reign of Murad II) was Michael Pylles, a native of Ephesus, "by training and occupation Secretary in the Prince's

---

Lampadarioi and Domestikoi of the Great Church, 1453–1821'), in Μνημοσύνη vol. II (1969), pp. 64–93.

[9] This exceptionally beautiful church, erected between 1292 and 1294, known in Turkish as Fetiye Cami, is still partially in use as a mosque. Some fine mosaics have been uncovered there in recent years.

[10] R. Guilland, 'Études sur l'histoire administrative de l'Empire byzantin, Titres et offices du Bas-Empire byzantin. Le Grand Interprète', ὁ μέγας διερμηνευτής, in 'Επετηρὶς "Εταιρείας Βυζαντινῶν Σπουδῶν (*Annual of the Society of Byzantine Studies*), vol. 36 (1968), pp. 17 ff.

[Sultan's] Palace, writer in Romaic [Greek] and Arabic letters".[11] Reference has already been made to Thomas Katavolinos and Demetrius Apokaukos. As Secretary (γραμμα-τικός), Greek Secretary (γραμματιστὴς "Ελλην) and Private Secretary (γραμματεὺς τῶν θυρῶν), Katavolinos undertook some very important missions, including one which had fateful consequences for the man himself, the embassy in 1461 to Prince Vlad the Impaler of Wallachia who put him to death. Apokaukos had been employed even before the Conquest to negotiate the treaty of 1446[12] with Venice. In 1454, at the request of the Italian humanist Francesco Filelfo, he was the intermediary with Mehmed II for the release from captivity of the mother-in-law of Manfredino Chrysoloras and her daughters.[13]

As the Empire expanded, diplomatic relations with the European powers became closer and with them, in consequence, the need for an Imperial Chancery grew. To meet this need the Porte employed European or Jewish renegades, Italians, Germans, Hungarians, Poles and others. Similarly, the foreign diplomatic missions in Constantinople also engaged interpreters. From the second half of the seventeenth century, the Sultans looked more and more exclusively to the Greeks and entrusted to them the duties of the Grand Dragoman. These men thus acquired very considerable power, but they never occupied what might be termed ministerial posts, which were open to Moslem subjects only.

The first Greek Grand Dragoman of whom there is mention is Panayiotis Nikousios, probably a native of Chios, born about the year 1613. He received a sound education in oriental languages and studied Latin, Italian, mathematics and

---

[11] Ducas, 'Historia Byzantina' (ed. Bekker), *CSHB*, Bonn, 1834, p. 186. Also in the ed. of B. Grecu, *Ducae Historia Turcobyzantina (1341–1462)*, Bucharest, 1958, p. 235. Cf. Sp. Lambros, 'Η Έλληνική ὡς ἐπίσημος γλῶσσα τῶν Σουλτάνων ('Greek as Official Language of the Sultans'), in *Νέος Έλληνομνήμων* vol. 5 (1968), pp. 56 ff.

[12] Franz Dölger, *Byzantinische Diplomatik*, Ettal, 1956, p. 269.

[13] Chr. Patrinelis, *Ο Θεόδωρος Άγαλλιανός*, op. cit., pp. 71 ff.

astronomy. At an early stage, from 1642, he was engaged as interpreter to the Ambassador Extraordinary of the Holy Roman Emperor at the Sublime Porte (*Interprete Cesareo presso la Porta Ottomanica*, as he styles himself). Letters are extant from his time at the Embassy, written in Italian and addressed to Ferdinand III and his advisers.[14] From 1661 we find Nikousios acting as Grand Dragoman. At the surrender of Candia (Iraklion) in 1669 he played an important part as the Ottoman representative in the negotiations with the Venetians. After the occupation of Crete, as Imperial Secretary and Interpreter (σεκρετάριος καὶ ἑρμηνεὺς τῆς Βασιλείας), he was granted the revenues of the island of Mykonos, which he collected through an agent.[15]

Up to the time of his death on 22 September 1673, Nikousios continued to exercise great influence on the foreign policy of the Ottoman Empire. Demetrius Cantemir (1673–1723) says that "he became so indispensable to the Ottoman Court and won such a reputation that no Christian ever played such a distinguished part there or ever will". Like all his fellow-countrymen in the Sultans' service, he was a great benefactor to the Greek nation and Church. It was he who established the rights enjoyed by the Greeks over the Holy Sepulchre and boldly upheld Christian doctrines against the Moslems. He was, besides, a collector of books and manuscripts. There is still preserved at Moscow, the Codex which he brought from Crete to Constantinople, and it is recorded that after his death Colbert instructed the French Ambassador at Constantinople,

---

[14] P. Zerlentis, Παναγιώτου Νικουσίου πρός Φερδινάνδον τὸν τρίτον, τὸν Γερμανῶν Αὐτοκράτορα καὶ τὸν αὐτοῦ μυστικὸν σύμβουλον 'Ερρῖκον Σχλίκιον 'Επιστολαί, ('The Letters of Panayiotis Nikousios to the Emperor of the Germans, Ferdinand III, and his Privy Counsellor Count Heinrich von Schlick'), in 'Ο ἐν Κωνσταντινουπόλει 'Ελληνικὸς Φιλολογικὸς Σύλλογος, Πεντηκονταετηρίς 1861–1911, (*The Greek Literary Society of Constantinople*, 50th Anniversary Pub. 1861–1911), Constantinople, 1913–21, pp. 221 ff.

[15] P. Zerlentis, Παναγιώτης Νικούσιος καί 'Αλέξανδρος Μαυροκορδᾶτος, ἄρχοντες Μυκονίων ('Panayiotos Nikousios and Alexander Mavrocordatos, Archons of Mykonos'), in Νησιωτικὴ 'Επετηρίς (*Yearbook of the Islands*), vol. I, Hermoupolis in Syros, 1918, pp. 161 ff.

the Marquis de Nointel, to acquire for the Royal Library some of the rare books and manuscripts from his estate.[16]

On the death of Nikousios, he was succeeded by Alexander Mavrocordato one of the most outstanding Greeks of the whole Turkish period.[17] Born at Constantinople in 1641 of a Chiote father and a highly cultured mother (Roxandra Skarlatos), he went as a boy to Italy, where he studied, first, in the Greek College at Rome (1657–60) and later, until 1664, at the University of Padua. He was then appointed a teacher of philosophy and medicine at Bologna, where he submitted a Latin treatise on the circulation of the blood (*Pneumaticum Instrumentum circulandi Sanguinis sive de Motu et Usu Pulmonum*).[18] Returning to Constantinople, he taught in the school of Manolakis of Kastoria, wrote essays on literary and philosophical subjects and rose in the service of the Patriarchate to be Grand Warden of the Treasury and Grand Logothete. Finally, in 1673, after serving for two years under Nikousios, he was called to replace him on his death. As Grand Dragoman, Mavrocordato in his turn took a leading part in the conduct of Turkish foreign policy. The disaster which overtook the Turks before Vienna in July and September 1683, led to his fall from power and to imprisonment and financial ruin. He nevertheless regained his post in 1685. The crowning achievement of his political career was the signature of the Treaty of Karlowitz (26 January 1699), after which the Sultan awarded him the title of Confidential Private Secretary (ἐξ ἀπορρήτων).

[16] Börje Knös, *L'Histoire de la Littérature néo-grecque. La période jusqu'en 1821*, Stockholm, 1962, p. 469.

[17] Const. Amantos, ʼΑλέξανδρος Μαυροκορδᾶτος ὁ ἐξ ἀπορρήτων (1641–1709) ('Alexander Mavrocordatos, The Confidential Private Secretary, 1641–1709'), in ʽΕλληνικά, vol. V 1932, pp. 335 ff. Nestor Camariano, *Alexandre Mavrocordato, le Grand Drogman. Son activité diplomatique (1673–1709)*, Salonica, 1970.

[18] M. Manoussacas, ʼΑνέκδοτα πατριαρχικὰ γράμματα (1547–1806) πρὸς τοὺς ἐν Βενετίᾳ μητροπολίτας Φιλαδελφείας καί τήν ʼΟρθόδοξον ʽΕλληνικήν ʼΑδελφότητα, *Lettere patriarcali inedite (1547–1806) agli Arcivescovi di Filadelfia in Venezia ed alla Confraternità dei Greci Ortodossi*, Venice, 1968, pp. 72 ff. It will be recalled that William Harvey, who had also studied at Padua, first pub. his treatise *De motu cordis et sanguinis in animalibus* in 1628.

Through his work as a writer Alexander Mavrocordato belongs to the Greek cultural renaissance of the seventeenth century.[19] It must suffice here to mention only his Φροντίσματα περὶ ἤθη καὶ πολιτείαν ('Thoughts on Morals and Politics'), which show the influence of Machiavelli and La Rochefoucauld, his Ἱστορία Ἱερὰ ἤτοι Ἰουδαϊκά ('Sacred History or Judaïca'), his Letters and his Diary of the events leading up to and following the Siege of Vienna.[20] He died in 1709 and was succeeded by his son Nicholas who was no less remarkable for his learning and for his political experience. Nicholas Mavrocordato was the first Greek to be officially appointed Prince of one of the Danubian Principalities and in fact only briefly held his post at Constantinople before ascending the throne, first of Moldavia and then of Wallachia. Thereafter the succession of Greek Grand Dragomans remained unbroken until the outbreak of the Greek Revolution in 1821. Of the three Greeks who held the post in that year, two, John Callimachi and Constantine Mourouzi, were summarily executed and the third, Stavrakis Aristarches, was exiled and later put to death.[21]

A post of lesser but still considerable distinction was that of Dragoman of the Fleet. This official was in the service of the Turkish High Admiral (Kapudan Pasha) and acted as liaison officer with the population of the islands, of whom he became in practice the administrator and patron. The core of this island province was the Cyclades and with these were grouped the islands of the Saronic and Argolic Gulfs (Aegina, Poros, Salamis, Spetsai and Hydra), the Northern Sporades (Skiathos, Skopelos and Skyros) and certain islands of the eastern Aegean

---

[19] Th. Livadas, Ἀλεξάνδρου Μαυρρκορδάτου τοῦ ἐξ ἀπορρήτων Ἐπιστολαί P', ('A Hundred Letters of Alexander Mavrokordatos the Confidential Private Secretary'), Trieste, 1879.

[20] Ἀλεξάνδρου Μαυροκορδάτου Ἱστορία, 1682–87 ('Alexander Mavrokordato, History, 1682–7'), ed. by A. Papadopoulos-Kerameus, in Eud. Hurmuzaki, *Documente privitoare la Istoria Românilor. Text Greceşti*, (*Documents concerning the history of the Romanians-Greek Texts*) vol. XIII, Bucharest, 1909, pp. 3–43.

[21] For the list of Greek Grand Dragomans see App. A.3 below.

(Samos, Patmos, Psará and Kasos). From 1774, Mani was detached from the administration of the Peloponnese and placed under the Kapudan Pasha, but the Dragoman's power of intervention in Maniote affairs was unimportant. His functions, generally, included the allocation and collection of taxes and the administration of justice, but at a very early stage they were extended to cover the communes, education and the Church.[22]

The first Dragoman of the Fleet is remembered chiefly because his period of office coincided with Kheireddin Barbarossa's exploits against the Venetians in the Adriatic and Ionian Seas.[23] But the High Admiral's grip on the Aegean tightened still further from the mid-seventeenth century onwards, and the Dragoman's post, which until then had been of little account, rose to be one of some importance. The first in the line of Greek Dragomans of the Fleet was Ioannakis Porphyrites in 1701: he was followed by Constantine Vendouras in 1713. The post came to be regarded as a stepping-stone towards appointment as Grand Dragoman and thereafter to one of the Danubian Princedoms, and in consequence members of the great Phanariote families (Mavroyeni, Demakis, Rosetti, Argyropoulos, Handjeris, Soutsos, Karadjà, Callimachi, Rhizos, Manos) were nominated to it.

Returning to the Grand Dragomans and their appointment to the thrones of Wallachia (since 1715) and Moldavia (since 1709) as the crown of their career, we may note that the official Turkish title of these Princes was Bey, a high but not the highest designation in the Turkish governmental hierarchy. *Vlachbey* is, for instance, the style given to the ruler of Wallachia in Greek texts of the eighteenth and early nineteenth centuries.[24]

---

[22] B. B. Sphyroeras, Οἱ Δραγομάνοι τοῦ Στόλου. Ὁ θεσμὸς καί οἱ φορεῖς του (*The Drogmans of the Fleet. The Post and its Holders*), Athens, 1965.

[23] See Ch. II, above, p. 34.

[24] See e.g. A. Papadopoulos—Kerameus, op. cit., pp. 119, 147, 541, 550. Cf. Sp. Lambros, ᾿Ενθυμήσεων ἤτοι χρονικῶν σημειωμάτων Συλλογὴ πρώτη, ('A first Collection of Recollections or Historical notes') *op. cit.*, in *Néos Ἑλληνομνήμων*, vol. VII, 1910, p. 236.

But side by side with this we also find in use the title of *Hospodar*, which was of Russian origin but extended to the Danubian princedoms as a result of the growing influence of Russian diplomacy, and another title, also of Slavonic origin but earlier accepted by the Turks, that of *Voivode* or *Grand Voivode*, which the native Romanian Princes had borne ever since the foundation of the two Principalities. The Greek Princes preferred to style themselves 'Lord and Prince' (αὐθέντης καὶ ἡγεμών) as some of their predecessors had also done, translated in Latin documents as *Princeps*.

The lands beyond the Danube, which the Greek Dragomans ruled from 1709, were not ordinary provinces of the Ottoman Empire but enjoyed self-government under the Sultan's suzerainty. Two principalities, originally vassal states of Hungary had been established in this area, that of Wallachia or Hungrowallachia by the early fourteenth century under Basarab (1314–52) and that of Moldavia or Moldovlachia in 1359. Their Romanian rulers, having come under the influence of Byzantium and as adherents of the Orthodox Church, took part in the resistance to the Turkish invasion of south-eastern Europe and inflicted some damaging defeats on the Turkish armies, but by the early years of the sixteenth century both principalities had been obliged to become tributaries of the Sultan, although on special conditions.[25] The Princes were obliged to obtain confirmation of their election from the Sultan, or in some cases were nominated directly by him, and like other vassals they were bound to supply military aid. In return they retained their own autonomous government and the relative independence of their countries. The agreements guaranteeing these privileges remained in force even in later times and were repeatedly renewed, as for example, after the expedition of Süleyman I against Moldavia in 1538.

[25] I.–R. Mircea, 'Sur les circonstances dans lesquelles les Turcs sont restés en Valachie jusqu'au début du XVIIe siècle', in *Revue des Études Sud-Est européennes*, vol. V (1967), pp. 77–86. General Survey: *Storia del Popolo Romeno*, (*History of the Romanian People*) a cura dell'accademico Andrei Oţetea, Rome, 1971, pp. 174 ff.

In spite of occasional infringements this special relationship proved highly beneficial. A strong ruling class developed at an early stage and some of the rulers of both Principalities— Stephen the Great (1457–1504), Neagoe Basarab (1512–21), Michael the Brave (1593–1601), Basil Lupu (1634–53)—were men of real mark. They were patrons of letters, they imposed the standards of Byzantine law and in a great variety of ways they were a tower of strength to the Patriarchate at Constantinople and to the Greek Church. They were also generous benefactors of the great monastic foundations of Mount Athos as well as of the monasteries of Meteora, Mount Sinai and Patmos.[26]

Under patronage of the Princes of Wallachia and Moldavia, Greek clergy, scholars, artists, administrators and merchants established themselves beyond the Danube. The country had for centuries been soaked in the Greek tradition and the beginnings of modern Romania are linked with Byzantium.[27] Recent excavations in the beautiful Prince's Church of Curtea de Argeş have brought to light coins of Theodore Angelus (1224–30) Andronicus II (1282–1328) and Michael IX (1294–1320).[28] In the second half of the fourteenth century the first Greek boyars appear at the Romanian courts.[29] The ancient

[26] P. Nasturel, 'Aperçu critique des rapports de la Valachie et du Mont Athos des origines au début du XVIᵉ siècle', in *Revue des Études Sud-Est européennes*, vol. II (1964), pp. 93–126. Maria Nystazopoulou-Pelekides, and R. Mircea, *'Ρουμανικὰ ἔγγραφα τοῦ 'Αρχείου τῆς ἐν Πάτμῳ Μονῆς* ('Romanian Documents in the Archives of Patmos Monastery'), ἵn *Σύμμεικτα (Miscellanea)* of the *Κέντρον Βυζαντινῶν 'Ερευνῶν (Centre of Byzantine Research)*, vol. II, Athens, 1970, pp. 255–320.

[27] Al. Elian, 'Byzance et les Roumains à la fin du Moyen Âge', *Proceedings of the XIIIth International Congress of Byzantine Studies*, Oxford, 5–10 September 1966, London, 1967, pp. 195–203. Cf. '*XIVᵉ Congrès International des Études Byzantines*', Bucharest 6–12 September 1971, *Rapports*, IV, Bucharest, 1971.

[28] N. Constantinescu, 'La résidence d'Argeş des voïvodes roumains des XIIIᵉ et XIVᵉ siècles. Problèmes de chronologie à la lumière des récentes recherches archéologiques', in *Revue des Études Sud-Est européennes*, vol. VIII, 1970, pp. 5–31.

[29] P. Nasturel, 'Sur quelques boyards roumains d'origine grecque aux XIVᵉ et XVᵉ siècles', *Revue de Études byzantines*, vol XXV 1967, pp. 107–11.

houses of Byzantium and the new Phanariot families formed connections with the local aristocracy and their princely dynasties, and eventually the two thrones themselves became accessible to the Greek ruling class. Without including among these the roving James Vasilikos who ended his adventurous life as Prince of Moldavia (1561–63), we may recall the Cantacuzene Princes of Greek descent, Şerban (1678–88)[30] and Demetrius (1674–5 and 1684–5).

The establishment of a Greek Church hierarchy also contributed greatly to the spread of Greek influence. In 1359 the first Greek Metropolitan was appointed in Wallachia and between 1381 and 1386 in Moldavia.[31] From the seventeenth century Greek education was organized in both countries, and Theophilus Korydaleus, Panteleimon Ligarides, and Ignatius Petritses set up two educational centres; the School of Greek and Latin Studies at Tîrgovişte in Wallachia and the School of the Three Hierarchs at Jassy (Iaşi) in Moldavia, both in 1646. There followed in 1679 the foundation by Şerban Cantacuzene of the Prince's School at Bucharest.[32] The introduction of a Western-type Greek and Latin education eclipsed the older Slavonic-based tradition.[33]

In these conditions Greek influence was already great in the countries which Greeks were called upon to administer in the Sultan's name. The Ottoman Government's decision to replace the local rulers by Greek administrators was forced on them by

---

[30] V. Cândea, 'Les Bibles grecque et roumaine de 1687–8 et les visées impériales de Serban Cantacuzène', in *Balkan Studies*, vol. X Salonica, 1969, pp. 351–76.

[31] V. Laurent, 'Aux origines de l'Église de Moldavie. Le métropolite Jérémie et l'évêque Joseph', in *Revue des Études byzantines*, vol. V (1947), pp. 158–69.

[32] Ariadna Camariano—Cioran, *Academiile domneşti din Bucureşti şi Iaşi,* (*The Princely Academies of Bucharest and Jassy*) Bucharest, 1971.

[33] Cl. Tsourkas, *Les débuts de l'enseignement philosophique et de la libre pensée dans les Balkans. La vie et l'oeuvre de Théophile Corydalée (1570–1646)*, 2nd ed., Salonica, 1967, pp. 129 ff., 378 ff. V. Papacostea, 'Les origines de l'enseignement supérieur en Valachie', *Revue des Études Sud-Est européennes*, vol. I (1963), pp. 7–39.

the special importance which the Danubian provinces had assumed in the light of recent international events—the wars of Peter the Great with Charles XII of Sweden and against the Turks, the wars between Turkey and Venice and the general trend of the eastern policies of the Central European powers. The Romanian princes of Wallachia and Moldavia had become undesirably involved in these conflicts and in international affairs generally, and this gave the Sultan a pretext for putting an end to their rule and entrusting the administration of the Danubian lands to his Greek Grand Dragomans.

The first reign of Nicholas Mavrocordato in Moldavia (he was able to claim descent from an earlier Romanian ruler of that Principality on his mother's side) lasted only from 1709 to 1710, his second from 1711 to 1715, when he was transferred to the richer Principality of Wallachia, in succession to Stephen Cantacuzene, who had reigned only a few months. In 1716 he had the misfortune to be taken prisoner by the Austrians, at that time in a state of war with Turkey, and was replaced *ad interim* by his brother John. In 1719, however, he regained his throne and continued as Prince until his death in 1730. Between 1709 and 1821 twenty-six Phanariot princes of the families of Mavrocordato, Ghika, Karadjà, Soutsos, Mourouzi, Callimachi, Hypsilanti, Rosetti and Mavroyeni, governed the two trans-Danubian territories, except for brief intervals of Russian or Austrian occupation.

These Greek princes were, in fact, Governors-General or Viceroys invested with the most far-reaching administrative powers. They were appointed and recalled, at frequent intervals, at the will of their sovereign, the Sultan; but since they were the successors of the native Princes, they took over from these not only the general structure of the princely Court, with its high officers drawn from the leading boyars, but also certain sovereign rights, some of them with the acquiescence of the Turks, others without their knowledge or consent. Thus, in spite of the precarious nature of their office, they managed to introduce the beginnings of a hereditary succession and to found what were, in fact, princely dynasties. Similarly, they employed locally recruited troops to maintain order, they issued decrees and collections of laws and maintained diplomatic relations with foreign powers. Their decrees, it should be noted, were not merely regulations governing purely routine questions but dealt with major problems of the community and in some cases introduced radical social reforms. An outstanding example was Constantine Mavrocordato who reigned intermittently in Wallachia between 1730 and 1748, for some twelve years in all, and three times in Moldavia (1733–5, 1741–1743 and 1748–9). His financial, agrarian and taxation reforms[34] were a genuine attempt to redress social injustice and, with his action in educational and other fields, rank him as one writer expresses it, "among the enlightened rulers of the eighteenth century".[35] In the legal sphere the most comprehensive collections of laws published during the reigns of the Phanariot princes were: the Νομικὸν Πρόχειρον (Law Manual) of Michael Photeinopoulos (1765); the Συνταγμάτιον Νομικόν (Collected Laws) of Alexander Hypsilanti (1780); the Κῶδιξ Πολιτικός (the Moldavian Civil Code) of Callimachi (1817); and the Βλαχικὸς Κῶδιξ (the Wallachian Civil Code) of Karadjà (1818).[36]

In the conduct of diplomatic relations the Greek Princes followed the precedents set by their predecessors, forming contacts more particularly with the Courts of St. Petersburg,

---

[34] Valentin Al. Georgesco and Emanuela Popesco, *La législation agraire de Valachie (1775–1782)*. *Le projet de Code agraire de M. Fotino—Lois pour les cultivateurs—établissements agraires antérieurs à 1780*, Bucharest, 1970. V. Mihordea, 'Les règlements fiscaux édictés par Constantin Mavrocordato en Valachie', in *Revue Roumaine d'Histoire*, vol. X, 1971, pp. 267–91. Pan. J. Zepos, 'La politique sociale des princes Phanariotes', in *Balkan Studies, vol.* XI (1970), pp. 81–90.

[35] V. Mihordea, op. cit., p. 291.

[36] Traian Ionascu and Valentin Al. Georgescu, 'Unité et diversité de la réception du Droit romain en Occident et du Droit byzantin en Orient', in *Revue des Études Sud-Est européennes*, vol. II, (1964), pp. 153–86. Pan J. Zepos, 'Byzantine Law in the Danubian Countries', in *Balkan Studies*, vol. VII (1966), pp. 343–56.

Vienna and Warsaw, as well as with leading political person-
alities in other parts of Europe. After the treaty of Kutchuk
Kainardji (Küçük Kainarca) of 1774 between Russia and
Turkey the position of the Danubian Princes was strengthened
by international agreements and in consequence their diplomatic activity—which did not always suit Turkish interests—
expanded notably.[37]

On the actions of the Greek Dragomans and Princes, conflicting judgements have been passed. Already in 1824 a
hostile study was published in Marseilles by a Greek writer and
since that date the record of their rule has been frequently
blackened.[38] According to one writer, for instance, "The rulers
of the Danubian Principalities were *des esclaves titrés*, to use the
phrase applied to them by one of their own ministers, Rhizos
Neroulos; but even as such they performed no lasting or
permanent service to the Greek nation and Greek literature."
Romanian writers have expressed equally unfavourable views.[39]

All these judgements, which had their origin in conflicting
schools of historical thought, were hasty and partial. In my
own view, in spite of the darker features of their careers, the
performance of the Greek Dragomans and Princes, when
viewed as a whole, forms the crowning achievement of Greek
culture during the Turkish period. Paparrhegopoulos was not
far from the mark when he observed that the achievements of
the Phanariots in the Danubian Principalities were great
enough to justify the claim that "if the government of these
principalities had continued in Greek hands throughout this
period, our nation might have boasted that, even while itself

[37] J. Filitti, *Lettres et extraits concernant les relations des principautés roumaines
avec la France de 1720 à 1810*, Bucharest, 1915, P. A. Argyropoulos, 'Une
correspondance diplomatique, 1816–18', *L'Hellénisme Contemporain*, 1952, pp.
293–329, 451–60; 1953, pp. 3–33, 99–130, 287–335, 459–74; 1954, pp. 54–
61, 137–45, 238–49.

[38] M. Ph. Zallony, *Traité sur les Princes de la Valachie et de la Moldavie sortis
de Constantinople, connus sous le nom de Phanariotes*, Paris, 1830 (1st ed.,
Marseilles, 1824).

[39] D. Thereianos, Ἀδαμάντιος Κοραῆς, vol. I, Trieste, 1889, p. 59.

remained in slavery, it had performed a feat which rivalled its greatest achievements at the height of its political power".[40]

The work of the Greek Dragomans and Princes has to be appraised from a number of angles.[41] That in a great variety of ways they protected Greek culture and Orthodoxy, that they supported the arts and contributed both directly and indirectly to the development and spread of Greek letters and became the regenerators of education: all this, I believe, is beyond doubt.[42] Yet this aspect, perhaps, although of great importance on its own account, is the least important for the history of the Greek nation. To my mind the main achievement of the administrative aristocracy which was reborn in and after the seventeenth century, so far as the Greeks were concerned, was that it gave the enslaved Greek people a political individuality, scope for a political career and a field within which it could radiate political, cultural and spiritual influence. In Constantinople,

[40] Constantine Paparrhegopoulos, *op. cit.*, vol. V, 2, p. 112.

[41] In general see the old biblio. of Epam. Stamatiades, Βιογραφίαι τῶν Ἑλλήνων μεγάλων διερμηνέων τοῦ Ὀθωμανικοῦ Κράτους (*Biographies of the Greek Great Dragomans of the Ottoman Empire*), Athens, 1865. Th. Blancard, *Les Mavroyéni. Histoire d'Orient de 1700 à nos jours*, in two vols., Paris, 1909. Émile Legrand, *Généalogie des Mavrocordato de Constantinople, rédigée d'après des documents inédits*, Paris, 1900. J.-C. Filitti, *Rôle diplomatique des Fanariotes de 1700 à 1821*, Paris, 1901. Alexandre Stourdza, *L'Europe orientale et le rôle historique des Maurocordato 1660–1830*, Paris, 1913. A brief, but spirited, defence of the Phanariots is to be found in an essay, by A. A. Pallis, included in his *Greek Miscellany*, Athens, 1964. Among more favourable opinions from Romanian scholars he quotes one by Nicholas Iorga. Today research into the Phanariot period has made considerable advances both in Greece and Romania, and the work of the Greek Princes has won greater recognition. Cf. C. Th. Dimaras, Περὶ Φαναριωτῶν. Εἰσαγωγή ('On the Phanariots. An Introduction', in Ἀρχεῖον Θράκης (*Archives of Thrace*), vol. XXXIV Athens, 1969, pp. 117 ff. R. Florescu, 'The Phanariot Regime in the Danubian Principalities', in *Balkan Studies*, vol. IX (1968), pp. 301 ff. More recently (21–5 October 1970) a Symposium has been held at Salonica on the Phanariot Period, with the participation of Greek and Romanian scholars.

[42] It is interesting to note that a modern historian, describing the social, ideological and general intellectual changes in south-eastern Europe in and after the seventeenth century, heads one chapter: 'L'Intellectuel Sud-Est Europeen: Le Drogman' (V. Cândea, 'Les Intellectuels du Sud-Est Européen au XVIIᵉ siècle', in *Revue des Études Sud-Est Européennes*, vol. VIII, 1970, pp. 637 ff.).

within the framework of the Ottoman State, combining, as they did in the highest degree, the Byzantine tradition with a knowledge of European affairs, the Grand Dragomans played a most significant role. One can say without exaggeration that by participating in the public business of the Sovereign Power they associated the Greek element of the population, to a certain degree, with the government of the State of which, historically and racially, they had come to form a part. So far as the Danubian lands were concerned, the Greek Princes, applying their Byzantine tradition to local realities and mingling both with the reviving breeze which came to them out of the West, created the necessary conditions for political life. This political life was a fruitful experience for the Greeks as a whole because it not only brought out the ability of the higher-ranking political and cultural leaders of the nation but also secured for Greeks a leading position in the Ottoman administration and among the other subject peoples. We cannot forget that the first wave of the Revolution broke in Moldavia, that Rhigas Velestinli had served under the Prince of Wallachia, that prominent figures in the Revolution like Soutsos, Mourouzi, the Hypsilantis and Mavrocordato came from that particular background. These considerations will be further developed later in our examination of the currents of thought which prevailed in the various centres of the Greek revival.

Besides the aristocracy which grew up in Constantinople and the Danubian countries, mention must be made of the economic, and also in part administrative, social class which flourished in the Ionian Islands, though in totally different circumstances.[43]

---

[43] The 'Seven Islands' or Heptanese: Corfù, Zante, Cephalonia, Levkas, Ithaca, Paxos, Cythera. The general reader will find historical particulars of the islands in *The Ionian Islands*, by Arthur Foss (London, 1969). An account of the history of the Heptanese will be found in D. A. Zakythinos, Αἱ ἱστορικαὶ τύχαι τῆς Ἑπτανήσου καί ἡ διαμόρφωσις τοῦ Ἑπτανησιακοῦ πολιτισμοῦ ('The Historical Fortunes of the Heptanese and the Formation of Ionian Culture'), in Πρακτικὰ τοῦ Τρίτου Πανιονίου Συνεδρίου, 23–29 Σεπτεμβρίου 1965 (*Proc. of the Third Panionian Congress*), September 23–9, 1965, vol. II, Athens, 1969, pp. 357–80.

After a long and varied history the islands of the Ionian Sea had come under Venetian rule, which had been firmly established in them since the end of the fifteenth century; with the exception of Levkas, which had been subject to the Turks for a longer period (1479–1684), they had known only brief and transitory spells of Turkish rule. When the Venetian Republic was dissolved by Bonaparte, the 'Seven Islands' fell to France under the treaty of Campo Formio (1797), but the French occupation lasted only a short while. The islands were seized by the allied fleets of Russia and Turkey and under the treaty of Constantinople (21 March 1800) were formed into the Septin-sular Republic under the suzerainty of the Sublime Porte—the first free Greek state of modern times. After a brief second French occupation (1807–9) they came into British possession and by the treaty of Paris (1815) passed under a British protectorate which lasted until 1864, when the 'Seven Islands' were united with Greece.

Under Venetian rule a unique social system developed. The Ionian Islands, following their historical traditions, were more powerful exposed to Western influence. A number of men of distinction devoted themselves to philosophy and to the arts and sciences—Evgenios Voulgaris, Nikephoros Theotokis, Ilias Miniatis, Nicodemus Metaxas, Vikentios Damodos, Iakovos Pylarinos and others.[44] In addition, under Venetian

[44] It is interesting to compare careers and interests exemplified in the short biographies below with those in footnote 27 to Chap. VII.

Evgenios Voulgaris. Born at Corfù (1716). Educated at Arta, Cephalonia, Ioannina and Padua. Taught in the Maroutsi School at Ioannina (1742–50), then at Kozani (Macedonia). Called by the Ecumenical Patriarch to direct the Academy on Athos, 1753. Forced by intrigues to leave, 1759. Went to Salonica and Constantinople, where he taught in the Patriarchal Academy (1759–61). His teaching methods proving too advanced, he resigned in 1761. After a stay in Wallachia, he went to Germany, where he published his *Logic* (Leipzig, 1766) and a Greek trans. of the *Essai historique et critique sur les dissensions des Eglises de Pologne* of Voltaire (Leipzig, 1768) Favoured by Frederick the Great and recommended by him to Catherine II, he went to Russia. He became Imperial Librarian in 1772 and in 1776 was promoted to the see of Slavinion and Cherson. Awarded the Order of St. Andrew and became a member of the St. Petersburg Academy. Being unwilling, owing

protection the islands developed a considerable merchant navy
and engaged in seaborne trade. The Venetian Government not
only gave them protection in the great Levantine trading

to advancing age, to continue his duties as Archbishop, he caused these to be
entrusted to Nikephoros Theotokis (q.v. below), 1779. At St. Petersburg, he
published *inter alia* his archaic hexameter translations of Virgil's *Georgics*
(1786) and *Aeneid* (1791). In old age withdrew to the Monastery of St.
Alexander Nevski, where he died, 1806. In the words of Koraës, he was
"one of those who contributed most practically to the moral revival of the
Greeks".

Nikephoros Theotokis (1731–1800). A Corfiote. Studied in Italian universities, particularly at Bologna. Returned to Corfu in 1756 and took Holy
Orders, becoming a monk in 1762. Called to Constantinople as a preacher
and a teacher of mathematics and Greek; he later went to Jassy, in Moldavia,
as headmaster of the Prince's Academy. At Leipzig, in 1766, he published a
two-volume *Elements of Physics*. In 1779 he succeeded Evgenios Voulgaris as
Archbishop of Slavinion and Cherson, being later transferred to the see of
Astrakhan and Stavropolis, where he converted many Moslems and pro-
cured the return of four thousand *Raskolniki* (Orthodox schismatics) to the
Church. On retirement he went to Moscow. After the *Elements of Physics*,
his best-known work is the *Kyriakodromion* (*Gospel Lectionary*), first pub. in
Moscow, in 1796.

Elias Miniatis (1669–1714). Born at Lixouri, Cephalonia. Educated at
Venice. His career was mainly that of a schoolteacher and an eloquent
preacher, with occasional excursions into diplomacy. He taught at Venice in
the Collegium Graecum Phlaginianum. Taken to Constantinople as Adviser
by the newly appointed Venetian Ambassador Lorenzo Soranzo, whose
two nephews he tutored. Later employed by Demetrius Cantemir, Prince of
Moldavia, on a special mission to Vienna in 1703. After seven years in
Constantinople (1699–1706), he retired to the Peloponnese as Bishop of
Kalavryta (since 1710). His chief significance in the Greek intellectual
revival, apart from his devotion to teaching, is as one of the outstanding
orators of the Greek Church and one of the earliest formative influences on
cultivated modern Greek. Among his works we mention *The Stumbling-block*
(1718) and *Sermons* (1716).

Nicodemus Metaxas (1585–1646). Born at Keramiés in Cephalonia. Nephew
of Nicodemus I Metaxas, Archbishop of Cephalonia and Zakynthos. Pupil
of Theophilus Corydaleus. At London he edited two of Corydaleus's works,
1624. In 1627 bought a Greek printing-press in England, which he trans-
ported to Constantinople under the protection of Sir Thomas Roe,
Ambassador of King Charles I. Largely engaged in printing refutations of
Roman Catholic theology, the Roman campaign for the conversion of the
Greeks being then at a moment of great activity. Imprisoned by the Turks
at the instance of the French Ambassador but subsequently released on the
intervention of the British Ambassador. Created Bishop of Neapolis and

centres but also, in some cases, employed Ionian islanders in its diplomatic and consular services. About the middle of the eighteenth century there was a substantial number of Venetian citizens of Ionian origin in Salonica.[45] After the proclamation of the semi-independent Septinsular Republic Ionian merchant-men sailed under their own flag.[46]

The special conditions of the Ionian Islands produced some of the leading figures in the intellectual and literary revival of Greece at the time of the Revolution, as well as a statesman of the international stature of Capodistria. The poets Solomos and Kalvos and the historian Mustoxides are examples of the great

Exarch for the towns and islands under Venetian rule, 1628. In the same year elected Archbishop of Cephalonia and Zakynthos (1628–46). Elected Metropolitan of Philadelphia, in 1634/1635, he declined the appointment.

Vikentios Damodos (1700–52). Born at Khavriata, Cephalonia, in 1700 (according to new evidence). Educated in Venice, at the Phlanginian School, and at Padua (Philosophy, Theology and Law). Practised as a lawyer in Cephalonia. In his birth-place he founded a celebrated School of Philosophy. Among his pupils was Evgenios Voulgaris (q.v. above). Two of his works were pub. after his death, an *Epitome of Aristotelian Logic* and an *Art of Rhetoric* (both in Venice, 1759). Many of his philosophical treatises remain unpub.: 'General and Special Physics', 'Metaphysics: First Philosophy and Natural Theology', 'Synopsis of Aristotles's Nicomachean Ethics', etc. His chief intellectual concern was with the expression of philosophical ideas in the common, as opposed to the learned, language of his time.

Iakovos Pylarinos (1659–1718). Born at Lixouri, Cephalonia. Studied in Venice and medicine in Padua. He travelled much in Europe and the Levant, Italy, Greece, Constantinople, Wallachia, Serbia, Russia, Egypt, Smyrna, Aleppo. Venetian Consul in Smyrna, 1712–18. Physician to a number of rulers, including Peter the Great. Wrote, in Italian, a *Defence of Medicine* (*La medicina difesa*, Venice, 1717). One of the pioneers of inoculation against smallpox, with the Chiote physician Timones. The latter communicated his experiments to Goodward at Oxford and Pylarinos to the naturalist Sherard, who also lived for a time at Smyrna. Their discovery was the subject of dispute until 1796, when Jenner devised its scientific application. Pylarinos's works on the subject were pub. in Latin: *Nova et tuta variolas excitandi per transplantationem methodus* (Venice, 1715) and *Tractatus de nova variolas per transplantationem excitandi methodo* (Leiden, 1721).

[45] K. Mertzios, Μνημεῖα Μακεδονικῆς Ἱστορίας, pp. 109 ff., 338 ff.

[46] M. Lascaris, Τὸ ᾽Ανατολικὸν Ζήτημα 1800–1923 (*The Eastern Question*), Salonica, 1948, pp. 183ff.

contribution to Greek culture and the development of the modern Greek language by Ionian writers and men of learning.

The Rise of the New Landed Aristocracy

It is still too soon to speak with any precision about the development of landed property in the Greek lands under Turkish rule; this will, however, become possible when the documentary material—the Turkish official documents, those relating to monastic and other Church property, and more especially notarial documents—comes to be published. A systematic attempt has been begun in recent years to examine and edit these basic historical sources. The Turkish lawbooks (*Kanunname*) of many Greek districts, towns and islands are now more easily accessible,[47] and the publication of Greek notarial documents is making progress. After the work of Skopeteas[48] and Visvizes[49], Professor George Petropoulos has made a fine contribution in his Μνημεῖα τοῦ Μεταβυζαντινοῦ Δικαίου (Monuments of post-Byzantine Law).[50] The Historical Research Centre for Greek

[47] Josef Kabrda, Ὁ Τουρκικὸς Κώδικας ('Kanunname') τῆς Λαμίας (Συμβολή στή μελέτη τῶν Τουρκικῶν ἱστορικῶν πηγῶν τῶν σχετικῶν μὲ τὴν Ἱστορία τῆς Ἑλλάδος) ('The Turkish Lawbook of Lamia. A Contribution to the Study of the Turkish Historical Sources relating to the History of Greece'), in Ἑλληνικά, vol. XVII (1962), pp. 202–18.

[48] S. Skopeteas, Ἔγγραφα ἰδιωτικά ἐκ Δυτικῆς Μάνης τῶν ἐτῶν 1547–1830 ('Private Documents from Western Mani, 1547–1830'), in Ἐπετηρὶς τοῦ Ἀρχείου τῆς Ἱστορίας τοῦ Ἑλληνικοῦ Δικαίου of the Academy of Athens, vol. III (1950), pp. 60–117.

[49] I. Visvizes, Ναξιακὰ νοταριακὰ ἔγγραφα τῶν τελευταίων χρόνων τοῦ Δουκάτου τοῦ Αἰγαίου (1538–1577) ('Notarial Documents of Naxos from the Last Years of the Duchy of the Archipelago, 1538–77'), in Ἐπετηρὶς τοῦ Ἀρχείου τῆς Ἱστορίας τοῦ Ἑλληνικοῦ Δικαίου of the Academy of Athens, vol. IV (1951), pp. 1–167, and Δικαστικαὶ ἀποφάσεις τοῦ 17ου αἰῶνος ἐκ τῆς νήσου Μυκόνου ('Judgments of the seventeenth Century from the Island of Mykonos'), ibid., vol. VII (1956), pp. 22–154.

[50] George A. Petropoulos, Ὁ κῶδιξ τοῦ νοταρίου Ἀθηνῶν Παναγῆ Πούλου 1822–33 (*The Codex of the Athenian Notary Panagis Poulos, 1822–33*), Athens, 1957.—Νοταριακαὶ πράξεις Παξῶν διαφόρων νοταρίων τῶν ἐτῶν 1658–1810, (*Notarial Documents of Different Notaries of Paxoi, 1658–1810*), Athens, 1958.—

Law of the Academy of Athens is pursuing a systematic programme of research in this field.[51]

The system of large Greek landed estates which prevailed in rural society during the last centuries of the Byzantine Empire began to break up with the extension of the timariot system and the transfer of land to Turkish owners.[52] This was a widespread development which is particularly observable in the first centuries after the Ottoman conquest but more detailed research will be needed before we can tell to what extent the great estates were preserved in the hands of individuals who had not gone over to the conqueror's religion. It is clear, for example, from the Klavazos Papers, that in the year 1572, in the region of Diakopton and Kalavryta in the northern Peloponnese, there were already considerable Greek Christian landowners— the Klavazos family (who belonged to the Peloponnesian family of the Asanai), the Zemnakoi, the Haralambes, the Khariti, and others.[53]

In the course of time an important change undoubtedly took place with regard to the acquisition of land by members of subject races. Agricultural land of greater or lesser extent came into Greek hands. The causes and stages of this development remain unknown. It is clear, however, that the general improvement in the demographic situation and the development of local industry and trade, as well as the decline of the Moslem settler population, contributed greatly to the expansion of

---

Νοταριακαὶ πράξεις Μυκόνου τῶν ἐτῶν 1663–1779 (*Notarial Documents of Mykonos of the years 1663–1779*), Athens, 1960.—Α'. Νοταριακαὶ πράξεις Κεφαλληνίας τῆς Συλλογῆς Ε. Μπλέσσα τῶν ἐτῶν 1701–1856 (*I. Notarial Documents of Cephalonia from the Collection E. Blessa, 1701–1856*); Β'. Ἔγγραφα τῆς 'Ηπείρου καί τῶν ἱερῶν μονῶν Αἰτωλίας τῶν ἐτῶν 1701–1887 (*II. Documents of Epirus and the monasteries of Aetolia of the Years 1701–1887*), Athens, 1962.—Α'. Νοταριακαὶ πράξεις Χίου τῶν ἐτῶν 1724–80 (*I. Notarial Documents of Chios 1724–80*); Β'. Ἔγγραφα 'Ρόδου καὶ Καστελλορίζου τῶν ἐτῶν 1847–74 (*II. Documents of Rhodes and Castellorizo 1847–74*), Athens, 1963.

[51] In general see D, Ghinis, Περίγραμμα τοῦ Μεταβυζαντινοῦ Δικαίου, (*Outline of post-Byzantine Law*) Athens, 1966.

[52] See Chap. II above.

[53] N. A. Bees, *op. cit.*, pp. 441 ff.

large estate holdings among the Greeks. Those who grew rich on trade and industry devoted large sums to the purchase of landed property. There are not a few cases of the sale of *tchifliks* (farm properties or small country estates) to Greeks by their Turkish owners. The increase in the acquisition of land was also helped by certain practices permitted by customary law whereby small freeholders ceded their holdings to big landowners with a view to 'protection' (προστασία).

Whatever the truth of the matter, it seems clear that in the eighteenth century Greek property holdings in the countryside showed a steady increase, particularly in the Morea. In other regions—Epirus, Thessaly and Macedonia—there were great Turkish estates, but many of these, as well as also the 'free villages' (ἐλευθεροχώρια) in Greek possession, later suffered encroachment by Ali Pasha of Ioannina.[54] Our information about the Morea is fuller. In northern and western Gortynia, for example, the family of the Syntykhi held forty *tchifliks* Large estates were also held by the families of Deliyannis and Kouriakos in Kalavryta and great tracts of land, in the eparchies (Departments) of Kalavryta and Karytaina and in the Eurotas valley, belonged to Greeks.

Greek landowners acquired considerable wealth and very soon became the ruling class in rural areas. They extended their power still further by taking on themselves the management of public business. Still confining ourselves to the affairs of the Morea, we note that in the last years of the Turkish regime great families flourished in this region, combining the power that accompanied land-ownership with the prestige derived from involvement in matters of public concern. Certain families exercised a wider influence throughout the entire Peloponnese and it was from these that the highest officials and representatives of the Greek community came.[55]

[54] D. Tsopotos, Γῆ καί γεωργοί τῆς Θεσσαλίας, (Land and Farmers in Thessaly) pp. 183 ff.

[55] M. Sakellariou, Ἡ Πελοπόννησος κατὰ τὴν Δευτέραν Τουρκοκρατίαν, *op. cit.*, pp. 48, 139 ff. Ibid., a list of influential Peloponnesian families, with their local connections. For the distribution of land between Greeks and Turks at

The landed aristocracy, who lost no time in seizing posts of advantage in the local government system, took part in the movements for national liberation and exercised in general an influence on the Greek revival. Some writers, both Greek and foreign, have passed very hostile judgements on the whole outlook of the great landowners and notables, based chiefly on the oppression to which their fellow-countrymen working the land were subjected. This caused them to be termed 'Turcophils' (τουρκίζοντες) and 'uncircumcised Turks'. The Frenchman Pouqueville speaks of them with a good deal of animosity, as also does Ubicini, quoting in support General Gordon's *History of the Greek Revolution.*[56] But, as Sakellariou has observed: "Up till now there has been a complete misunderstanding of the part played by the Greek notables, particularly in the Peloponnese, since our sources have led us to view the problem through the troubled atmosphere of the time." Again, according to the same writer, the Greek landowners "felt no class solidarity with the Turks; on the contrary, it was between them and the Turks that a violent national antipathy arose". The Greek landowners, in waging their struggle for economic domination against the Turkish timariot, were bound to bring pressure to bear on their own compatriots, but this struggle was vital to the national existence. In this way "the economic and racial antagonisms between Greek and Turkish landowners became one and the same. Every acquisition in the economic field became at the same time a step forward for the nation. Conversely, awareness grew that national independence would

---

the end of the Turkish period, see also the table at the end of Chap. II above, taken from the 'Memorandum of Capodistria to the Protecting Powers (1828)'. On the general question of redistribution of land see B. B. Alivisatos, *La Réforme agraire en Grèce au point de vue économique et social*, Paris, 1932, pp. 94 ff. G. P. Nakos, Αἱ "Μεγάλαι Δυνάμεις" καὶ τὰ "ἐθνικὰ κτήματα" τῆς Ἑλλάδος (1821–1832) ('The "Great Powers" and the "National Lands" of Greece, 1821–1832'), in Ἀριστοτέλειον Πανεπιστήμιον Θεσσαλονίκης. Ἐπιστημονικὴ Ἐπετηρίς Σχολῆς Νομικῶν καί Οἰκονομικῶν Ἐπιστημῶν (University of Salonica. *Scientific Yearbook of the Faculty of Law and Economics*), vol. IX (1970), pp. 467–546.
[56] M. A. Ubicini, *Lettres sur la Turquie*, vol. II, Paris, 1854, pp. 191 ff.

bring with it economic freedom as well. For this reason the Greek landowning class stood out as the revolutionary element *par excellence* in the situation. It was this class which prepared the ground for two insurrections. The first, particularly that of 1770, was above all its handiwork. . . . The landowning class, favoured by the prevailing system of local self-government, had also in its hands the political leadership of its fellow-countrymen. They had concentrated in themselves the whole of such authority as was allowed to the subject race and showed themselves in all respects its manifest leaders. A further asset, gained in the exercise of local government, was their political experience and their feel for politics. . . ."[57]

[57] Quotations from M. Sakellariou, *op. cit.*, pp. 136 ff., 137, note 3.

VII

The Rebirth of the Greek Nation: II. The Greeks of the Dispersion and the New Urban Upper Class

The Greeks of the Dispersion

Even before the fall of Constantinople, but chiefly after it, a strong current of Greek emigration set in to the West.[1] The first phase of this movement was aristocratic in character. Scholars and political or military leaders left their enslaved country and took refuge in the Christian countries of Europe. especially Italy. But not long after, the stream became a torrent and Greeks started to arrive as refugees in substantial numbers. This happened after the conquest of the Despotate of the Morea in 1460, after the Turco-Venetian war of 1463–79 and later still after the collapse of Venetian colonial power in Greece with the

[1] The biblio. of Greek settlement overseas and in Europe is a long one. Only a few titles can be mentioned here. For biblio information on individual Greek settlements see footnotes below. M. Dendias, *Αἱ Ἑλληνικαὶ παροικίαι τοῦ Ἐξωτερικοῦ*, Athens, 1919. Tr, Evangelides *et al.*, *Ὁ Ἑλληνισμὸς τῆς Διασπορᾶς* ('The Greeks of the Dispersion'), in *Μεγάλη Ἑλληνικὴ Ἐγκυκλοπαιδεία*, (*Great Greek Encyclopaedia*), vol. X (1934), pp. 729 ff. N. B. Tomadakis, *Ἡ συμβολὴ τῶν Ἑλληνικῶν κοινοτήτων τοῦ Ἐξωτερικοῦ εἰς τόν Ἀγῶνα τῆς Ἀνεξαρτησίας* (*The Contribution of Greek Communities abroad to the Struggle for Freedom*), Athens, 1953. J. Irmscher and M. Mineemi (eds.), *Ὁ Ἑλληνισμός εἰς τό Ἐξωτερικόν*. 'Uber Beziehungen des Griechentums zum Ausland in der neueren Zeit', *Berliner Byzantinische Arbeiten*, vol. 40, Deutsche Akademie der Wissenschaften zu Berlin, Berlin, 1968. See also review by C. P. Kyrris, 'The Greeks of the Diaspora', in *Balkan Studies*, vol. X (1969), pp. 377–92.

loss of Lepanto in 1499, of Modon and Coron in 1500, of Nauplia and Monemvasia in 1540, of Cyprus in 1571 and finally of Crete in 1669. The war of 1684–1718 between Turkey and Venice provoked a new crisis. The character of these successive waves of emigration was different from that of the earlier ones. These later emigrants came more from the common people and their settlements abroad were agricultural and military. From the end of the fifteenth century bodies of Greek soldiery, the so-called *Stradiotti* or Estradiots, served as mercenaries under Venetian, French and other foreign commanders and had their effect on European tactical ideas.[2]

These repeated emigrations led to the formation of the Greek colonies and communities in the West. The main bulk of the refugees settled in Italy. The princes and states of that country maintained closer relations with Greece and their importance for the fate of Greece was considerable. The Roman Church paid particular attention to the refugees, hoping to find support among them in gaining its age-old objective, the union of the Churches under the aegis of the Pope. Sicily and the southern provinces of Italy received a large number of Greek- and Albanian-speaking immigrants who began to reinforce the Greek element which had been settled there since ancient and medieval times. Even in our own days the Greek language is to be heard in these regions.[3]

The most significant of all the overseas urban communities of Greeks at this time was undoubtedly that of Venice.[4] Its

[2] C. Oman, *A History of the Art of War in the sixteenth Century*, London, 1937, p. 92. Cf. above, Chap. V, n. 1, p. 70.

[3] Stam. C. Caratzas, *L'origine des dialectes néo-grecs de l'Italie méridionale*, Collection de l'Institut d'Études Byzantines et Néo-helléniques de l'Université de Paris, Fasc. 18, Paris, 1958. Benito Spano, *La grecità bizantina e i suoi reflessi geografici nell'Italia meridionale e insulare. Pubblicazioni dell'Instituto di Geografia dell'Università di Pisa*, 12, Pisa, 1965.

[4] J. Veloudos, Ἑλλήνων ὀρθοδόξων ἀποικία ἐν Βενετίᾳ. Ἱστορικὸν ὑπόμνημα (*The Colony of Orthodox Greeks in Venice. A Historical Dissertation*'), second ed., Venice, 1893. Deno John Geanakoplos, *Greek Scholars in Venice. Studies in the Dissemination of Greek Learning from Byzantium to Western Europe*, Cambridge, Mass., 1962. G. Fedalto, *Ricerche storiche sulla posizione giuridica ed ecclesiastica*

history dates from before the fall of Constantinople but its systematic organization came later. We have no exact evidence of the number of Greek refugees in the city, but in 1478 the Greek colony there totalled more than four thousand and by 1580, according to one source, which may, however, be exaggerating, there were fifteen thousand Greeks living in Venice.[5] The first licence from the Venetian Senate for the building of a Greek church was granted on 18 June 1456, but no action was taken on it. Final sanction was given on 28 November 1498, and this led to the foundation of the Scuola di San Nicolò della Nazione Greca. The still existing church of San Giorgio dei Greci was founded in 1539 and rebuilt in 1573; it became the centre of the Greek community in Venice[6], and in 1578 an Orthodox archbishopric was established in the city, the first appointment to it being that of Gabriel Severus, Metropolitan of Philadelphia (1577–1616).[7]

dei Greci a Venezia nei secoli XV e XVI, Florence, 1967. G. S. Ploumidis, *Αἱ βοῦλλαι τῶν παπῶν περὶ τῶν Ἑλλήνων ὀρθοδόξων τῆς Βενετίας* (1445–1782) ('The Papal Bulls regarding the Orthodox Greeks of Venice, 1445–1782'), in *Θησαυρίσματα*, vol. VII 1970, pp. 228–66.

[5] D. J. Geanakoplos, *op. cit.*, pp. 60 ff.

[6] M. I. Manoussacas, *Ἡ πρώτη ἄδεια* (1456) *τῆς Βενετικῆς Γερουσίας γιά τὸ ναὸ τῶν Ἑλλήνων τῆς Βενετίας καί ὁ καρδινάλιος Ἰσίδωρος* ('The First Licence, 1456, given by the Venetian Senate for the Greek Church in Venice, and Cardinal Isidore'), in *Θησαυρίσματα*, vol. I (1962), pp. 109–18. N. G. Moschonas, 'I Greci a Venezia e la loro posizione religiosa nel XVo secolo. Studio su documenti veneziani', in *Ὁ Ἐρανιστής*, vol. V (1967), pp. 105–37. Phanè Mavroeidis—Ploumidis, *Ἔγγραφα ἀναφερόμενα στὶς ἔριδες τῶν Ἑλλήνων τῆς Βενετίας στά τέλη τοῦ ΙΕ′ αἰῶνα* ('Documents relating to the Quarrels of the Greeks of Venice at the end of the Fifteenth Century'), in *Θησαυρίσματα*, vol. VIII (1971), pp. 115–87.

[7] M. I. Manoussacas, *Ἀνέκδοτα πατριαρχικὰ γράμματα* (1547–1806) *πρὸς τοὺς ἐν Βενετίᾳ μητροπολίτας Φιλαδελφείας καί τήν Ὀρθόδοξον Ἑλληνικὴν Ἀδελφότητα*, ('"Unpublished Patriarchal letters (1547–1806) to the Metropolitans of Philadelphia at Venice and the Greek Orthodox Fraternity"), *Venice*, 1968 Id., *Συλλογὴ ἀνεκδότων ἐγγράφων* (1578–1685) *ἀναφερομένων εἰς τοὺς ἐν Βενετίᾳ μητροπολίτας Φιλαδελφείας* ('Collection of Unpublished Documents, 1578–1685, relating to the Metropolitans of Philadelphia in Venice'), in *Θησαυρίσματα*, vol. VI (1969), pp. 7–112. Id., *Ἡ ἐν Βενετίᾳ Ἑλληνικὴ κοινότης καί οἱ μητροπολῖται Φιλαδελφείας* ('The Greek Community in Venice and the Metropolitans of Philadelpheia'), in *Ἐπετηρὶς Ἑταιρείας Βυζαντινῶν Σπουδῶν*, vol. XXXVII (1969–70), pp. 170–210.

The Greek community in Venice developed into the most important cultural centre of Greece overseas and one from which Greek civilization spread all over Europe. In late Byzantine times Venice was already noted for humanist studies. It was there that Guarino of Verona, the pupil of Manuel Chrysoloras, introduced the systematic study of Greek letters (1414–18)[8] and it was to Venice, as 'another Byzantium' that Cardinal Bessarion left his rich collection of manuscripts (1468).[9] From the presses of Venice there issued, besides the great masterpieces of Antiquity, the works of later Greek writers, theological, educational, ethical and secular. The first Greek book published in Venice is thought to have appeared in 1471. In 1486 the Cretan Laonikos published the pseudo-Homeric *Batrachomyomachia* ('The Battle of the Frogs and Mice') and the first book from the Greek press of Zacharias Kallergis (also a Cretan) saw the light in 1499. The greatest international force in spreading the Venetian study of Greek was however, the press set up by Aldo Manuzio in 1494/5 and the consequent foundation of the Aldine New Academy.[10]

In 1405, the city of Padua whose university, founded in 1222, was the great mediator of European education to the Greek and even to the whole Christian East, had been added to the Venetian Republic. In the Chair of Greek Letters which was founded there in 1463 the first appointment was that of Demetrius Chalkokondyles, followed later by Markos Mousouros. In this second revival of a new Greece, both Venice and Padua threw open their doors to a wider section of the community. In Venice, beside the Church of San Giorgio, there was founded, in 1593, a school which had some distinguished

[8] D. J. Geanakoplos, *op. cit.*, pp. 28 ff.

[9] For the commemoration of the fifth centenary of the foundation of the *Biblioteca Marciana*, an exhibition was organized in Venice, May 1968. *Cento codici Bessarionei. Catalogo di mostra a cura di Tullia Gasparrini Leporace ed E. Mioni*, Venice, 1968.

[10] For this same commemoration an exhibition of books was prepared. *La stampa greca a Venezia nei secoli XV e XVI. Catalogo di mostra a cura di Marcello Finazzi*, Venice, 1968.

teachers, and from 1662 to 1797 there was a flourishing Greek High School (Φροντιστήριον) at Venice, the Phlanginianon: founded by a Corfiote benefactor, a patriot and man of learning, Thomas Phlangines.[11] Similarly, in 1653 the Macedonian scholar, John Kottounios (1572–1657) Professor of Greek and Philosophy at the Universities of Bologna and Padua, founded in the latter city the Kottounian College.[12] From the second half of the seventeenth century the new Greek presses of Venice were at their height, their publications being directed first and foremost to the rising Greek community. The most important of these presses were those set up by the Glykys family of Ioannina in 1670 and by Demetrius and Panos Theodosios from the same city (1755–1824).[13]

After the Second World War, the scanty Greek community in Venice devoted its resources and its works of post-Byzantine art to founding the Hellenic Institute of Byzantine and Post-Byzantine Studies, which was established by law in 1951 and started its activity in 1955.[14]

[11] C. Mertzios, Θωμᾶς Φλαγγίνης καί ὁ Μικρὸς Ἑλληνομνήμων ('Thomas Phlangines and the 'Mikros Hellenomnemon'), Πραγματεῖαι τῆς Ἀκαδημίας Ἀθηνῶν (Dissertations of the Academy of Athens), vol. IX, Athens, 1939.

[12] Artist. P. Sterghellis, Τὰ δημοσιεύματα τῶν Ἑλλήνων σπουδαστῶν τοῦ Πανεπιστημίου τῆς Πάδοβας τὸν 17° καί 18° αἰῶνα (The Publications of Greek Students at the University of Padua in the Seventeenth and Eighteenth Centuries), Athens, 1970. See also Giov. Fabris, Gli Scolari illustri della Università di Padova, Padua, 1941. Id. 'Professori e Scolari Greci all'Università di Padova', in Archivio Veneto, Serie 6, vol. XXX (1942), pp. 121–65. Cl. Tsourkas, Gli scolari greci di Padova nel rinnovamento culturale dell'Oriente Ortodosso, Università di Padova, 1958.

[13] N. Kontosopoulos, Τὰ ἐν Βενετίᾳ τυπογραφεῖα Ἑλληνικῶν βιβλίων κατὰ τὴν Τουρκοκρατίαν ('The Printing of Greek Books at Venice during the Period of Turkish Rule in Greece'), in Ἀθῆνα vol. LVIII (1954), pp. 286–342. G. S. Ploumidis, Τὸ Βενετικὸν τυπογραφεῖον τοῦ Δημητρίου καὶ τοῦ Πάνου Θεοδοσίου (1775–1824) (The Venetian Printing-Press of Demetrius and Panos Theodosios, 1775–1824), Athens, 1969. N. B. Tomadakis, Ἡ ἐν Ἰταλίᾳ ἔκδοσις Ἑλληνικῶν ἐκκλησιαστικῶν βιβλίων (κυρίως λειτουργικῶν) γενομένη ἐπιμελείᾳ Ἑλλήνων Ὀρθοδόξων κληρικῶν κατὰ τοὺς ΙΕ΄–Ιϛ΄ αἰῶνας (The Publication of Greek Ecclesiastic Books, particularly Liturgical, in Italy, edited by Greek Orthodox Clergy in the Fifteenth and Sixteenth Centuries), in Ἐπετηρὶς Ἑταιρείας Βυζαντινῶν Σπουδῶν, vol. XXXVII (1969–70), pp. 3–33.

[14] The Institute publishes a yearly periodical entitled Θησαυρίσματα. The

Of the other earlier Greek settlements in Italy mention must be made of those at Naples and Leghorn. Already from the seventies of the fifteenth century, men of note had begun to arrive in the Kingdom of Naples as refugees from Greece, especially from the Peloponnese.[15] Owing to their origin and to the political ties between Greece and the country in which they had found hospitality, these exiles in Naples were particularly active in helping the various movements of revolt against Ottoman rule.[16] The Greek church in Naples was founded in 1518.[17]

In Leghorn the first nucleus of a Greek community is found in 1572–4. The first Greek church there was founded in 1601 and a later building in 1757.[18] To these early settlements must be added those of the Maniotes who left their homes under the pressure of poverty and tyranny and emigrated in groups to the Venetian islands of the Ionian Sea, particularly Zante.[19] Large scale emigrations of Maniotes also took place in 1670 to Tuscany and in 1675 to Corsica, first to Paomia and later to Cargèse, the Greek inhabitants of which speak a special dialect.[20]

first issue appeared in 1962. For its museum of Byzantine and Post-Byzantine Art see Manolis Chatzidakis, *Icônes de Saint-Georges des Grecs et de la Collection de l'Institut*, Bibliothèque de l'Institut Hellénique d'Études Byzantines et Post-byzantines de Venise, No. 1, Venice, 1962.

[15] Sp. Lambros, Μετανάστευσις Ἑλλήνων ἰδίως Πελοποννησίων ἐποίκων εἰς τό Βασίλειον τῆς Νεαπόλεως (Emigration of Greek Settlers, particularly from Peloponnese, to the Kingdom of Naples), in *Νέος Ἑλληνομνήμων*, vol. VIII (1911), pp. 377–461.

[16] J. K. Hassiotis, 'La communità greca di Napoli e i moti insurrezionali nella Penisola Balcanica meridionale durante la seconda metà del XVI secolo', in *Balkan Studies*, vol. X (1969), pp. 279–88.

[17] Sp. Lambros, 'Ἡ Ἑλληνικὴ Ἐκκλησία Νεαπόλεως ('The Greek Church of Naples'), in *Νέος Ἑλληνομνήμων*, pp. 3–19 and 158–81.

[18] N. B. Tomadakis, Ναοί καί θεσμοί τῆς Ἑλληνικῆς κοινότητος τοῦ Λιβόρνου ('Churches and Institutions of the Greek Community in Leghorn'), in *Ἐπετηρίς Ἑταιρείας Βυζαντινῶν Σπουδῶν*, vol. XVI (1940), pp. 81–127.

[19] D. Vayiakakos, Μανιᾶται εἰς Ζάκυνθον ἐπὶ τῇ βάσει ἀνεκδότων ἐγγράφων τοῦ Ἀρχειοφυλακείου Ζακύνθου ('The Maniotes in Zante according to Unpublished Documents from the Archives of Zante'), in *Ἐπετηρὶς τοῦ Ἀρχείου τῆς Ἱστορίας τοῦ Ἑλληνικοῦ Δικαίου τῆς Ἀκαδημίας Ἀθηνῶν* (Annual of the Archives of the History of Greek Law, Academy of Athens), vol. V, 1954, pp. 3–96 and VI (1955), pp. 3–92.

[20] Sp. Lambros, Ὁ κατὰ τὸν δέκατον ἕβδομον αἰῶνα εἰς τὴν Τοσκάναν ἐξοικισμός

The first great wave of Greek emigration was launched by the Turkish conquest and by Turkish acts of oppression. The emigrants were inspired by the ideal of an anti-Turkish crusade, But from the mid-seventeenth century, and during the eighteenth, the Greek Dispersion entered a second phase of its history. A new and powerful stream of emigrants can now be seen making for western and central Europe, but inspired to a lesser degree by the motives which had produced the first emigration; they had other and more material reasons. This emigration was obviously connected with the great economic revival which had begun to appear both in the Greek lands under Turkish rule and among the Greeks living outside them.

These new Greek elements came to reinforce and to rejuvenate the old settlements. Venice, Leghorn, Ancona and other Italian cities had proved to be important centres of Greek trade. Northern Greece carries on an intensive exchange with the cities of Italy and the transhipment centres, such as Durazzo, are for the most part in Greek hands. But besides the older settlements which thus acquire new life, vigorous new communities are created in countries where until this moment Greek activities had been limited or non-existent. The main thrust of the emigrants was directed towards Austria and Hungary and other lands of the Habsburg Empire. Austria's growing interest in the countries to the east and south-east, and the stabilization of relations with Turkey by the treaties of Karlowitz (1699), Passarowitz (1718) and Belgrade (1739), opened up the great international highways to Greek traders and contributed indirectly to the development of local centres of production in the enslaved countries. The Danube, brought under an international regime, became a great waterway from

τῶν Μανιατῶν (The Emigration of the Maniotes to Tuscany in the Seventeenth Century), in Νέος Ἑλληνομνήμων, vol. II (1905), pp. 396–434. D. Vayiakakos, Οἱ Μανιᾶται τῆς Διασπορᾶς. Α΄. Οἱ Μανιᾶται τῆς Κορσικῆς (The Maniotes of the Diaspora. I. The Maniotes in Corsica), vols. I and II, 1, Athens, 1970. See also G. H. Blanken, Introduction à une étude du dialecte grec de Cargèse (Corse), Leiden, 1947, and 'Les Grecs de Cargèse (Corse)' Recherches sur leur langue et leur histoire, vol. I, Leiden, 1951.

central to south-eastern Europe. In these conditions an immense network of Greek settlements, developed in Austria, Hungary, Germany, France, Britain, the Low Countries, Spain, the Balearic Islands and Malta, and the spread of Greek colonies extended to the Danubian Principalities and Russia.

The oldest Greek settlements in Hungary[21] dating from this period were in the domains of the Transylvanian princes of the house of Rákóczy, where the Orthodox were accorded their first privileges as early as 1636. This early settlement, mostly of Macedonian Greeks, was agricultural in character, but it was not long before trading centres were established. According to recent research the number of Greek settlements in Hungary of some importance was a hundred and twenty-five, including a substantial Greek colony at Tokay, which included settlers from Kozani; its surviving records from the years 1725–71 are an interesting illustration of the life of such communities. Spyridon Lambros writes:

> the chief of these from south to north, were Semlin [now Zemun], Neusatz [now Novi Sad], Temesvar [now Timişoara], Szegedin [now Szeged], Szentes, Kecskemét, Debrecen, Budapest, Miskolcz and Pressburg [now Bratislava]. I have intentionally named these towns from the south northwards since such an arrangement shows clearly the route taken by those coming from the region of Macedonia where most of the emigrants originated and most probably the order, more or

[21] Sp. Lambros, Σελίδες ἐκ τῆς ἱστορίας τοῦ ἐν Οὑγγαρίᾳ καί Αὐστρίᾳ Μακεδονικοῦ Ἑλληνισμοῦ ('Pages from the History of the Macedonian Greeks in Hungary and Austria'), in Νέος Ἑλληνομνήμων, vol. VIII (1912), pp. 257–300. N. B. Tomadakis, 'Les communautés helléniques en Autriche', in Festschrift zur 200—Jahrfeier des Österreichischen Haus-, Hof- und Staatsarchivs, vol. II, Vienna, 1952, pp. 452–61 (with a bibliogr. on the subject), reprinted in N. B. Tomadakis, Miscellanea Byzantina—Neohellenica, Modena (in press). Ödön Füves, 'Stand und Aufgaben der Forschungen zur Geschichte der Griechen in Ungarn', in Irmscher and Mineemi, Ὁ Ἑλληνισμός εἰς τὸ Ἐξωτερικόν, pp. 313–38. See also by Ödön Füves, Οἱ Ἕλληνες τῆς Οὑγγαρίας (The Greeks in Hungary), Salonica, 1965, and Ἐπιτύμβιοι ἐπιγραφαὶ Ἑλλήνων εἰς τὴν Οὑγγαρίαν ('Epitaphs of Greeks in Hungary'), in Ἑλληνικά, vol. XIX (1966), pp. 296–347.

less, in which they established themselves in these Hungarian towns, wandering steadily further northwards from their homelands. . . . Actually, Semlin, which until the early decades of the nineteenth century was the main transhipment centre for Greek trade with Hungary and Austria, lies on the banks of the Danube almost directly opposite Belgrade. It was therefore through Serbia that the emigration route to Hungary and Austria lay for the Greeks of Macedonia or for the other inhabitants of the Balkan Peninsula. . . .[22]

The Greek communities of Buda and Pest grew to be considerable. They were made up chiefly of merchants and the representatives of commercial houses: hence the word *görög*, meaning originally a Greek, means in present-day Hungarian, a trader in general. At first the Greeks of Pest worshipped in the Serbian Church of St. George, but in 1790 they founded the Church of the Dormition. The scholar George Zaviras (1744–1804) lived and died in Pest. A native of Siatista in Macedonia, his book *Nea Hellas* (New Greece) is an attempt to write the history "of those cultured Greeks who flourished after the grievous tribulation of our nation".[23] Andras Graf, in 1935, published a catalogue of Zaviras's library and Endre Horváth, in 1937, wrote a study of his life and work.[24]

Of the Greek communities in Austria the most important was that of Vienna.[25] It reached a peak of its development in the

---

[22] Sp. Lambros, *op. cit.* in preceding footnote, p. 272.

[23] Ed. by G. Kremos: Γεωργίου Ἰωάννου Ζαβίρα, Ἀνέκδοτα συγγράμματα, Νέα Ἑλλὰς ἢ Ἑλληνικὸν Θέατρον (*'G. V. Zaviras. Unpublished Writings'*). Athens, 1872.

[24] Andras Graf, Κατάλογος τῆς ἐν Βουδαπέστῃ Βιβλιοθήκης Γεωργίου Ζαβίρα, Budapest, 1935. Endre Horváth, Ἡ ζωὴ καί τὰ ἔργα τοῦ Γεωργίου Ζαβίρα (*Life and Works of G. Zaviras*), Budapest, 1937. The Greek manuscripts of the Zaviras Collection form part of the University Library of Budapest.

[25] The Ὑπόμνημα ἱστορικὸν περὶ ἀρχῆς καί προόδου καί τῆς σημερινῆς ἀκμῆς τοῦ ἐν Βιέννῃ Ἑλληνικοῦ Συνοικισμοῦ ('Memoir on the Beginnings and Progress and the Present Flourishing State of the Greek Community in Vienna') by Dr. A. Pallatides, pub. in Vienna in 1845, has lately been reprinted in the Βιβλιοθήκη Ἱστορικῶν Μελετῶν (*Library of Historical Studies*), No. 25, Athens, 1968.

second half of the eighteenth and the first decades of the nineteenth century. For a long time the Greeks found themselves at variance with the Serbs over Church affairs. In 1776 Maria Theresa granted them their first privileges, which were renewed in 1782, 1791 and 1794 and constituted the basic charter of the community. The Greek subjects of Turkey thus obtained in 1776 their own parish church of St George, built eventually in 1802. The Austrian Greeks had also built a church of their own in the Fleischmarkt, in 1787, dedicated to the Holy Trinity.[26] Vienna eventually became the foremost national, cultural and economic centre of the Greek Dispersion, in succession to Venice, and Greeks of some distinction—Anthimos Gazis, Neophytos Doukas, Theoklitos Pharmakides, Baron Sina[27]—

[26] Sp. Loukatos, 'Ο πολιτικὸς βίος τῶν 'Ελλήνων τῆς Βιέννης κατὰ τὴν Τουρκοκρατίαν καί τά αὐτοκρατορικὰ πρὸς αὐτοὺς προνόμια ('The Political Life of the Greeks of Vienna during the Period of Turkish Rule and the Imperial Grants of Privilege to Them'), in Δελτίον τῆς 'Ιστορικῆς καί 'Εθνολογικῆς 'Εταιρείας, vol. XV (1961), pp. 287–350.

[27] *Anthimos Gazis* (1764–1828). Born at Miliès in Thessaly. Took Holy Orders in Constantinople. Sent in 1798, as Archimandrite, to take charge of the Greek Church in Vienna. Forbidden by the Turks to found a school in his home town, he combined with others (see below) to start the Λόγιος 'Ερμῆς. In 1817 he returned to Greece and became a member of the revolutionary society, the *Philiki Hetaireia*. Aided the Greek insurrection in Thessaly, Macedonia and eastern Greece. His works include *Greek Library* (Βιβλιοθήκης 'Ελληνικῆς βιβλία δύο) in two vols., Venice, 1807, and the *Greek Dictionary* (Λεξικὸν 'Ελληνικόν), in three vols., Venice, 1809, 1812, 1816.

Neophytos Doukas (ca. 1760–1845). Cleric, teacher and commentator on the classics. Born in Epirus. Educated at Metsovon and Bucharest. Priest-in-charge of the Greek Church at Vienna in 1803. Taught at Bucharest 1815–17, but resigned owing to an attempt on his life over the language question. During the Greek Revolution he went as a national missionary (ἐθναπόστολος) to Transylvania. Summoned to Greece by Capodistria, taught in the Orphanage founded by the Governor in Aegina. Kolettis called him to Athens as a member of the Committee supervising the new Church laws, and he helped to found the Rizareion School of which he was made Director. Among his works we mention the *Tetraktys* (Τετρακτύς), a compendium of Rhetoric, Logic, Metaphysics and Ethics, written in 1817/1818 and published at Aegina in 1834, and the editions of ancient Greek authors, Thucydides, Aeschylus, Euripides, Sophocles, the Attic Orators, etc.

Theocletos Pharmakides (1784–1860). Born in Thessaly. Educated at Larissa (where he entered the Church as a Deacon in 1802), Constantinople, Cydoni (Aivali) in Asia Minor, Jassy and Bucharest. Appointed archpriest

made reputations there. Vienna too was closely, if tragically, associated with Rhigas Velestinlis in his struggle for Greek freedom. It was in Vienna that the press of the Zantiote Vendotis was set up and also that of the brothers Markides Pouliou, from Siatista in Macedonia, who published the first Greek newspaper, the *Ephemeris*, in 1790–7, but among the various Greek periodicals published in the city the most outstanding was the *Learned Mercury* (*Λόγιος 'Ερμῆς*) started by Anthimos Gazis and other writers and scholars, which appeared

---

at Vienna in 1811 and helped to edit *Logios Hermes* (1816–19). Invited by Lord Guilford in 1819 to become Prof. of Theology in the Ionian Academy, he went first to Göttingen to study modern theology but on the outbreak of the Revolution hastened back to Greece. In 1823 he took up his duties at the Ionian Academy. In 1825 he was made director of the Greek National Press and of the Official Gazette, but in 1827 he resigned and lived as a private citizen during the whole period of Capodistria's administration. In 1832 he became Superintendent (*ἔφορος*) of schools in Aegina, and in the following year the Regency appointed him Secretary of the Synod, in which post he supported the movement for the autocephaly of the Greek Church. In 1837 he was made honorary Prof. of the Theological Faculty in the newly founded University. In 1839, having been falsely accused of sympathy with the doctrines of the brilliant, but politically and ecclesiastically unorthodox, teacher and philosopher Theophilos Kaïris of Andros, he was moved to the Chair of Greek Philology and ceased to be Secretary of the Synod. He published his defence against these charges (*'Απολογία*, Athens, 1840). He was restored to his former posts of Prof. of Theology (1843–60) and Secretary of the Synod (1844–50).

Simon Sina (1753–1822). A Greek from Moschopolis in Macedonia, who settled in Vienna and concentrated on trade exchanges between Austria and Turkey. When the French Revolution broke out and communications between Austria and the Balkans were interrupted, Sina organized convoys for the protection of traders and paid particular attention to the traffic in cotton and textiles. He became extremely wealthy and was created a Baron by the Emperor Francis I in 1816. His son, *George Sina* (1783–1856), who took over after his father's death, was founder and director of the Austrian National Bank and founded also the first railway company in Austria, as well as initiating steam navigation on the Danube and promoting the textile industry and the cultivation of tobacco in Austria and Hungary. In 1834 he was appointed Greek Consul-General in Austria. Among other benefactions to the new kingdom of Greece, he presented to the city of Athens in 1842 the Observatory on the Hill of the Nymphs to the west of the Acropolis. This splendid building was erected in the days of his son, *Simon Sina jr.*, between 1859 and 1885.

from 1811 until the outbreak of the Greek Revolution in 1821.[28]

The Greek colony at Trieste was hardly less important in its influence and numbers. After the Peace of Passarowitz in 1718, Trieste was proclaimed a Free Port and became of special significance in the transit trade between south-east Europe and the Levant and central Europe. The first Greek church there was built in 1751, under Maria Theresa, who granted the Greek community their official privileges. Here again the late eighteenth and early nineteenth centuries marked the period of highest development. The Greeks used not only the overland but also the sea routes for their trade, the former being more convenient for northern Greece, the latter for the Peloponnese, western Greece and the islands. Contact with Trieste played a notable part in the development and growth of the Ionian merchant navy.[29]

In addition to the Greek settlements already mentioned and the Greek minorities and communities within the territories under Turkish rule, many similar centres were to be found both in western and in eastern Europe—in Russia and Poland, in Germany, France, England the Balearic Islands and Holland. The roots of both Byzantine and post-Byzantine Greek culture struck deepest in Orthodox Russia. From the conversion of Russia to Christianity in 989, the presence of Greek clergy and artists in Kiev played a fundamental part in the organization of the Russian Church, the development of Russian culture, the formation of Russian law and the philosophy of government and the promotion of art and letters. This old tradition per-

[28] See Catherine Coumarianou, 'Cosmopolitisme et Hellénisme dans le "Mercure Savant", première revue grecque, 1811–1821', in *Actes du IVe Congrès de l'Association internationale de Littérature Comparée*, Fribourg, 1964, The Hague-Paris, 1966, pp. 601–8.

[29] Διήγησις τῶν περὶ τήν ἐν Τεργέστῃ Ἑλληνικὴν Κοινότητα σπουδαιοτέρων συμβάντων ἀπὸ τῆς συστάσεως αὐτῆς μέχρι τῶν καθ' ἡμᾶς χρόνων ('An Account of the Affairs of the Greek Community in Trieste, from its Foundation to the Present Time'), Trieste, 1882. Reproduced in the Βιβλιοθήκη Ἱστορικῶν Μελετῶν (*Library of Historical Studies*), No. 48. G. Stefani, *I Greci a Trieste nel Settecento*, Trieste, 1960.

sisted until the rise of Muscovite Russia. About the year 1370 Theophanes the Greek, an outstanding artist—an early El Greco of the East—was among the creative artists working in Moscow and Novgorod.[30]

With the marriage of Ivan III with the Princess Zoë-Sophia, —daughter of Thomas Palaeologus, Despot of the Peloponnese —in 1472, Russia was laid wide open to Greek influence. Members of the great Byzantine families, churchmen and intellectuals sought refuge there and Russia was led towards the doctrine of Moscow as the Third Rome and autocracy.[31] But, beside the Byzantine tradition, many of these Greek refugees also brought with them the cultural experience of the West. A remarkable illustration of this is provided by the career of the monk Michael Trivolis (c. 1475–1556), the celebrated 'Maximos the Greek', educated in Italy and a follower of Politian, Marsilius of Padua, Pico della Mirandola, Janos Lascaris and Savonarola.[32] Trivolis was certainly among those who helped to stimulate and revive the intellectual life of the Russians, as the great Russian historian, Klyuchevsky, observes: "To him resorted many members of the Muscovite aristocracy who had a taste for letters, until such was the throng of visitors who assembled to argue with him 'concerning the books and customs of Tsargorod (Constantinople)' that his cell in the suburban monastery of St. Simeon came to resemble a regular literary club".[33] The growth of economic life in the eighteenth century led to the formation of new Greek settlements in southern Russia, which proliferated still further after the Russo-Turkish

[30] V. Lazarev, *Theophanes der Grieche und seine Schule*, Vienna and Munich, 1968.

[31] Hildegard Schaeder, *Moskau das Dritte Rom. Studien zur Geschichte der politischen Theorien in der Slawischen Welt*, ed., Darmstadt, 1957.

[32] E. Denissoff, *Maxime le Grec et l'Occident. Contribution à l'histoire de la pensée religieuse et philosophique de Michel Trivolis*, Paris–Louvain, 1943.

[33] Klyuchkevsky, *History of Russia*, trans. Hogarth, vol. II, London, 1912, p. 62. See also William K. Medlin and Christos G. Patrinelis, *Renaissance Influences and Reforms in Russia. Western and Post-Byzantine Impacts on Culture and Education (Sixteenth–Seventeenth Centuries)*, Geneva, 1971.

war of 1769–74. On the orders of Catherine II, Greeks were allowed to settle in the Crimea and in the territory of Azov.

In Germany we find Greek settlements in the major trading cities. Both Leipzig, the scene of the great annual trade fair, and Breslau had Greek communities from the middle of the eighteenth century.[34] In France the most flourishing Greek centres were Marseilles and Paris: at the time of the Greek revival scholars and copyists of Greek manuscripts took refuge in the French capital and at the turn of the eighteenth and nineteenth centuries there were several Greeks of the first rank there—Adamantios Koraïs, Constantine Nikolopoulos, Panayiotis Kodrikas and others. The Greek colony in London was of old standing. Joseph Georgeirenes, Metropolitan of Samos, had founded the Church of the Dormition there in 1677, and about the same time Greeks were studying at the University of Oxford.[35]

In the Low Countries two Greek clerics, the Archimandrite Hierotheos Abbatios from Cephalonia and Meletios Pantogalos, formerly Metropolitan of Ephesus, were enrolled at the University of Leiden.[36] By the middle of the eighteenth century, the Greek community at Amsterdam included a substantial number of merchants. One of these, John Pringos, from Zagora in Pelion, wrote an account of the Greek colony and its doings from 1753 to 1764. Besides this *Chronicle*, the same naïve historian set down in popular Greek the events of the Russo-Turkish war of 1768–74 and a number of lesser works.[37]

---

[34] Em. Turczynski, *Die deutsch-griechischen Kulturbeziehungen bis zur Berufung König Ottos*, Munich, 1959.

[35] Ep. Stamatiades, Ἐπιστολιμαία διατριβὴ περὶ Ἰωσὴρ Γεωργειρήνου, ἀρχιεπισκόπου Σάμου, 1666–1671 (Letters regarding Joseph Georgeirenes, Archbishop of Samos, 1666–71), Samos, 1892. See also J. Gennadius, *Hellenism in England*, London, 1915. Steven Runciman, *op. cit.*, pp. 296 ff., 300 ff.

[36] Keetje Rozemond, *Archimandrite Hierotheos Abbatios 1599–1664*, Leiden, 1966.

[37] V. Skouvaras, Ἰωάννης Πρίγγος (1725–1789). Ἡ Ἑλληνικὴ παροικία τοῦ Ἀμστερνταμ. Ἡ Σχολὴ καί ἡ Βιβλιοθήκη Ζαγορᾶς (*John Pringos, 1725–89, The Greek Colony at Amsterdam. The School and Library of Zagora*), Athens, 1964.

In Minorca, Greeks received permission to settle in 1745 and built their church there in 1751-2.[38] In Malta, Greeks had been settled since the sixteenth century and the community was further strengthened in the two succeeding centuries.

Up to a certain point the expatriation of Greeks had an adverse effect on their enslaved country. In saying this, I am not thinking mainly of the departure of the leading class but of the mass emigrations. Paparrhegopoulos writes on this point:

> We repeat that these men proved of use to the intellectual development of the West and helped to foster the goodwill of the European community towards Greece. But we doubt whether, in emigrating in large numbers to other countries, they fulfilled their principal duty to their own. Not only did nearly all of them become westernized [the Greek word used means 'Latinized'] either from the start or in the process of time; but in their absence the schools of Greece were left without teachers and most were closed, while the affairs of Church and State were mishandled for lack of men of learning and experience.[39]

One cannot accept this absolute verdict in its entirety. In contradiction to the historian's assertion, we can claim that the emigration of scholars and other eminent men did help to preserve the leaders of Greece who would have been exposed to the greatest dangers if they had remained in their conquered country. The influence of these leading minds on European affairs was considerable and in general their political and intellectual activity had an important effect during the first phase of Turkish domination. Finally, we ought not to forget that the first emigrants prepared the ground for the commercial emigration, which Paparrhegopoulos considers from quite a different angle.

---

[38] N. Svoronos, Ἡ Ἑλληνικὴ παροικία τῆς Μινόρκας. Συμβολὴ στὴν ἱστορία τοῦ Ἑλληνικοῦ Ἐμπορικοῦ Ναυτικοῦ τὸν 18ον αἰῶνα ('The Greek Colony in Minorca. Contribution to the History of the Greek Navy in the Eighteenth Century'), in *Mélanges Octave et Melpo Merlier*, vol. II (Athens, 1956), pp. 323-49.

[39] C. Paparrhegopoulos, *op. cit.*, vol. V, 2, p. 27.

In other ways too the Greeks of the Dispersion, both the earlier and the later emigrants, had a very great influence on the fortunes of the whole Greek nation in the period of Turkish rule. The great highways of Europe, the sea routes, opened up before them limitless fields of activity in which the potentialities of the Greek mind and spirit could be displayed. As time went on, their piecemeal action was co-ordinated, their individual regrets for their homeland were transformed into creative energy and the fragmentary Dispersion developed into a solid, organic body, the radiation of which, back into the inner heart of Greece, moved at last the immovable mass of that oppressed country. An economic ruling class was forged in the free Greek communities abroad. Itself subject to the Greek tradition and in turn adapting foreign traditions to its own spirit, it laid the foundations not only of an economic revival but also of educational reform. Further, the economic leadership became the bearer of ideas and of cultural and spiritual trends, which fertilized the national mind and turned the nation towards new and creative achievements.

Forming in truth a 'Third Estate' over and against the ecclesiastical and secular leaders of Greek society in Greece and Constantinople, the Greeks living abroad broke through the constricting limits of the Conqueror's administrative and fiscal system but also through those of the small-scale structure of the Commune. They gave a new direction to the fiery imagination of the Greeks and recalled them to the true sources of their inspiration. They deliberately turned back to the models of Antiquity. Although they remained firmly attached to their religious tradition, their secret inclination was towards secularization. Like sensitive recorders, they registered every turn and tremor of European thought and assimilated whatever in it was assimilable. More conservative in some cases, more progressive in others, they injected into all their concerns—their own language question, the great international conflicts of their day, all their philosophical and political arguments—bold plans for the revival of Greece. These 'new men', who lived abroad, combined in a masterly fashion a passion for moneymaking with a passion for their country, the practice of commerce with an enthusiasm for letters. Themselves totally representative of the rising urban class, they swept along with them to decisive victories the lethargic landed aristocracy and the leaders of Church and Administration.[40]

The Development of Economic Life and of the Greek Navy

The peak development of the Greek communities abroad is, as has been said, directly linked with the revival of economic life which first became evident in the second half of the seventeenth century and reached its height in the eighteenth. This period of economic growth was due to the improvement of living conditions throughout Europe and to the conditions which, in the main, prevailed in the Ottoman Empire generally and in the Greek lands; but it was due also to a special cause. Great changes had taken place in the markets of the East at the end of the seventeenth and the beginning of the eighteenth century. The progressive weakening of the Ottoman Empire and the strain of its Persian wars created an extremely confused situation in the eastern Mediterranean at this time. The ports and markets of Syria and Egypt fell into decay and, as a result, the axis of international trade shifted towards the north. Thus Smyrna and Salonica became great centres of the transit trade. Secondary trading posts sprang up in the Archipelago, in Crete, the Morea, Attica, Arta, Ioannina, Valona, Durazzo and elsewhere. Parallel with this development consulates and consular agencies of European powers (France, Russia, Britain, Austria, the Netherlands, Venice, Ragusa and others) were established in Greek cities and islands.[41]

As an illustration of the movements of trade and the general

[40] See also D. A. Zakythinos, Ὁ Ἑλληνισμὸς τῆς Διασπορᾶς ('The Hellenism of the Diaspora'), in Παρνασσός, vol. XIII (1971), pp. 389 ff.

[41] Félix Beaujour, *Tableau du Commerce de la Grèce, formé d'après une année moyenne depuis 1787 jusqu'en 1797*, Two vols., Paris, 1800. P. Masson, *Le commerce français dans le Levant pendant le XVIIᵉ siècle*, Paris, 1897, and *Le*

trend of economic activity, some typical figures are given below[42]: they refer to imports into and exports from Salonica.[43]

In the years 1700–18 the trade turnover of the city amounted to 300,000 Venetian ducats or sequins.[44] Later on, up to 1786, there follows a steady increase—from 1722 to 1737, 320,000 sequins, from 1738 to 1743 440,000 sequins; from 1744 to 1749, 400,000 sequins; from 1750 to 1770, 875,000 sequins; from 1771 to 1777, 1,500,000 sequins; from 1778 to 1786, 1,800,000 sequins; and from 1786 to 1800, 1,250,000 sequins. The falling off in the last period was due to the repercussions of the French Revolution.

Equally noteworthy are the figures given by Félix Beaujour— French Consul at Salonica from 1794 to 1797, and an expert in commercial matters—for the overall trade of Greece. On his showing this amounted to 13,791,000 piastres[45]; 8,821,320 for exports; 4,970,670 for imports. The same writer states elsewhere that before the French Revolution the import and export figures for Smyrna reached 16,000,000 piastres; for Constantinople 4,000,000 piastres; for Salonica 6,500,000 piastres; for the Morea 1,500,000 piastres and for Cyprus and Crete the same. The figure given for Salonica has been thought exaggerated. So far as the Morea is concerned, we know from other sources that, about the end of the eighteenth century, the value of goods exported amounted to 3,745,255 piastres and that of imports to 3,380,208 piastres.

---

commerce français dans le Levant au XVIIIe siècle, Paris, 1911. D. A. Zakythinos, Εἰδήσεις περὶ τῆς ἐμπορικῆς κινήσεως τῶν λιμένων τῆς Ἀττικῆς κατὰ τὰ μέσα τοῦ IZ' αἰῶνος ('Information on the Movement of Trade in the ports of Attica in the mid-18th Century'), in Ἑλληνικά, vol. VII (1934), pp. 253–65. M. Lascaris, Salonique à la fin du XVIIIe siècle, Athens, 1939. N. G. Svoronos, Le commerce de Salonique au XVIIIe siècle, Paris, 1956.

[42] In view of eighteenth-century statistical methods, these figures cannot be taken as wholly accurate. They can, however, be taken as indicative.

[43] N. G. Svoronos, op. cit., p. 323.

[44] The Venetian ducat or sequin (Zecchino) was a gold coin weighing 3,494 grammes.

[45] The piastre was a Turkish coin, the value of which fluctuated greatly in the eighteenth century. In 1787–1800 the sequin was rated at 6.75 piastres.

All these figures, looked at comparatively, indicate the change which had come over the economic life of the Greek lands. The main bulk of both the export and import trade was in the hands of Europeans. At the head of these were the French who at a certain period, from 1771 to 1777, handled about half the entire trade of Salonica. But other trading nations were Britain, Venice and the citizens of other Italian cities, Ragusa, Holland, Denmark and Sweden, Germany and Austria, Russia and the Jews. The French Revolution destroyed the preponderance which French trade had enjoyed in the East. Beaujour, speaking of the years 1787–97, rates the share of the leading European countries in the Greek market as follows:

Greek Exports

British, 558,320 piastres;	Germans, 4,663,000 piastres;
Italians, 1,150,000 piastres;	Dutch, 140,000 piastres;
Russians, 1,000,000 piastres;	French, 1,310,000 piastres.

Greek Imports.

British, 558,320 piastres;	Germans, 1,544,550 piastres;
Italians, 644,400 piastres;	Dutch, 100,400 piastres;
Russians, 960,000 piastres;	French, 1,163,000 piastres.

This economic activity had both a direct and an indirect influence on the fortunes of the Greeks. They took a vigorous part in the internal trade, in which they were outstandingly successful, and also in the external trade, in which they continuously improved their position. They cooperated with the other nationalities and also channelled Greek and Turkish produce through the Greek settlements abroad. Durazzo, Trieste and Semlin were the main outlets through which they communicated with the great markets of Europe. From the mid-eighteenth century the Greeks, released from foreign tutelage, increased their activity to such a point that they became dangerous rivals to the larger foreign firms. According to the information of Arasy, French Consul at Salonica in 1776, the Greeks of Turkey controlled the wool and cotton trade, and Austrian firms were unable to cope with these competitors. The Consul remarks:

It should also be noted, that a substantial part of the internal trade of the Viennese and other Austrian markets is in the hands of Greek merchants from Turkey, some residing in the country and others going to and fro. They possess very considerable liquid assets and contribute to the general flow of money. It would therefore be risky to forbid them to carry on their country's trade here in this way, thus forcing them to quit Vienna and carry their capital elsewhere, since the result would be a serious vacuum and harmful to the trade of that city. The Austrian Court had a taste of this experience when it promulgated a law limiting the freedom which the Greeks had constantly enjoyed in Vienna and in the territories of the Empire. It soon became noticeable that the leading merchants of this nation [viz. the Greeks] were transferring their capital to Leipzig and other German commercial centres and that they had begun to filter it away to the detriment of Austrian trade. To stop this leakage, which might have become general, the Court at once annulled the dangerous law and further granted these people the right to build a church, a right which the Greeks had never succeeded in obtaining until then.[46]

The great events of the last quarter of the eighteenth century —the French Revolution, the Russo-Turkish war, the great European conflicts—strengthened the Greek position still further. A large part of the declining French trade fell to them. So long as the Continental Blockade of 1806 lasted, the Greeks played a highly important role. "The Greeks", a French Consul at Salonica wrote in 1812, "are the most active agents in the trade [in 'colonial' products] and our chief rivals." And as a scholar interested in the trade of the Macedonian city has concluded, the Greeks "had in their hands, in the last quarter of

---

[46] N. G. Svoronos, *op. cit.*, p. 198.

the eighteenth century, not only the internal but also half the foreign trade. After the French Revolution this proportion grew still further and we can state almost with certainty that seventy five per cent or more of the oriental trade was carried on by Greeks."[47]

The expansion of Greek economic life ran parallel with the revival of the Greek merchant navy. We saw earlier how piracy trained the manpower for the manning of the fleet. In the eighteenth century the latter was systematically organized. Greek ships sailed the eastern Mediterranean, flying the Turkish, Venetian and Ragusan flags.[48]

The international situation in the second half of the century favoured the expansion of Greek shipping, and that of the merchant navy was particularly affected by the Russo-Turkish war of 1768–74 and by the treaty of Kutchuk Kainardji (Kücük Kainarca) which concluded it. Under Article 7 of that treaty "the Sublime Porte undertakes to give continual protection to the Christian religion and its churches". Article 17 makes provision for the inhabitants of the Aegean islands, who are granted an amnesty; freedom of worship; two years' remission of taxes and the right to emigrate with their possessions within a year. By the Interpretative Agreement of 10 March 1779, fresh commercial privileges were granted, by virtue of which the island Greeks obtained the right to sail the

---

[47] Ibid., p. 354.

[48] Anastase Orlandos, Ναυτικά, ἤτοι ἱστορία τῶν κατὰ τὸν ὑπὲρ Ἀνεξαρτησίας τῆς Ἑλλάδος ἀγῶνα πεπραγμένων ὑπὸ τῶν τριῶν ναυτικῶν νήσων, ἰδίᾳ δὲ τῶν Σπετσῶν (Nautica, or a History of the Achievements of the three Naval Islands, particularly Spetsai, during the Greek War of Independence), Two vols., Athens, 1869. A. Jurien de la Gravière, La Station du Levant, Two vols., Paris, 1876. C. Rados, La marine grecque pendant la Guerre de l'Indépendance, Athens, 1907. Ant. Lignos, Ἱστορία τῆς νήσου Ὕδρας (History of the Island of Hydra), Two vols., Athens, 1946–53. R. Matton, Hydra et la guerre maritime (1821–1827), Athens, 1953. C. A. Alexandris, Ἡ ἀναβίωσις τῆς θαλασσίας μας δυνάμεως κατά τήν Τουρκοκρατίαν (The Revival of our Sea power during the Turkish Period), Athens, 1960. See also the excellently illustrated book Ἑλληνική Ἐμπορική Ναυτιλία (1453–1850) (The Greek Mercantile Marine, 1453–1850), pub. by the National Bank of Greece, under the direction of St. A. Papadopoulos, Athens, 1972 (also in English).

Black Sea under the Russian flag. These favourable clauses were also included in the Treaty of Jassy (9 January 1972). Later on, at the time of the Napoleonic wars, and the Continental Blockade, the islanders, in the face of innumerable dangers and of clashes with pirates from Africa, "took part in this extremely hazardous form of trade and contrived by this means within a short space of time to amass those huge financial resources which Divine Providence, in its unsearchable dispensation, destined for the liberation of the Greeks".[49]

Under these international agreements the Greek navy came into being and expanded. The islands of the Ionian and Aegean Seas, the Cyclades, the rocky islets of the eastern coast of the Peloponnese and certain coastal towns of mainland Greece, notably Missolonghi and Galaxidi, provided the bases for these miniature armadas. From about the middle of the eighteenth century our sources begin to give us the first definite figures. In 1745 Missolonghi harboured upwards of fifty ships, the largest of which were of up to 180 tons. Galaxidi boasted a long maritime tradition which a later document dates back to the thirteenth century; be that as it may, this little town on the Gulf of Corinth certainly disposed, in 1702, of a sizeable naval force.[50]

A document of 1764 supplies more detailed figures. According to this, the merchant navy of the Aegean islands and some of the mainland towns numbered 615 ships with a total tonnage of 153,580 tons, with crews totalling 37,526 men. The following are some typical figures: Galaxidi, 50 ships totalling 10,000 tons; Andros, 40 ships totalling 2,2,800 tons; Skopelos, 35 ships totalling 6,300 tons; Thera (Santorin), 32 ships totalling 2,560 tons; Lemnos, 15 ships totalling 3,900 tons; Mykonos, 22 ships totalling 3,300 tons.[51] Mykonos, Hydra, Spetsai and Psarà were the chief Aegean bases.[52] In 1786, Hydra had 78 large and 42

---

[49] A. Orlandos, *op. cit.*, vol. I, p. 36.
[50] C. A. Alexandris, *op. cit.*, pp. 153 ff.
[51] *Ibid.*, pp. 181 ff.
[52] *Ibid.*, pp. 159 ff., 216 ff.

small ships; in 1806 this number was reduced to 72 large and 14 small ships. The larger vessels exceeded 90 tons, the smallest were under 19; two of the larger ships were, respectively, of 400 and of 450 tons. In 1812 the Hydriotes fleet numbered 126 ships with a total tonnage of 27,413 tons, thirteen of these being of between 400 and 548 tons. At the outbreak of the War of Independence in 1821 Spetsai had about 50 large ships. Other islands—Chios, Psarà, Kasos and others—also had considerable fleets.

Félix Beaujour, already mentioned, had been obliged to admit that the French Navy had found new antagonists in the Greek islanders and, more particularly, in the Hydriotes. Again, Adamantios Koraïs, in his *Mémoire sur l'état actuel de la civilisation dans la Grèce* (1803), treats the islanders of the Aegean with a good deal of sympathy, and especially those of the little town of Hydra; there was keen competition between them in enlarging their merchantmen and extending the length of their voyages. These modern Argonauts were to be seen in every harbour of Italy and France, which countries they provisioned in times of dearth, and in the Baltic and even in America. These ocean voyages presuppose at least a certain professional skill equal to the perils of long-distance navigation; but the islanders appear to have been, properly speaking, quite without any technical training, the lack of which they supplied, only so far as first entry into a foreign harbour was concerned, by the use of European pilots and in other eventualities by their own courage and daring, these two qualities being the product of their own peculiar brand of seamanship and of their highly individual apprenticeship to the sea, which in all probability did not differ greatly from that of the ancient Greek seafarers. Koraïs writes most prophetically when, noting the Sultan's apparent benevolence towards the assembling of a Greek navy, he says: "There can be no doubt that if the [Ottoman] Government could only have foreseen that one day the Greeks would contrive to have a merchant navy of several hundred vessels, mostly piratical, they would have sunk it at birth. Now, however, they do not dare to check its progress because of the assistance it renders to their own merchantmen. . . ."[53]

The result of the expansion of Greek economic life was to create a certain primitive industry or light manufacture and, indirectly, to raise the standard of living. A great reputation was acquired by the cooperative society at Ambelakia, already mentioned[54], but this was not the only example of Greek industrial enterprise. Local industries flourished also in the Pelion region and still more in Epirus and Macedonia as well as in the islands, particularly Chios.

The raising of the standard of living helped to break the monotony of life in the Greek communities. Little by little the population began to develop social differences and a certain class hierarchy began to appear. The birth of this urban class was a fact of prime significance in the history of modern Greece. The confused view of this subject caused by the one-sided theories, which have unfortunately been supported by our Marxist historians from time to time, in no way robs the historian whose views are scientifically based of his right to his own opinion on this new factor in the social development of our country and his right to stress the contribution which it made.

The economic leadership of Greece came to birth within the structure of the Ottoman Empire and in close connection with the economy of Europe and the plutocracy which sprang from it. It therefore operated within limits set, first, by the administrative methods and the oppressive actions of the imperial power and secondly, by the protectionist policies of foreign governments. The latter sometimes, and the former often, went to lengths which amounted to persecution. This basic feature, which is seldom encountered in the economic history of Europe, is an essential mark of the history of the Greek urban class under Turkish rule, whether within Turkey itself or in the Dispersion abroad, in contrast to the urban class in other countries. In other words, while the middle class elsewhere, owing to its

---

[53] D. Thereianos, 'Ἀδαμάντιος Κοραῆς, vol. III, Trieste, 1890.
[54] See Chap. IV above, pp. 61–2.

economic preponderance, was able, directly or indirectly, to bring the power of government under its control and in some degree to take a share of that power, the corresponding class of Greeks remained subject to persecution and at the stage at which the Conquest had left them. Precisely for this reason the Greek urban class, while following in its own upward course that of its European counterparts, displayed tendencies different from theirs and motives and ideals of its own which were also totally different—ideals which strove for the attainment of power by a nation, not by a class.

The result of the great economic revival and of the development of a navy was the rise of a new generation of men. These were the bearers of a new spirit and of new ways of life. The reconquest of the sea opened up the closed horizons, it led the Greeks back to the sources of their inspiration in their own past. The Greek thinking of earlier centuries, freed from Byzantine formalism, became a factor in their intellectual rebirth, while Greek contacts with Western culture stimulated intellectual enquiry. The whole of the Mediterranean East was transformed by this Greek initiative. As Arnold Toynbee observed: "Greece served them [the peoples of the Balkans and the Levant] as a gate through which Western influence forced an entry into the Orthodox Christian world."[55] How this came about is the theme of the chapter which follows.

[55] A. Toynbee, *A Study of History*, vol. II, Oxford, 1939, pp. 81–2.

VIII

Political Trends
and the Clash of Ideas

After giving a general outline of Greek political and economic development during the period of Turkish domination, it is time to consider the various trends of political thought which were current during the closing years of that period and not only led to the War of Independence but strongly influenced later thinking on the character and destiny of Free Greece. This enquiry, however, will be limited to the political field and does not attempt to cover the development of Greek education, literature or philosophy, although these are relevant to the general theme and require mention at certain points. Some of the works in which they can be more closely studied are named in the footnote below.[1]

---

[1] Émile Legrand, *Bibliographie Hellénique ou Description raisonnée des ouvrages publiés en grec par des Grecs aux XVe et XVIe siècles,* four vols., Paris, 1885–1906; *Bibliographie Hellénique ou Description raisonnée des ouvrages publiés par des Grecs au XVIIe siècle,* five vols., Paris, 1894–1904; Émile Legrand, L. Petit, H. Pernot, *Bibliographie Hellénique ou Description raisonnée des ouvrages publiés par des Grecs au XVIIIe siècle,* two vols., Paris, 1918–28 (until 1790), Modern Reprint, Paris, 1962 Émile Legrand, H. Pernot, *Bibliographie Ionienne du XVe siècle à 1900,* two vols., Paris, 1910; D. Ghinis, V. G. Mexas, Ἑλληνικὴ Βιβλιογραφία 1800–63 (*Greek Bibliography 1800–63*), three vols., Πραγματεῖαι τῆς Ἀκαδημίας Ἀθηνῶν, Athens, 1939–57; G. E. Voumvlinopoulos, *Bibliographie critique de la Philosophie grecque depuis la chute de Constantinople à nos jours 1453–1953,* Athens, 1966; C. Th. Dimaras, C. Koumarianou, L. Droulia, *Modern Greek Culture. A Selected Bibliography,* 3rd. rev. ed., Athens, 1970; Constantin N. Sathas, Νεοελληνικὴ Φιλολογία. Βιογραφίαι τῶν ἐν τοῖς Γράμμασι διαλαμψάντων Ἑλλήνων, ἀπὸ τῆς καταλύσεως τῆς Βυζαντινῆς Αὐτοκρατορίας μέχρι τῆς

Greece entered upon the Turkish period at a time when its intellectual reputation and influence were at their height. We know of few instances in which nations which had lost their political independence and had been brought under the rule of another nation of different race and religion took with them into a new, prolonged and gloomy phase of their history so great a heritage of intellectual and artistic activity. This extraordinary spectacle of the political decline of Byzantium, during the fourteenth and fifteenth centuries, running parallel with the intellectual revival of Greece is, in itself, one of the most fascinating problems history has to offer.[2] As Steven Runciman has recently written: "In strange contrast with the political decline, the intellectual life of Byzantium never shone so brilliantly as in those two sad centuries."[3]

The intellectual life of the Greeks under Turkish rule was grounded in the tradition handed down from those last Byzantine centuries. This derivation may be more obvious in the visual arts; it was no less decisive in other spheres, and its many-sided influence often foreshadowed future developments. Both in the field of general culture and in that of literature, the existence side by side of the 'two languages' (in Greek, *Diglossia*) created both a 'learned' and a 'popular' tradition; both a vigorous Hellenic humanism and the attractive grace of popular poetry and fiction. In theology and philosophy the contrasts

---

Ἑλληνικῆς Ἐθνεγερσίας (1453–1821) (*Modern Greek Literature. Biographies of Greeks of literary distinction from the Destruction of the Byzantine Empire to the National Revival, 1453–1821*), Athens, 1868; Tr. Evanghelides, Ἡ παιδεία ἐπὶ Τουρκοκρατίας (*The Education in the Turkish Period*), two vols., Athens, 1936; C. Th. Dimaras, Ἱστορία τῆς Νεοελληνικῆς Λογοτεχνίας (*History of Modern Greek Literature*), 4th ed., Athens, 1968, French trans., *Histoire de la Littérature Néo-hellénique des origines à nos jours*, Athens, 1966; Börje Knös, *L'Histoire de la Littérature Néo-grecque. La période jusqu'en 1821*, Stockholm—Göteborg—Uppsala, 1962; Bruno Lavagnini, *La letteratura neoellenica*, new ed., Milan, 1969.

[2] D. A. Zakythinos, Βυζάντιον. Κράτος καί κοινωνία. Ἱστορικὴ ἐπισκόπησις (*Byzantium. State and Society. A Historical Survey*), Athens, 1951, pp. 139 ff.

[3] Steven Runciman, *The Last Byzantine Renaissance*, Cambridge, 1970, pp. 1 ff.

between Aristotelian and Platonic thinking and between Hellenic rationalism and Christian mysticism had marked out the two parallel channels of Byzantine thought, and in dealing with the acutest problems of the time—the union of the Eastern and Western Churches, the defence of the beleaguered Empire and the possibility of a European Crusade—these conflicts of opinion had divided the Greek community into two opposed ideological camps. Out of them there emerged the clash, which had long been latent, between the old universalist principle of the Empire and the national idea, resolved eventually in favour of the latter.[4]

One feature in the general landscape of Byzantine decline is particularly worthy of note. Intellectual activity is divided between a number of centres—Constantinople, Trebizond, Athos, Salonica, Epirus, the Peloponnese, even the Latin-held islands of Cyprus and Crete. As was already the case with the existing or newly emerging schools of art and architecture, so each of these new centres in time developed its own local style in other ways also. As Runciman observes: "The Greek world of the last two centuries of Byzantium had shrunk now to become little more than a group of city-states, Constantinople, Thessalonica, Trebizond and Mistra. It had become, far more truly than in its grand imperial days, the descendant of the city-states of the ancient Hellenic world, and it showed the same intellectual vitality and bustle."[5]

The first Greek humanism of the years following the Conquest had been bound up with the wider movement of the Italian and European Renaissance but it faded with the second generation of Greek scholars in the West. A 'second humanism' was soon to refresh Greek thinking: it would be the fruit of the

---

[4] Emm. Kriaras, 'Die Besonderheiten der letzten Periode der mittelalterlichen griechischen Literatur', in *Jahrbuch der Österreichischen Byzantinischen Gesellschaft*, vol. VIII (1959), pp. 69–85. Id. 'Diglossie des derniers siècles de Byzance: Naissance de la Littérature néohellénique', in *Proceedings of the XIIIth International Congress of Byzantine Studies, Oxford, 5–10 September 1966*, London, 1967, pp. 281–99.

[5] Steven Runciman, *The Last Byzantine Renaissance* p. 23.

great social restructuring described in previous chapters. In the years which followed the fall of Constantinople Greek society, after first being levelled out under the common disaster, began in the course of time to show some differentiations. Thus a certain upper class grew up, some of it elevated from the lower, popular strata of the nation, some based on the surviving elements of the older Byzantine society. These social classes formed and developed under the eyes of the occupying power in a way which arouses one's astonishment and bears witness to the extraordinary adaptability of the Greeks. Internal differences of opinion were not carried as far as the open ruptures which were to be found in other societies. One might say that love of their country kept the separate parts of the whole community in unison with each other and forced them to advance together within the framework of a harmonious common life. Nevertheless, because of their differing individualities and because of the isolation in which each community existed, to a greater or lesser extent each of these sectors of the Greek population developed its own peculiar characteristics and evolved its own individual ways of thought and its independent cast of mind. All these various streams, converging into the one river-bed, enriched and fertilized Greek life.

I. Neo-Byzantine Universalism and the Idea of a Universal State

The various lines of thought which developed within the reviving Greek culture of the Turkish period had their common basis in this 'second humanism' a term used here to denote one of the great periods of post-Byzantine Greek civilization. We may place its earliest manifestations in the first decades of the seventeenth century, and symbolically in the year 1622. It was at that date that the Athenian philosopher Korydaleus began to teach in the Patriarchal Academy at Constantinople. It was the time of the stormy but brilliant Patriarchate of Cyril I Loukaris and the rise of the new administrative aristocracy. In contrast to the First Humanism, the Second was aimed at a far wider section of the community and extended its influence to a greater number of centres, both within and outside the frontiers of the Ottoman Empire—Venice, Padua, Rome, Cephalonia, Crete and Cyprus, and before long to Ioannina and such towns of Northern Greece as Moschopolis and Kastoria. But its chief centres of influence were Constantinople itself and the Danubian Principalities, where the School of the Three Hierarchs was founded at Jassy in 1644 and the Bucharest Academy in 1679. In these the Second Humanism passed by degrees and without a break into the Greek equivalent of the western Age of Enlightenment.[6]

In this way, from the seventeenth century onwards, Greek thought moved towards the gradual formulation of two distinct lines of political thinking. Their distribution over a wide variety of centres and of social strata ensured that there was nothing uniform about the process. The ecclesiastical hierarchy of Constantinople, for instance, and a large part of the aristocracy which was linked with it, were essentially a conservative element. They saw co-operation with the ruling power as a necessity and submission to it as a means of acquiring a dominant influence within it. Over the centuries this class fluctuated between an attempt to achieve some sort of balance in their difficult relationship with the sovereign power and a struggle for supremacy within the framework of the Ottoman Empire; between vigorous opposition to the interventions of foreign Churches, particularly the Church of Rome, and their own expansionist policy on their own home ground of the East Christian world; and between the universalist traditions of Byzantium and the narrower antagonism of a Greek Church struggling within the Orthodox fold against the superior weight of the Slav element within Orthodoxy. All these considerations explain and excuse the vacillations, the contradictions, the occasional vicious reactions, but at the same time they account for the noble actions too.

[6] C. G. Dimaras, *La Grèce au temps des Lumières*, Geneva, 1969. G. P. Henderson, *The Revival of Greek Thought 1620–1830*, Albany, 1970.

This new spirit bore fruit throughout south-eastern Europe, most of all in the developing Greek culture of the Danubian Principalities, where an intellectual merger of East and West, of still wider importance was in preparation.[16] In these countries the Phanariotes were shortly to undertake still greater experiments.[17] Originally conservative in temperament, the Greek administrative aristocracy established in Moldavia and Wallachia became open to the flood of liberal ideas. The Princes themselves embraced humanistic and progressive principles, became votaries of 'Enlightened Despotism' and, as true 'philosopher-kings', favoured the founding of schools, acted as the patrons of scholars, and wrote philosophical and moral treatises. Nicholas Mavrocordato—Prince of Moldavia from 1709 and of Wallachia from 1715—following the example of his illustrious father, Alexander the Sultan's Confidential Private Secretary[18], wrote a $Bίβλον$ $περὶ$ $τῶν$ $Καθηκόντων$ (Book of Duties) (published in Bucharest in 1719) and $Φιλοθέου$ $Πάρεργα$ (The Thoughts of Philotheus). "His general allegiance to Plato is new, and if Plato be counted a liberating influence, then Mavrocordato did his best to open up Greek education in this respect."[19] Among the foremost examples of the Greek mingling of cultures in south-eastern Europe were the sons of Constantine Brâncoveanu, Prince of Wallachia (1688–1714), Stephen and Constantine, Gregory Brâncoveanu and the greatest of the Romanian humanists, Demetrius Cantemir—Prince of Moldavia (1710–11), son of a Greek mother, who was educated by Greek teachers. Speaking of the Greek scholars of his time, he was to write later, in 1714–16, that Greece "produced intellects who might be compared with the sages of Antiquity".[20]

But whether conservative or progressive, the leading class of

---

[16] Virgil Cândea, op. cit., pp. 181–230, 623–68.
[17] See Chap. VII above, pp. 103–6.
[18] See Chap. VII, above, pp. 97, 107.
[19] G. P. Henderson, op. cit., p. 25.
[20] Quoted by Cl. Tsourkas, op. cit., pp. 378 ff.

the Church hierarchy and the administrative aristocracy, who had grown up under the rule of the Sultan in Constantinople or in Wallachia and Moldavia, were all inspired by the universalist ideal of Byzantium which they invoked to justify both their blacker and their more commendable actions. Fluctuating between contradictory schools of thought, they framed an early version of the 'Great Idea' which one might call neo-Byzantine.[21] According to this theory, Greek influences, attacking from within, would emerge as the dominant force at the heart of the Turkish Empire, and the Greeks would become co-rulers of the 'mighty Monarchy' and would transform this into a multiracial state, thus realizing their own liberating, political dream through the Turkish Empire which would be transfigured as an 'Ottoman State of the Greek Nation'.

This line of thought was obscure but very widespread. The idea that the Greek nation, forming a peculiar unit within the Ottoman State, already had a part in its government through Greek ecclesiastical and political leaders, through the Grand Dragoman and the Danubian Princes, is to be found as a developing conception in a document written about the year 1783. Rejecting the pronouncements of Voltaire and inspired by Aristotle and Montesquieu, Demetrius Katartzes (Catargiu) Grand Logothete of Wallachia, became the champion of these views in his Συμβουλὴ στοὺς Νέους (Advice to the Young).[22] In the last years before the Revolution the rival faction was to dub those who professed these views 'Greco-Turks'.[23]

Connected with this ideological line were the plans and reforms of some of the Danubian Princes—Alexander Hypsilanti

[21] Steven Runciman, op. cit., pp. 378 ff.

[22] C. Th. Dimaras, ed., (Demetrius Katartzis, The Extant Works), Athens, 1970, pp. 44 ff. On Demetrius Katartzis see also C. Th. Dimaras, La Grèce au temps des Lumières, pp. 26 ff. Stephen G. Xydis, 'Modern Greek Nationalism', in Peter F. Sugar, Ivo J. Lederer, Nationalism in Eastern Europe, Univ. of Washington Press, 1969, pp. 224 ff.

[23] L. Vranousis, 'Ρήγας. Ἔρευνα, συναγωγὴ καὶ μελέτη ('Rhigas. An Introduction, a Compilation and a Study'), in the series Βασικὴ Βιβλιοθήκη (Basic Library), No. 10, Athens, 1953, p. 111. 2nd ed., Athens 1963.

(Prince of Wallachia, 1774–82 and 1796–7, and of Moldavia, 1787–8), and his son Constantine (Grand Dragoman 1796–9, Prince of Moldavia 1799–1801 and of Wallachia 1802–6 and 1806–7). Alexander reorganized the armed forces of the Danubian Principalities. Constantine, the father of the Hypsilanti leaders of the Revolution, a man of passionately held views and a bold innovator, played an important part in the major issues of the critical period at the end of the eighteenth and the beginning of the nineteenth century. His general policy appears in his continuance of the military reorganization begun by his father, in the establishment of the Septinsular (Ionian) Republic tributary to the Sultan, in his support of the Serbian revolt of 1804 and in his plan for the merging of the two Danubian Principalities into a single 'Dacian' state. Constantine Hypsilanti's policy favoured the extension of the system of autonomous principalities under Ottoman suzerainty. It is impossible to tell whether this would have led to "the disintegration of the Empire into a number of states or whether a single unitary state would have replaced it".[24]

A Greek jurist has described as a 'multinational state' the kind of polity towards which the conservative Church and administrative aristocracy were drawn in their vision of the future restoration of Greece.[25] These optimistic views were based not only on the universal spread of Greek culture throughout eastern Europe but also on the lessons of a long experience. The co-existence of the political and administrative system of the sovereign power with another, parallel system, ecclesiastical and political—a real *imperium in imperio*—strengthened by the elevation of Greek officials for some time past to high offices of State and further reinforced regionally by organs of partial self-government, created in practice a kind

[24] Notis Botzaris, *Visions balkaniques dans la prèparation de la Révolution Grecque (1789–1821)*, Geneva—Paris, 1962, pp. 66 ff. See also pp. 18, 43 ff., 64 ff.

[25] N. Pantazopoulos, ῾Ρήγας Βελεστινλῆς. ῾Η πολιτικὴ ἰδεολογία τοῦ ῾Ελληνισμοῦ πρόαγγελος τῆς ᾽Επαναστάσεως (*Rhigas Velestinlis. Greek Political Thinking as a Forerunner of the Revolution*), Salonica, 1964, pp. 27 ff.

of tacit condominium. Katartzes had rightly diagnosed the long-term significance of these facts.[26]

II. The Progressive Forces in Greek Thinking. The National Idea and the National State

The same Greek jurist, an expert in medieval and modern Greek law, has described as 'a multiracial state of the Greek nation' the version of the national state which was the ideal of the progressive and democratic thinkers. He terms this ideal 'multiracial' because it was based on the autonomy and self-sufficiency of the various political units of which it was to be composed. He terms it 'uniracial', i.e. 'of the Greek nation', inasmuch as its aim was the establishment of a Greek national state, based on the idea of the revival, continuation and wider extension of the Greek cultural heritage.[27]

This inclination towards a national state arose from a renewal of the idea of a Greek nation. In Greek tradition there are no gaps in the Greeks' consciousness of their own nationhood. It took definite shape in the last age of Byzantium (1204–1453).[28] Thereafter the idea of 'the Nation' was preserved and developed by the Greek scholars of the Renaissance, who linked it with the conception of a crusade against the Turks. The second and third generation of their successors—whether they belonged to the guardians of the Greek tradition—as, for instance, Nicholas Sophianos or Antony Eparchos in the sixteenth century; or to the pro-Latin school of thought, like Leo Allatius in the sixteenth and Francis Skouphos in the seventeenth century—handed down the national idea without a

[26] D. A. Zakythinos, Ἡ Ἐπανάστασις τῶν Παραδουναβίων Ἡγεμονιῶν καὶ ἡ ἔναρξις τοῦ Ἀγῶνος τῆς Ἀνεξαρτησίας ('The Revolution of the Danubian Principalities and the Outbreak of the Struggle for the Independence'), in Πρακτικὰ τῆς Ἀκαδημίας Ἀθηνῶν, vol. XLVI (1971), p. 50.

[27] N. Pantazopoulos, op. cit., in 25 above, pp. 28 ff.

[28] Stephen G. Xydis, 'Mediaeval Origins of Modern Greek Nationalism', in Balkan Studies, vol. IX (1968), pp. 1–20.

break to the representatives of the 'Second Humanism' and the Enlightenment.[29]

This conception found its final formulation among the Greeks of the Dispersion and those of the rising urban class and was closely linked with the revival of Greek education, with the return to the springs of Classical Greece and with the new currents of thought which flowed from the west European Enlightenment and the French Revolution.[30] But whereas in the west there was a conflict between the universal character of the ideas of the Enlightenment and the particularism of the nationalist ideal, in south-eastern Europe the Enlightenment was one of the chief motive forces which helped to shape national consciousness among the various peoples.[31] As in earlier periods, Greek thinking played a leading part in this development.[32] The Greek schools, both inside and outside Greece, had more than a narrowly national character and helped to form an intelligentsia, Orthodox and non-Orthodox, in the Levant and the Balkans. They thus acted as power-houses radiating a humane and inspiring Greek culture. Men of the highest calibre, who distinguished themselves in politics and in letters and the sciences, and who contributed in a great variety of ways to the regeneration of their own countries,

[29] Stephen G. Xydis, 'Modern Greek Nationalism', in P. F. Sugar—I. Lederer, *op. cit.*, pp. 207 ff.

[30] The connections between the Enlightenment and the formation of national consciousness among the peoples of south-eastern Europe were examined in an international discussion in Paris in 1968, see *Association Internationale D'Études du Sud-Est Européen. Les Lumières et la Formation de la Conscience nationale chez les peuples du Sud-Est Européen*, Bucharest, 1970.

[31] Valentin A. Georgescu, 'La Philosophie des Lumières et la formation de la conscience nationale dans le Sud-Est de l'Europe', in *Les Lumières et la formation de la Conscience nationale*, *op. cit.*, in preceding footnote, pp. 23–42.

[32] D. A. Zakythinos, Ὑπερεθνικαὶ ἀξίαι τοῦ Ἑλληνικοῦ Πολιτισμοῦ τῆς Τουρκοκρατίας ('Supranational Concepts in the Greek Culture of the Turkish Period'), in Νέα Ἑστία, Christmas, 1970, pp. 5–12. See also W. T. Elwert, 'Zur griechisch-rumänische Symbiose der Phanariotenzeit', in *Beiträge zur Südosteuropa—Forschung anlässlich des I. Internationalen Balkanologenkongresses in Sofia*, Munich, 1966, pp. 391–402. D. A. Zakythinos, Ἡ Ἐπανάστασις τῶν Παραδουναβίων Ἡγεμονιῶν, *op. cit.*, pp. 42 ff.

were pupils of the Greeks. Thus, Prince Demetrius Cantemir, who has already been mentioned, and who wrote, among other things, a valuable history of the rise and decline of the Turkish Empire,[33] studied before 1700 at the Patriarchal Academy in Constantinople. Another intellectual leader of the Balkans, the Serb Dositej Obradović (1743–1811), was at school in Greece and at Smyrna in the years 1765 and 1766. Bulgarians who afterwards led the way in creating a new Bulgaria— Hilarion Stoyanovitch, Ivan Dobrovski, George Rakovski and others—studied at Andros, Ioannina and Athens, as well as in the Greek schools of Romania.

Considered in detail, the spread of the Greek language and literature is seen to have taken a great variety of forms: (a) translations or arrangements of Greek works in foreign languages; (b) imitations of Greek originals; (c) Greek translations of works of European literature which were then translated from the Greek into Balkan and other languages; (d) translations of works of European literature into Greek or of works of Ancient Greek literature into modern Greek, executed by non-Greek translators; (e) the transmission of the Greek language to scholarly circles not of Greek origin. In general it may be said that in the intellectual formation of south-eastern Europe, in the late eighteenth and early nineteenth century, Greek thought and the Greek language performed a service very like that which had been discharged by post-Byzantine art in the wide field of eastern and south-eastern Europe and the Levant.

The Greek Enlightenment may be defined chronologically as extending from 1766 to 1821. In 1766, Evgenios Voulgaris published his *Logic* at Leipzig as well as his verse translation of the *Memnon ou la Sagesse Humaine* of Voltaire, the first known translation of the French philosopher's work into Greek. Other typical features of this new age are the spread of education and of an interest in culture to wider sections of society and the attention paid to the editing, annotating and wide circulation

[33] An English trans. was pub. by the Rev. N. Tindal in London in 1734.

of the masterpieces of Greek literature, a turning towards the natural sciences, language research and the growing influences of the West.

The problem of the Greek language was not a new one. The existence side by side of 'learned' and 'popular' forms is a native characteristic of Greek, which from a theoretical point of view engaged the attention of the scholars of the Turkish period. Nicholas Sophianos, who flourished in the first half of the sixteenth century, was the first to pose the question of written modern Greek in his *Grammar*. But what was new about the situation in the period with which we are concerned was that the language controversy became part of the advance towards national self-awareness. Whether they were 'Atticisers' (i.e. classical purists), like Voulgaris or Neophytos Doukas, or devotees of the 'popular' form of the language, like Katartzes, Moisiodax, Daniel Philippides or Gregory Constantas; or whether they were somewhere between these two extremes, like Adamantios Koraïs and his followers who were in favour of the evolutionary purifying of the spoken language; all the contestants in the language dispute regarded the Greek tongue as an instrument of national unity and of national and social regeneration. As Koraïs himself wrote in the preface to his edition of the *Ethiopica* (1804): "Our language is one of the most inalienable possessions of our race. Every member of our nation shares it, so to speak, in democratic unity ..." And again: "The character of a whole nation may be known from its language."[34]

Arnold Toynbee remarked that "Greece has served as a water-gate through which Western influence has forced an entry into the Orthodox Christian world".[35] Western influence did indeed force an entry into that world, and not into it alone, through Greece. In this great mission Greece did not merely

[34] V. Rotolo, *A. Korais e la Questione della Lingua in Grecia*, Quaderni dell' Istituto di Filologia Greca della Università di Palermo, 4, Palermo, 1965.

[35] Arnold Toynbee, *A Study of History*, vol. II, Oxford, 1962, pp. 81 ff.

play the part of a passive intermediary, it created a broad and noble synthesis of East and West.[36]

After Theophilos Korydaleus, Vikentios Damadós (1679–1752), Methodius Anthrakites (c.1660–c.1749), Evgenios Voulgaris (1716–1806), and Nicephorus Theotokes (1731–1800) —very different characters—continued the tradition of philosopher-teachers.[37] Voulgaris was beyond dispute the commanding personality of his age, advancing "new ideas in an old language".[38] In addition to his knowledge of classical, Christian and Byzantine philosophy he had the closest affinity with the philosophers of western Europe. Having been taught by the Zantiote philosopher Antony Katephoros, the translator of Locke, Voulgaris made extensive use of Locke's works, as also of those of Descartes, Newton, Leibnitz and Wolf. At the beginning of his career he was an admirer of Voltaire, whose first Greek translator he became. Locke's work was already widely known in the Greek world, since, apart from Katephoros, the latter's fellow-Zantiote John Litinos had published a *Handbook of Metaphysic and Dialectic or a most accurate Summary of Mr. Locke, the celebrated Philosopher, on the Human Understanding* (᾿Εγχειρίδιον μεταφυσικὸ διαλεκτικὸν ἢ ᾿Επιτομὴ ἀκριβεστάτη τοῦ κυρίου Λοκκίου περιβοήτου φιλοσόφου περὶ τῆς ἀνθρωπίνης διανοίας) which appeared in Venice in 1796, and Gabriel Kallonas (1724–95), and Moisiodax (c.1730–1800) had drawn largely on Locke's *Some Thoughts on Education*.[39] Katartzes has

---

[36] One must remark here that any enquiry into the facts, on the basis of the written evidence alone, conveys a misleading impression of the proportions and extent of this great cultural achievement. To the written evidence must be added that of the spoken word. We know that the oral instruction of the teachers of the Greek Enlightenment had very significant repercussions throughout the East.

[37] G. P. Henderson, *op. cit.*, pp. 28 ff.

[38] *Ibid.*, pp.. 41 ff.

[39] A. Anghelou, 'Comment la Pensée néo—hellénique a fait la connaissance de l' "Essai" de John Locke', in *L'Hellénisme Contemporain*, Athens, 1955, pp. 230–49. See also Emm. Kriaras, Γαβριὴλ Καλλονᾶς, μεταφραστὴς ἔργων τοῦ Locke καὶ τοῦ Gracián ('Gabriel Kallonas, trans. of Works by Locke and Gracian'), in ῾Ελληνικά, vol. XIII (1954), pp. 294–314. Ariadna Camariano-

been called a "typical representative of his time, the first advocate of the ideas of the Encyclopaedists in the Greek East".[40] Athanasius Psalidas (1764–1829) studied Descartes, Leibnitz and Condillac and, most of all, Kant.[41]

The intellectual line which both positively and negatively—but more negatively than positively—influenced the thinking of the Greek world was that of Voltaire. Voulgaris's translation of *Memnon* was followed by others of the *Essai historique et critique sur les Dissensions des Églises de Pologne* (1768), the *Traduction du Poème de Jean Plokof, Conseiller de Holstein, sur les affaires présentes* and *Le Tocsin des Rois aux Souverains de l'Europe*. In addition to these some of Voltaire's major works appeared in Greek translation, the *Essai sur les Moeurs et l'Esprit des Nations, Le siècle de Louis XIV*, the *Histoire de Charles XII*. We possess also translations of Voltaire's tragedies, some of which were staged in Corfu, Bucharest and Odessa.[42]

It was on this soil of the Greek Enlightenment, so fertile in so many ways, that the National Idea was nurtured and fed from the twin streams of classical culture and the liberal principles of European thought. Its forceful nationalist spirit was active over an enormous area stretching from Paris, Vienna, Budapest, Venice, Leghorn and Rome to Constantinople, Bucharest, Jassy, Odessa, Moscow and St. Petersburg. The generations who were inspired by this ideal stood resolutely against the conquering Power, the "Tyrant". Any co-existence or reconciliation with him was unthinkable. As it matured through

Cioran, 'Un directeur éclairé à l'Académie de Jassy il y a deux sièckes: Iosip Moisiodax', in *Balkan Studies*, vol. VII (1966), pp. 297–332.

[40] C. Th. Dimaras, *La Grèce au temps des Lumières*, p. 36.

[41] L. Vranoussis, 'Ἀθανάσιος Ψαλίδας, ὁ Διδάσκαλος τοῦ Γένους (*Athanasius Psalidas, Teacher of the Nation*), Ioannina, 1952. Raphael Demos presented an abridged trans. in English of the philosophical Treatise of Psalidas *The True Happiness*, written in Greek and Latin: *Vera felicitas, sive fundamentum omnis religionis* (Vienna, 1791). R. Demos, 'True Happiness, or the Basis of all Religion', by Athanasios P. Psalidas, in *Journal of the History of Ideas*, vol. XXI, N. 4 (Oct.–Dec. 1960), pp. 481–96. See also G. P. Henderson, *op. cit.*, pp. 99 ff.

[42] C. Th. Dimaras, *La Grèce au temps des Lumières*, pp. 61 ff, 95 ff.

education the nation must seek its liberation by its own strength. On all other points there was a cleavage between Greek nationalism and Byzantine universalism with its still surviving ecclesiastical machinery of the Patriarchate of Constantinople. If there was any touch of Byzantium about it, its presence was the palest shadow. Certain writers like Koraïs were clearly hostile to the medieval Greek Empire.[43] This religious faith, which colours every thought and every action, becomes something more spiritual and rises, as it were, above the confinement of the ecclesiastical apparatus and its ministers. As has been observed, we are confronted with a movement towards the secularisation of national policy.[44]

The master policy of Greek nationalism was the establishment of a unitary state, independent and under liberal government. It was to embrace all the political, intellectual and cultural activities of the nation. In his *Advice to the Young*, Katartzes was the first to analyse the concept of the Nation and to try to harmonize it with the realities of Greek nationality. When he turns to the historic past he lists the great Byzantine emperors and commanders side by side with Pericles and Themistocles.[45] But it is rather Koraïs who is *par excellence* the true representative of Greek nationalism. Brought up on the study of humane letters, grown to manhood among the French Encyclopaedists, a student of Edward Gibbon, taught by Karl Schlegel that Nation and Language are synonymous, he became the prophet of the new doctrine.[46] His voice was heard above all those which resounded from every point of the compass in these years of the Greek revival.

So far as the trend of thought outside the larger towns is concerned, we have to note that here the opposing currents,

---

[43] D. A. Zakythinos, 'Le monde de Byzance dans la pensée historique de l'Europe à partir du XVIIᵉ siècle: Le point de vue des Épigones', in *Jahrbuch der Österreichischen Byzantinischen Gesellschaft*, vol. XV (1966), pp. 92 ff.

[44] Stephen G. Xydis, 'Modern Greek Nationalism', *op. cit.*, pp. 223 ff.

[45] See n. 22 above.

[46] Steven Runciman, *The Great Church in Captivity*, pp. 392 ff, 396 ff.

those coming from Constantinople and those coming from the major centres outside Greece, often clashed. Certain regions of Greece—Epirus, where Ioannina had become a centre of cultural and intellectual movement, the Ionian Islands, Crete, Cyprus, the larger Macedonian towns, Pelion, Athens—were wide open to the ideas of reform and progress. In other areas, on the other hand, it was the native element which prevailed and in this way local tensions were created—tensions which in some places were non-clerical in character and had their origin among the laity—and it was these which shaped Greek patriotism in the narrower provincial sense. General Makriyannis (1797–1864), the author of the well-known *Memoirs*,[47] is perhaps the most characteristic figure of grassroots nationalism.

III. Rhigas and the Vision of a Universal State in the East. The Universalist Ideal and the Multiracial State of the Greek Nation

Into the tangled and disorderly growth of the Greek Enlightenment the systematic thinking of Rhigas, the first martyr to the cause of Greek freedom, brought some constructive elements.[48] From a period of chaotic searching after new forms we emerge into clarity and advance from theory to practice. For this reason Rhigas "is justly recognized as a great and noble revolutionary figure, whose historical stature is visible beyond

[47] For a recent (abr.) trans. in English, see *Makriyannis, The Memoirs* (ed. and trans. by H. A. Lidderdale), Oxford, 1966.

[48] On the life and work of Rhigas see: Ap. B. Daskalakis, *Rhigas Velestinlis, la Révolution Française et les préludes de l'Indépendance hellénique*, Paris, 1937. L. I. Vranoussis, op. cit. Ar. J. Manessis, 'L'activité et les projets politiques d'un patriote grec dans les Balkans vers la fin du XVIIIᵉ siècle', in *Balkan Studies*, vol. III (1962), pp. 75–118.—Ap. B. Daskalakis, Μελέται περὶ 'Ρήγα Βελεστινλῆ (*Studies on Rhigas Velestinlis*), Athens, 1964. N. Pantazopoulos, 'Ρήγας Βελεστινλῆς. *op. cit.* in footnote 25 above. A new ed. of the works of Rhigas: L. I. Vranousis, 'Ρήγας Βελεστινλῆς—Φεραῖος, Συναγωγὴ κειμένων, φιλολογικὴ ἐπεξεργασία καὶ παρουσίαση ('Rhigas Velestinlis-Pheraios. Texts collected, critically assessed and presented by L. I. Vranousis'), in the series ˝Απαντα 'Ελλήνων Κλασσικῶν, Athens, 1968–9.

the frontiers of Greece, rises above the Balkans and embraces mankind at large".[49]

Rhigas was a many-sided personality. He was born, probably in 1757, at Velestinon in Thessaly, the ancient Pherae, whence his afternames Velestinli(s) or Pheraios. He received his general education at Zagora in Pelion. At Constantinople, where he established himself between 1777 and 1780, he was engaged in trade and acted as secretary to Alexander Hypsilanti the elder. About 1786 he moved to Wallachia where he continued as a merchant and probably served as secretary to Prince Nicholas Mavroyeni. As a clerk in the service of Christodoulos Kirlianos, Baron Langelfeld, he visited Vienna from June 1790 to January, 1791, and there launched the publication of his earliest works. Returning to Wallachia, he worked with the French consular authorities. His literary work and his revolutionary plans took him again to Vienna in August, 1796 and December, 1797. On his way back to Greece he was arrested at Trieste on 19 December 1797, brought to Vienna and handed over by the Austrians to the Turkish authorities. On 24 June 1798, he was executed at Belgrade with seven of his associates.

Rhigas's work as writer and translator was published in the last years of his brief life and was at first concerned with the compilation and interpretation of foreign authors (Restif de la Bretonne, Marmontel, Metastasio, Gessner and the *Voyage du Jeune Anacharsis en Grèce* of the Abbé Barthélémy), but later rose to original poetry in Greek of a noble patriotic fervour, the most famous example being his War-Hymn (Θούριος). Yet another aspect of his more serious work was educational and in this must be included his cartographical publications and his Νέα Πολιτικὴ Διοίκησις (*New Political Dispensation*), both of which deserve more particular mention. His cartographical work consisted of a *New Map of Wallachia* (1797), a *General Map of Moldavia* (1797) and a *Plan of Constantinople* (1796) which,

[49] Ar. J. Manessis, *op. cit.*, p. 118. See also Hans Kohn, *The Idea of Nationalism. A Study in its Origins and Background*, New York, 1961, pp. 537 ff.

with eleven other sheets, made up his *Map of Greece*, published in 1797. This has been called "a real monument of its time . . . a publishing feat and a work of indefatigable patience and industry, long study and astonishing erudition".[50] Its chief aim was to link the past with the present in a single huge portrayal.

The *New Political Dispensation of the Inhabitants of Rumelia, Asia Minor, the Mediterranean Islands and Vlachobogdania* [i.e. Wallachia and Moldavia] (*Νέα Πολιτικὴ Διοίκησις τῶν κατοίκων τῆς Ρούμελης, τῆς Μικρᾶς 'Ασίας, τῶν Μεσογείων Νήσων καὶ τῆς Βλαχομπογδανίας*), published in 1797, contains a Revolutionary Proclamation, the Rights of Man, the Constitution and the *War-Hymn*. The Proclamation and the Constitution are in fact elaborated versions of the French *Déclaration des Droits de l'Homme et du Citoyen* of 24 June 1793, and of the *Acte Constitutionnel* of the same year. The variations from these texts constitute the original elements in Rhigas's scheme.

The work, the political ideas and plans of Rhigas are clearly bound up with the lines of thought coming from the West. The influence of the French Enlightenment and the French Revolution was powerful, and even went as far as textual imitation. Two fundamental principles were, in addition, grafted on to the body of French revolutionary thought: the modern Greek view of history in its earliest form and the universalist idea.

Of the universalist idea and its various nuances something has already been said and more will be said later. By the new Greek view of Greek history is meant that intellectual movement which by historical study linked the new Greece with the national past, and more particularly with Antiquity. This new strain of thought was undoubtedly a constant feature of the thinking of the modern Greeks, whether they belonged to the highly educated or to the more popular classes, and the expression "in its earliest form" has been deliberately used in order to distinguish this from both the older and the fully developed

[50] L. I. Vranousis, *'Ρήγας*, p. 49.

form of the movement. The older form, which had its roots in the Greek historical theory of the last Byzantine centuries, lasted on into the generations of the Greek scholars of the Renaissance and their immediate successors. The later and more mature form, which, after the period of historical writing about the Revolution was over, developed through the *Philosophical Essay on the Rise and Fall of Ancient Greece* (1839) (Φιλοσοφικὸν Δοκίμιον περὶ τῆς προόδου καὶ τῆς πτώσεως τῆς παλαιᾶς ῾Ελλάδος), of George Typaldos-Kozakis, the *Philosophy of History* (Φιλοσοφία τῆς ῾Ιστοριάς) of Markos Renieris (1841) and the *Folksongs of Greece* (῎Ασματα δημοτικὰ τῆς ῾Ελλάδος) (1852) and *Byzantine Studies* (Βυζαντιναὶ Μελεταὶ) (1857) of Spyridon Zambelios, and came to an end with the *History of the Greek Nation* (῾Ιστορία τοῦ ῾Ελληνικοῦ ῎Εθνους) (1860–74) of Constantine Paparrhegopoulos.

Between these earlier and later forms, differing both in their essential character and in the sources of their inspiration, lies the early version of the modern Greek theory of history. This was the product of a new school of Greek historians who were moving away from both the Byzantine type of chronicle and from local histories. The work of George Kontaris from Macedonia, *The Ancient and Most Instructive History of the famous City of Athens* (῾Ιστορίαι παλαιαὶ καὶ πάνυ ᾿ωφέλιμοι τῆς περιφήμου πόλεως τῆς ᾿Αθήνης), published at Venice in 1675, does indeed belong to this latter class but it derives a special importance from its subject and marks a turning-point. The interest shown by the Greeks of the eighteenth century in their country's history is closely connected with the appearance, in the form of translations and compilations, of works relating to the past. So far as classical Greece is concerned, mention must be made of the *Histoire Ancienne* of Charles Rollin in the translation by Alexander Kankellarios of Athens (in sixteen volumes, published at Venice in 1750). On Byzantine history there was the Βίβλος χρονικὴ περιέχουσα τὴν ῾Ιστορίαν τῆς Βυζαντίδος (*Book of Annals containing the History of Byzantium*) by John Stanos and Agapios Loverdos (in six volumes, published at Venice in 1767) which contained translations of Byzantine texts into current Greek.[51]

Drawing its initial impulse from the winds of change which were coming out of the west from the centres of 'enlightened Europe'[52], Rhigas's political theory was directed against the lines of thought which had hitherto prevailed in Greek circles. Regarding the form of this new "Greek Republic" as it was imagined by this bold visionary, I venture to quote below some extracts from a study which I published in 1948, on the one hundred and fiftieth aniversary of Rhigas's execution.[53] As the reader will note, I reject the view that there lay hid in Rhigas's plan the germ of the eventual Balkan Alliance. Since then other scholars have rallied to my support.[54] My thesis in regard to the form of the new state is that, as against the federal conception ($\pi o\lambda v\kappa\rho a\tau\iota\kappa\grave{o}v$ $K\rho\acute{a}\tau os$ $\tau o\hat{v}$ $\Gamma\acute{e}vovs$) and the conception of the unitary, multiracial state ($\pi o\lambda v\epsilon\theta v\iota\kappa\grave{o}v$ $K\rho\acute{a}\tau os$ $\tau o\hat{v}$ $\Gamma\acute{e}vovs$), the new state was to be based on the participation of all the subject races and on the equal status of the national groups composing it, without regard to their racial origin or religious belief. Outwardly, therefore, it would present the appearance of a single, supra-national state.[55] The description of it which is given in the heading to the present section of this chapter summarizes my view; it is based on the distinction to be made between the term 'nationality' ($'E\theta v\acute{o}\tau\eta s$) and the term 'nation' ($"E\theta vos$). I have taken this distinction as defined in Lalande's *Vocabulaire*, where it is phrased as follows:

Nationality. (in French, *Ethnie*) A social group united by a

---

[51] C. Th. Dimaras, *Histoire de la Littérature Néo-hellénique*, pp. 177 ff., and *La Grèce au temps des Lumières*, pp. 103 ff. D. A. Zakythinos, *op. cit.*, in footnote 43 above.

[52] C. Th. Dimaras, 'Η φωτισμένη Εὐρώπη (The Europe of the Enlightenment), in *Νέα Ἑστία*, vol. LI (15 Feb. 1952), pp. 225 ff. Reprinted in his Φροντίσματα, P. I, Athens, 1962, pp. 3–23.

[53] Reprint in D. A. Zakythinos, 'Η Ἅλωσις τῆς Κωνσταντινουπόλεως καὶ ἡ Τουρκοκρατία (*The Taking of Constantinople and the Turkish Domination*), Athens, 1954, pp. 127–35.

[54] See e.g. Ar. J. Manessis, *op. cit.*, pp. 107 ff.

[55] N. Pantazopoulos, *op. cit.* in footnote 25 above pp. 29 ff.

community of race or at least of civilisation, by a historic tradition and by common aspirations (even when this group does not form a state). *Nation* (in the French text the same word): the totality of the individuals who make up a state, considered as a society as opposed to a Government.[56]

Rhigas, although a follower of the doctrines of the French Revolution and modern ideas and an admirer of Greek Antiquity, came no less under the spell of Byzantium. Born and brought up within the Ottoman Empire and the Orthodox Church, he had seen at close quarters, in Constantinople and Bucharest, the co-existence of different nationalities and was well aware of the great variety of ideas that were in circulation about the restoration of Greece and Greek culture. His system embraced all their conflicting demands. "The Hellenic Republic of Rhigas, haunted by a vision of a new Byzantium" was to include the Balkan Peninsula and the Levant "in a unitary Greek state".[57] It is also worth recalling that thirty years later, in the critical years 1825 and 1826, the Greek Administration entered into negotiations with the Serbs and Montenegrins. According to the Greek view, these latter, having regained their liberty, ought to be considered Hellenes and reckoned as members of the 'Hellenic race', forming a single state.[58] But at this point we may look at the extracts from my earlier study.

"... The Greek democracy which is to emerge from the revolution and from the fall of Ottoman tyranny is a single whole, no matter how many races and religions it may embrace." Its sovereign people will include all the inhabitants of this state without regard to differences of religion or language. "All men, Christians and Turks, are by nature equal" and "the

---

[56] André Lalande, *Vocabulaire technique et critique de la Philosophie*, 6th ed., Paris, 1951, p. 665.

[57] Valentin A. Georgescu, *op. cit.*, p. 38.

[58] Sp. D. Loukatos, Σχέσεις Ἑλλήνων μετὰ Σέρβων καί Μαυροβουνίων κατὰ τὴν Ἑλληνικὴν Ἐπανάστασιν 1823–26 (*Relations of the Greeks with the Serbs and Montenegrins during the Greek Revolution, 1823–26*), Salonica, 1970, pp. 61 ff.

freedom of all types of religion—Christianity, Islam, Judaism and the rest—will be unrestricted under this Dispensation". Clearly, the principle governing Rhigas's state is to be a racial and religious tolerance which will lead to such a degree of joint solidarity that "the Bulgar must feel himself roused when the Greek suffers and the Greek in his turn must feel for the Bulgar and both for the Albanian and the Vlach". It is precisely for this reason that the revolutionary poet turns in his *War-Hymn* to all the peoples who groan under Ottoman tyranny and to all of them—Greeks and Bulgars, Albanians and Armenians, dwellers by the Danube and the Sava, Lazes and Georgians, and even the more distant Moslems of Egypt—he addresses his call to the struggle for deliverance and reconstruction.

This message, however, directed to a variety of uncoordinated national and religious groups, proceeded from a single, well-coordinated motive force:

Greece calls thee, Greece longs for thee, Greece feels for thee . . .

We shall meet this dominant, vibrant force in Rhigas's vision of the new state. The Greek Republic will be the successor state to the Ottoman Empire and its people will include the people, descendants or successors of the Greeks, who inhabit Rumelia, Asia Minor, the Mediterranean islands, Vlachobogdania (i.e. Wallachia and Moldavia). In the attempt to define the citizen of the new state the Greek contribution is positively and heavily stressed: "Whoever speaks the plain [i.e. popular] or Greek [i.e. educated Greek] tongue and helps Greece, though he live in the Antipodes (since the Greek leaven has spread to both the hemispheres) is a Greek and a citizen" [i.e. of the new state]. Rhigas insists on the significance of the Greek language as the organ of communication and the unifying factor between the races that are to live together. All laws and ordinances all legal documents and other public acts will be drawn up in the common speech of Greece. The inspired paragraph which stresses the necessity for all citizens without exception to become literate and the duty of the State to establish schools everywhere and which proclaims that "from literacy comes that progress by which free nations shine" lays down explicitly that "the old historians are to be expounded, the French and Italian languages are to be taught in the larger towns, but Greek is essential".

But while the particulars given in the *New Dispensation* are so detailed in regard to the structure of the new state, they do not fully disclose Rhigas's views on its character. They do, however, allow us to form some definite conclusions. They rule out, in the first place, the view that Rhigas, as a pan-Balkan figure, represented in his person the desires of all the Balkan peoples, and that he conceived of his new state as a federal union of the Balkan nations. From a comparison of his writings it is un-mistakably clear that the political amalgam which was to emerge from the Revolution was to be neither Balkan nor a federation. One precondition of federation is the integration of individual political units with a view to the composition of a single whole. Further, Rhigas's plan went beyond the limits of the Balkan Peninsula and included the Greeks of Asia Minor as well as other oriental peoples, more particularly the Armenians. His plan for a democracy would therefore have had a more universal character in so far as its national components went, although from another point of view its framework would have been more restricted.

What Rhigas dreamed of was a Greek state and it was as such that his contemporaries understood it, even the Austrian authorities who were so attentive to Balkan affairs. He wanted it one, unitary and universal from the start, not made up in part of autonomous units. He inserted into the framework the national and religious units which he included under the common name 'Greece', and he allowed them political equality of rights. But above all these distinctions Rhigas set, as the governing and cohesive force, the Greek element and its spiritual and intellectual riches. He was fully aware of their significance and of their historic mission. Highly typical is the

164

phrase which he slips into his definition of the new citizen ". . . since the Greek leaven has spread to both the hemispheres". The Greek element is revealed as the 'leaven' of the new state and its spiritual and intellectual resources—from the simplest form of the Greek language to the memories of the historic past and the ancient writers—are called upon, with all their educational value, to give the new world rising into existence the broad-based support of tradition and the basic lines of its future course. Politically equal, the various racial and religious groups would thus be drawn into the shining orbit of the Greek world.

Rhigas's theoretical construction, a curious mixture of prophetic vision and political practicality, emerges in the last analysis as a composite of living Greek traditions and modern ideas about the rights of peoples and about human life and freedom. This mixture of ideals corresponds to the two sources of the author's spiritual and ideological inspiration—the French Revolution and the Greek 'Great Idea'. Our knowledge of his life is so scanty that we are left completely in the dark as to how he arrived at these twin poles of his thought. His thirst for freedom and his loathing of oppression inclined him in any case towards his French models, but he must have needed long intellectual training to break free from the narrowly Greek horizons of his native Thessalian plain and to rise to the conception of a universal Empire of the East. It is precisely in his amalgamation of the two ideals that the originality of his thought lies. To him the Enlightenment meant the raising of the peoples of the Balkans and Asia Minor in the scale of human worth and gave a solid moral content to the idea of a universal state. For the first time the ideals of the French Revolution really fertilized Greek thinking; the dream of a universal state was already familiar to the leading minds of Greece or to the broader strata of the Greek nation. It is therefore of particular relevance to our subject to reconstruct the stages by which Rhigas rose to his vision of a 'Greek Republic.'

During the eighteenth century the rise of Russia had suggested, both to the political and religious leaders of the Phanar and to the imaginations of the Greek people at large, possibilities of action against a weakening Ottoman Empire and even of the restoration of some form of Greek Eastern Empire. Yet even in this same period there was also a small section of the Greek leadership which disliked the idea of foreign intervention and looked rather to the internal corrosion and eventual absorption of the Ottoman Empire. This counter-scheme allowed the union of the Balkan Slavs with the Greek nation through the administration of the Church, but set as its ultimate objective their assimilation, and indeed the inclusion of the Ottomans themselves, within the national structure. These views were nothing new to the spirit of Greek tradition and, at that particular moment of history, faint indications suggested a hope that the empire of the Sultans might indeed be transformed into an "Ottoman Empire of the Greek Nation".

Undoubtedly Rhigas's vision is directly bound up with this line of thought about Greek liberation. Although he was by origin and temperament far removed from the ruling classes, he had received his schooling in that milieu and had received from that schooling the seeds of the 'Great Idea'. At the time when his own political thought was being shaped, a certain slackening and fatigue were observable in these higher circles. "If then, at the time appointed by prophecy," wrote Athanasius Comnenus Hypsilanti, "after such great victories of the Muscovites over the Ottomans and at such a favourable moment, we Romans were not liberated, it would be very hard for the resurrection of the Greek Empire to take place thereafter. . . ."[59] Rhigas caught up and made his own the flagging 'Idea' and made too his own synthesis of the differing lines of thought. A new ideology, originating in the French Revolution,

---

[59] Athanasius Comnenos Hypsilantes, Ἐκκλησιαστικῶν καὶ Πολιτικῶν τῶν εἰς Δώδεκα Βιβλίον Η', Θ' καί Ι' ἤτοι Τὰ μετὰ τὴν Ἅλωσιν (1453–1789), ed. by Archim. Germanos Aphthonides Sinaïtes, Constantinople, 1870, p. 534. (Vols. VIII, IX and X of Twelve Books on Church and Political Affairs, or Events since the Conquest.)

and more in accordance with his own temperament and way of thinking, brought him closer to the mass of his people. The breach with tradition had been accomplished and Rhigas, fixing his gaze on a newer, modern Greece, drifted away from Byzantine traditions.

IV. The Clash of Ideas

Thus in the second half of the eighteenth century the two systems of Greek political thought attain their full definition. As against the more fluid forms of the other ideologies—fluid both because of their intrinsic lack of clarity and because of the differences between their objectives—the Church, then at the height of its authority, built up the traditional body of Orthodox doctrine. This, naturally, related chiefly to faith and morals, but it had its reflection too in the great contemporary political and cultural issues. Although conservative in matters of doctrine, this Orthodox *Summa* was wide open to educational ideas from abroad; it admitted the foundation of schools and the circulation of the printed word. Major Church leaders like Dositheos Notaras, Patriarch of Jerusalem (1669–1707) and his nephew Chrysanthos (1707–31), sons of a Peloponnesian family, drafted the new spiritual synthesis of Orthodoxy and the leading directives of the Church's view of its own Faith and of the Church's view of its own Faith and of the world.[60]

By the end of the eighteenth century and the beginning of the nineteenth the clash between the two rival schools of thought had reached its height. This whole period was one of the most critical in the history of mankind. The events of fifteen years had upset the world balance of power, had stirred society to its depths and had changed its ways of life, its thinking and its human relationships between man and man. This radical international disturbance had spread to eastern and south-eastern Europe, where it had already gained some foothold: the second

[60] Steven Runciman, *The Great Church in Captivity*, pp. 338 ff.

167

Russo-Turkish War (1787–92), the Russian and Austrian invasion of the Danubian Principalities in 1788, the naval activities of Lambros Katsonis, the Treaty of Jassy in 1792, the French Revolution, Bonaparte's Italian campaigns and the Peace of Campoformio (1797), the French occupation of the Ionian Islands in the same year, Bonaparte's Egyptian campaign, the alliance between Russia and Turkey, the Treaty of Constantinople (1800) had all profoundly affected the situation in the East. Beyond any doubt the moment which Rhigas had chosen for action was a unique opportunity.

Leaving out of account minor deviations from the general pattern, one may define the clash of ideas within the Greek world as a conflict between neo-Byzantine universalism and the reviving spirit of nationalism. The battlefield between the two sides was now the question of the national and political restoration of Greece. It will help towards an understanding of what was afoot if one compares certain documents which distinguish the views of either side as formulated by them. These texts include certain synodical and Patriarchal documents, encyclicals, decisions by Church authorities, denunciations, and a variety of publications, polemical pamphlets in prose and verse, proclamations, admonitions, dialogues and letters. All of these have one characteristic in common; they aim at a wide distribution, and this literature has been aptly given the general title of 'The Battle of the Pamphlets'.[61] One may add that this outburst of publicity represents one form of the Greek journalism which was beginning to flourish at the time. Some of the publications were printed on the newly installed Patriarchal press.

The contest appears to be a confrontation between conservative and liberal ideas—outwardly at least between 'Ancients' and 'Moderns'; but at a deeper level the facts suggest another view. The wide distribution given to the works of Western thinkers, viewed in the light of local political and social developments, was causing lively anxiety in Church

[61] C. Th. Dimaras, *Histoire de la Littèrature Néo-hellénique*, pp. 174 ff.

circles and among the conservative aristocracy associated with them. The figure of Voltaire again takes the limelight as a target for denunciation. In a letter of 1790, published in the following year[62], Evgenios Voulgaris renounced his allegiance to the French philosopher, but this recantation, by Voltaire's first Greek translator, was due not only to the hardening of Voltaire's intransigence in the matter of religion but also to a shift in the Russian attitude towards him. Athanasius Psalidas followed suit in his Ἀληθὴς Εὐδαιμονία (*True Happiness*), written in Greek and Latin and published at Vienna in 1791. In the Τρόπαιον τῆς Ὀρθοδόξου Πίστεως (*Triumph of the Orthodox Faith*), also published at Vienna in the same year, Antony Manuel likewise aims at demonstrating the virtues of piety and refuting the babblings of the impious. The pamphlet entitled Ἡ ἀθλιότης τῶν δοκησισόφων, ἤτοι ἀπολογία ὑπὲρ τῆς πίστεως τῶν Χριστιανῶν πρὸς ἀναίρεσιν τινῶν φιλοσοφικῶν ληρημάτων (*The Miserable Mind of the Pseudo-Sages or a Defence of the Christian Faith to the Putting Down of certain philosophic Babblings*), published at Trieste in 1793, was written, ostensibly by Celestine of Rhodes, a *nom de plume* which probably concealed a certain Spyridon Zorzelas, who also reprehends Voltaire. The same year saw the publication at Vienna of the pamphlet in verse Νεκρικοὶ Διάλογοι (*Dialogues of the Dead*) by Polyzoës Kontos, in which the author attacks the French Revolution and the slackening of morals. In 1794 there was published, with introduction and commentary, a Greek translation of a book by Joseph Guillaume Clémence, *L'Authenticité des Livres tant du Nouveau que de l'Ancien Testament démontrée et leur Véracité défendue, ou Réfutation de "La Bible enfin expliquée" de V(oltaire)* Paris, 1782. The translator's name is not given but he may have been Nicephorus Theotokes.[63] Finally, two further works may be

---

[62] Ἐπιστολὴ Εὐγενίου τοῦ Βουλγάρεως .... πρὸς ἀναίρεσιν τινὸς φληνάφου δυσσεβοῦς (*Letter of Eugenios Voulgaris ... in Refutation of a Certain Impious Prattler*), Vienna, 1791.

[63] The title of the Greek trans. is: Ἀπόδειξις τοῦ κύρους τῶν τῆς Νέας καὶ Παλαιᾶς Διαθήκης Βιβλίων καὶ τῆς ἐν αὐτοῖς Ἀληθείας ὑπεράσπισις, Ἡ ἀνασκευὴ τῆς τοῦ Βολτέρου Βίβλου τῆς καλουμένης Τελευταῖον Διερμηνευθείσης Διαθήκης. Ἐκ τῆς

mentioned from the continuing blasts of anti-French and anti-Voltairean polemic, the Ἀντιφώνησις πρὸς τὸν παράλογον ζῆλον τῶν ἀπὸ τῆς Εὐρώπης ἐρχομένων φιλοσόφων (*Reply to the Irrational Zeal of the Philosophers coming from Europe*), published at Trieste in 1802, by Athanasius of Paros, writing under the assumed name of Nathaniel of Neocaesarea, and the Λόγος παραινετικὸς πρὸς τοὺς ἰδίους μαθητὰς ἢ κατὰ Οὐαλταίρου καὶ τῶν ὀπαδῶν (Word of Advice to his own Pupils, or Against Voltaire and his followers) by Makarios Kavvadias (Venice, 1802).[64]

The official attitude of the Church towards the new ideas is illustrated by the Patriarchal encyclicals.[65] Already in an encyclical of 1777 Patriarch Sophronius II was condemning those who read the works of Voltaire. In 1793 Neophytus VII, excommunicating Christodoulos of Acarnania, named Voltaire, Rousseau and Spinoza as "the agents of utter impiety and godlessness". The great events of the end of the eighteenth century and the beginning of the nineteenth required still more severe action on the Patriarch's part. In July 1797 and July 1798 encyclicals were issued charging Christian congregations "not to be deceived involuntarily and through lack of attention and not to be decoyed by that Satanic snare which they spread

---

τῶν Γάλλων φωνῆς μεταφρασθεῖσα, ᾗ προσετέθησαν καί τινες σημειώσεις, Vienna, 1794.

[64] C. Th. Dimaras, *La Grèce au temps des Lumières* pp. 72 ff. This propaganda campaign against the French and Voltaire coincided with the affair of Christodoulos of Acarnania (his surname was Pamblekis) whom the Church excommunicated in 1793. He had written a book entitled Περί Φιλοσόφου, Φιλοσοφίας, Φυσικῶν, Μεταφυσικῶν, Πνευματικῶν καί Θείων Ἀρχῶν (*On Philosophers, Philosophy, Physical, Metaphysical, Spiritual and Divine Principles*), pub. in Vienna in 1786. See C. Th. Dimaras, *op. cit.*, pp. 40 ff.

[65] L. I. Vranousis, Ἄγνωστα πατριωτικά φυλλάδια καί ἀνέκδοτα κείμενα τῆς ἐποχῆς τοῦ Ῥήγα καί τοῦ Κοραῆ. Ἡ φιλογαλλική καί ἀντιγαλλική προπαγάνδα ('Unknown Patriotic Pamphlets and unedited Texts of the Time of Rhigas and Koraïs. Pro- and Anti-French Propaganda'). This will appear in the forthcoming number of the Ἐπετηρὶς Μεσαιωνικοῦ Ἀρχείου (*Yearbook of Medieval Archives*), Academy of Athens, vols. XV/XVI, Athens, 1965–66), pp. 183 ff. See also Bernard Lewis, 'The Impact of the French Revolution on Turkey. Some Notes on the Transmission of Ideas', in *Cahiers d'Histoire Mondiale—Journal of World History*, vol I, No. 1 (1953), pp. 105–25.

covertly and craftily in the name of Liberty". At the beginning of September 1798 Patriarch Gregory V issued his encyclical to the Ionian Islanders, in which he wrote: ". . . the wicked serpent, the source of all evil . . . finding the French nation the readiest to harbour such wickedness, has of late poured plentifully into their souls the poison of rebellion aginst God, and after having brought them to civil war and to miserable regicide, he has plunged them forthwith into utter atheism and impiety". And when, in addition, the French attempted their "robbers' raid" against Egypt, this "mighty Empire", namely Turkey, "justly declared war by land and sea, in order to punish, with God's help, these destroyers of mankind, rebels against God and violators of the common order and peace". He summoned to this war "powerful kings, our allies, those of Russia and Britain, who are also in accord with this Divine purpose, to deliver humanity from the woes to come and to keep the royal governments of the world within their boundaries".[66]

Other anti-French texts were also being circulated in print and manuscript. Special mention may be made of Patriarch Gregory's encyclical of 1 December 1798, to all Metropolitans in which the *New Political Dispensation* (Νέα Πολιτικὴ Διοίκησις) of Rhigas is denounced as a work "full of rottenness in the confusion of its thought and contrary to the doctrines of our Orthodox Faith".[67] Clearly all these documents were directed to the great international conflicts of the day; the expedition against Egypt; the French occupation of Malta and Alexandria; the Battle of the Nile; the official declaration of war between France and Turkey (4 September 1798); Turkey's recourse to an alliance with Russia, Britain and Austria. This 'battle of the pamphlets' was carried on as a means of spreading rumours and slogans in regard to international affairs, not only against the French but also in support of them. Beside certain works of Koraïs of which more will be said later, two pro-French

---

[66] L. I. Vranousis, *op. cit.*, 179 ff., 242 ff.
[67] *Ibid.* pp. 195 ff.

publications may be cited, whose significance has been emphasized by recent research. One is the proclamation *To the Romans* [i.e. Greeks] *of Greece* (Πρὸς τοὺς Ρωμαίους τῆς 'Ελλάδος), published at Constantinople on 4 October 1798, the writer of which calls himself Philopatris Eleutheriades (Patriot Son of Freedom): the other is entitled *Thoughts of a Philhellene* (Στοχασμοὶ ἑνὸς Φιλέλληνος). It was published in Vienna and is undated. The first pamphlet was in fact the work of a well-known patriot and Francophil, a writer and translator named Constantine Stamatis of Constantinople (1764–1817). The second was by Émile Gauden, a French diplomatist who had served in Constantinople, Bucharest and Vienna, a jurist and author according to Stamatis his translator. Both pamphlets had been printed in Paris.[68]

There can be no doubt today that exceptional pressures and political aims, and not merely a spirit of conservatism, made these anti-French activities necessary.[69] In the great European conflicts of that tempestuous time the official attitude of the Constantinople Patriarchate had perforce to be pro-Turkish. The fact that Russia was Turkey's ally helped considerably to remove all hesitations. The Patriarch's writings extolled the 'Mighty Empire' and the 'mightiest of Emperors' and the Greek nation's absolute duty of submission to the Sultan's orders. The monarch is represented as one ordained by God to rule over Christians and obedience to him is enjoined by apostolic precepts, "and likewise we are under the greatest obligation to observe such obedience to our most mighty Emperor whom Almighty God has appointed to be over us, since the holy Apostles command us to observe such obedience to our Ruler. . . . Therefore we ought to call upon the Lord our God with all our heart and soul to grant our most mighty Emperor a long life and much strength and to confound, destroy and root out the enemies of his most mighty Empire."

[68] *Ibid.*, pp. 125 ff., 144ff. The texts will be found on pp. 209–37, together with the French originals in parallel. These latter are preserved in the Archives of the French Ministry of Foreign Affairs.

[69] *Ibid.* pp. 186 ff.

Both the propaganda lines, pro-French and anti-French, correspond to the more general lines of thought among the Greeks during the last years of Turkish rule. All those concerned—Church circles, the Phanariot aristocracy, Rhigas and Constantine Stamatis in his endeavours to help the French in their Eastern expeditions—all dreamed of the creation of a strong Greek state.[70]

Returning to the attitude of Gregory V, we note that one of the documents of the anti-French campaign, and the best known, was the *Paternal Instruction* (Διδασκαλία Πατρική) which appeared, spuriously, under the name of Anthimos, Patriarch of Jerusalem, and was published at Constantinople in 1798.[71] It is more than probable that the author of this pamphlet was Athanasius of Paros (c.1723–1813), a much-travelled teacher and a controversial and pugnacious theologian and writer, to whom we owe a further work, hitherto unpublished, a rejoinder to the *Fraternal Instruction* of Koraïs[72] The following is a typical extract from the *Paternal Instruction*:

Here yet again, beloved Christians, we must see and marvel at God's boundless love towards us. Behold most clearly what our Lord, infinite in mercy and all-wise, has decreed, to preserve yet again unspotted the Holy Orthodox Faith of us, His worshippers, and to save us all. He raised up from nothing this strong Empire of the Ottomans in the place of our Roman Empire, which had begun in some respects to halt in the doctrines of the Orthodox Faith, and He exalted this Empire of the Ottomans above all others, that He might show beyond doubt that this had come to pass by God's will and

---

[70] *Ibid.* pp. 157 ff. See also Catherine Coumarianou, Ἐνέργειες τοῦ Κωνσταντίνου Σταμάτη γιὰ τὴν ἀπελευθέρωση τῆς Ἑλλάδος 1798–1799 ('The Efforts of Constantine Stamatis for the Liberation of Greece, 1798–9'), in the Πρακτικὰ τοῦ Τρίτου Πανιονίου Συνεδρίου, 23–29 Σεπτεμβρίου 1965 (*Proceedings of the Third Panionian Congress*), vol. I, Athens, 1967, pp. 154–74.

[71] For a recent study of the *Paternal Instruction* see the article of Richard Clogg, 'The "Dhidhaskalia Patriki" (1798): An Orthodox Reaction to French Revolutionary Propaganda', in *Middle Eastern Studies*, vol. V, London, 1969, pp. 87–115.

[72] L. I. Vranoussis, Ἄγνωστα πατριωτικὰ φυλλάδια, pp. 251 ff.

not through the power of men and that He might assure all the faithful that it was His pleasure to order in this way a great mystery, namely the salvation of His chosen people. The Almighty Lord, therefore, set this lofty Empire over us (for there is no power but of God) that it might be, as it were, a bridle upon the West and to us in the East an agent of salvation. Therefore too He put it into the heart of the Emperor of these Ottomans to keep our Orthodox Faith in liberty and to give it exceeding authority, so that at times it might instruct even Christians who had turned out of the way to have the fear of God ever before their eyes.

The *Paternal Instruction* gave Adamantios Koraïs his chance to intervene in the controversy. A brief reference has already been made to the place which this great reformer of Greek letters holds in the reshaping of the political thought of modern Greece. He had already begun his career as a writer in 1782 by publishing, besides books on medical subjects, works on catechetics and philology, but the year 1798 was to remain a turning-point in his intellectual development.[73] In reply to the *"Paternal Instruction* falsely published at Constantinople under the name of *His Beatitude the Patriarch of Jerusalem"* Koraïs published anonymously at Paris (not at Rome, as recorded on the title-page) his *Fraternal Instruction to the Greeks living all over the Ottoman Empire* ('Αδελφικὴ Διδασκαλία πρὸς τοὺς εὑρισκομένους κατὰ πᾶσαν τὴν 'Οθωμανικὴν 'Επικράτειαν Γραικούς).[74] In this work Koraïs denounces the "foolish and irreligious teaching" of the

---

[73] For Greek studies on Koraïs see: D. Thereianos, 'Αδαμάντιος Κοραῆς, Three vols., Trieste, 1889–90. C. Th. Dimaras, 'Ο Κοραῆς καί ἡ ἐποχή του (Koraïs and his Time'), in the series Βασικὴ Βιβλιοθήκη (*Basic Library*), No. 9, Athens, 1953. *Idem*, 'Α. Κοραῆ, Τρεῖς Διάλογοι ('*Three Dialogues 'of A. Koraïs*), Athens, 1960. Ap. B. Daskalakis, 'Ο 'Αδαμάντιος Κοραῆς καί ἡ ἐλευθερία τῶν 'Ελλήνων (*A. Koraïs and the Liberty of the Greeks*), Athens, 1965, and Κοραῆς καί Κοδρικᾶς. 'Η μεγάλη φιλολογικὴ διαμάχη τῶν 'Ελλήνων 1815–21 (*Koraïs and Kodrikas. The Great Literary Debate of the Greeks*), Athens, 1966.

[74] Both *Didaskaliai* were reproduced by G. Valetas, Κοραῆς. "Απαντα τὰ πρωτότυπα ἔργα (*Koraïs, All the original Works*), vol I, Pt. I, Athens, 1964, pp. 39 ff.

Turcophil writer who "seeing the hatred of the barbarian tyrants of Greece increasing more and more", wished "to lull the righteous indignation of the Greeks and to deter them from imitating the present movements of many nations of Europe in the cause of liberty". In contrast to the earlier writer he paints the conqueror's tyranny in black colours: "It is well known to everyone what a pitch the tyranny of the Turks has reached today. The wretched Greeks no longer own lands or children or their own wives. Their honour and their lives depend on the will not only of the Chief Tyrant himself but on that of each one of his slaves." Reversing the doctrine of apostolic command, he writes: "Therefore, according to the teaching of the Apostles, such lawless rulers are owed, not blind, unreasoning submission, but valiant resistance." In conclusion, the victims of tyranny "have the inalienable right to seek in every way to break the yoke of tyranny and to recover this priceless gift of self-government".

After the *Fraternal Instruction* Koraïs continued until his death in 1833 to occupy himself with the themes of national restoration and education and the national language as well as with major Greek and international problems. To this end he made use of pamphlets and letters but he liked also to insert his own thoughts into the long introductions to his literary publications and translations. It was in this way that there appeared the prefaces to his edition of the Hippocratic treatise on *Varieties of Air, Water and Situation* (Περὶ 'Αέρων, 'Υδάτων, Τόπων) (Paris, 1800); his translation of Beccaria's *Dei Delitti e delle Pene* (Paris, 1802); his edition of the *Aethiopica* of Heliodorus (Paris, 1804); his own 'Random Thoughts on Greek Education and the Greek Language' (Αὐτοσχέδιοι Στοχασμοὶ περὶ τῆς 'Ελληνικῆς παιδείας καὶ γλώσσης) in his *Preliminary Notice of the 'Greek Library'* (Πρόδρομος 'Ελληνικῆς Βιβλιοθήκης), published in Paris in 1805.[75]

---

[75] The *Greek Library* ('Ελληνικὴ Βιβλιοθήκη) was the general title of a series of sixteen vols. (Paris 1807–26), in which several classical authors were edited.

More directly connected with our subject and with the period under examination are Koraïs' *Trumpet Call to War* (Σάλπισμα πολεμιστήριον), nominally published in Alexandria but actually in Paris, 1801, and his dialogue, *What should the Greeks do in the present situation? A Conversation between two Greeks living in Venice on hearing of the brilliant victories of the Emperor Napoleon* (Τί πρέπει νὰ κάμωσιν οἱ Γραικοί, εἰς τὰς παρούσας περιστάσεις; Διάλογος δύο Γραικῶν κατοίκων τῆς Βενετίας, ὅταν ἤκουσαν τὰς λαμπρὰς νίκας τοῦ Αὐτοκράτορος Ναπολέοντος), nominally published in Venice but actually in Paris, December 1805. The *Trumpet Call*, which is in the form of a circular letter, summons all Greeks living in Greece, Egypt or elsewhere to take part in the Egyptian expedition and to assist the French in every way. But the chief work of Koraïs in this field was written in French, the *Mémoire sur l'État actuel de la Civilisation dans la Grèce*[76] which he read to the Société des Observateurs de l'Homme on 6 January 1803. It bears witness to the writer's keen historical insight, to a wide-ranging knowledge of Greek affairs and not least to a certain prophetic vision of the future. Taken as a whole, these writings of Koraïs, with others which cannot find mention here, but more especially the *Mémoire*, the *Random Thoughts* and the letters, form a solid contribution to the study of the great political, religious, educational and intellectual problems of Greece at the time and form a master-plan for national reform, in which Koraïs envisaged the restoration of Greece and Greek culture as resting on the spread of education and the creation of a generally accepted form of the Greek language. Of a milder disposition than Rhigas, he disapproved of premature rebellion. J. K. Orelli, in 1823, called him "the literary architect of his nation" and compared him to Fichte. "Koraïs was not a radical, filled with the impetuosity of revolution; he was humanitarian, realistic and moderate", an "enlightened philanthropist deeply imbued with middle-class liberalism".[77] He admired the great

[76] Greek trans. by D. Thereianos, *op. cit.*, vol. III, German trans. by C. Iken.
[77] Hans Kohn, *op. cit.*, p. 543.

nations of the West but believed that Greece would return to life by its own native strength. In 1818 he wrote: "Having foreseen long ago the present violent agitation in the spirit of Greece and fearing that such a transformation might be attributed to the progressive Powers and not recognised as our own spontaneous movement, I tried to anticipate and destroy any such preconception, partly by my *Random Thoughts* and partly by my treatise on the present state of civilisation in Greece."[78]

It remains to add a few words about the book Ἑλληνικὴ Νομαρχία ἤτοι Λόγος περὶ Ἐλευθερίας (*Greeks and the Rule of Law, or A Discourse on Freedom*), which describes itself as "having been composed and printed at his own expense by an anonymous Greek for the benefit of Greeks"; it was published in Italy, at Pisa, in 1806.[79] The writer is thought by some to have been Spyridon Spakhos of Ioannina, by others John Kolettis and by others again George Kalaras of Corinth. It is influenced by the general views of the Enlightenment and the French Revolution and is permeated with a spirit of rationalism. At the same time it contains severe criticism of the various components of Greek society and a fierily optimistic call to revolution. In its theoretical parts there is some discussion of freedom, war and mankind and about the way in which peoples live in slavery. This is followed by an examination of the Greeks under Turkish rule, the causes of their subjection and, finally, the question whether their liberation is possible. It is perhaps akin to the outlook created, especially in the Danubian Principalities, by the study and practice of law. We recall the drafting of legal codes, and the accompanying treatises, particularly the Δικανικὴ Τέχνη ('The Art of Jurisprudence'), by Demetrius Katartzes (1793).[80]

The causes of Greek subjection are, according to the writer, the "ignorant priesthood" and "the expatriation of the best citizens". He speaks with harshness of the higher clergy, whom

---

[78] See D. Thereianos, *op. cit.*, vol. I, p. 340.
[79] Eds. by N. Tomadakis, Athens, 1948; G. Valetas, Athens, 1957.
[80] C. Th. Dimaras, Δημήτριος Καταρτζῆς, Τὰ Εὑρισκόμενα, pp. 262 ff.

he condemns for their ignorance and avarice. He does not spare the expatriate Greeks, whom he calls upon to return to their homeland. The notables of subject Greece, "the hereditary and worthless archons, the money-loving and ignorant archbishops, the insolent and truly barbarous headmen" are content to enjoy the fruits of their wealth and are indifferent to the liberation of the nation, saying that such an enterprise is impossible. But the revival of Greece is possible. The first reason why this is so is the decrepitude of the Ottoman tyranny. Other reasons are "the progress made by our race in education" and the "morals of the Greeks". "All Greeks", he says, "and particularly the country folk, have a great inclination to arms ... and they are, in general, endowed by nature with a generous and upright spirit. Among their natural virtues, so to speak, hospitality is common to them all. Finally, they are lovers of their religion and bitterly opposed to the Turks. The special qualities of their diet and the clear spring water which they drink keep them permanently in a state of robust health and in superb physical condition. Their openness and honesty are indeed worthy of the Golden Age. In their respect for the old and their love of fame they resemble the Spartans. They have the utmost contempt for their oppressors and a keen desire to be free. They wait only for a chief to lead them, that they may all become his followers and regain their liberty. . . . The Ottoman State", the anonymous author goes on, "is foredoomed to fall by one means or another. But woe to our nation if it is mastered by some foreign monarchy. In that case the Greeks will cease to remain Greeks. . . . For our honour's sake, think carefully of this. Do not be led astray by the promises of the representatives and emissaries of foreign rulers. They are no less slaves than we are and to mitigate their own shame they wish to add to their numbers. They worship only their own ruler and gold. Do not imagine, brothers, that any of them will sacrifice money and soldiers to drive out the Turk and then leave us free! Oh, better that an earthquake or a flood should destroy all of us Greeks than that we should bow any longer beneath a foreign sceptre. . . . Further,

178

do not let our inexperience make cowards of you, but look at the Serbs. Look, again, at the sailors of our race at this time, how, unlettered as they are, they travel with the greatest ease on every sea and work single-handed the finest and swiftest ships. Do not think that centuries are needed to beautify our nation as we should. No, Greeks, to be free is to be beautiful, the one will follow the other in the same moment. . . . The good sailor sails with all winds. Even so, whatever the circumstances Chance decrees for him, the man who would free Greece can always manage well enough since he has before him one aim and one goal, I mean the common good. Ottoman tyranny has risen to such a pitch that itself foreshadows its own destruction. Freedom has drawn near to her former home!" The writer of the book failed to understand and therefore misjudged the chief agents of the national tradition and the chief factors in the real situation of Greece. But his work is a flaming message of hope and this hopefulness he drew from the clear springs of the Greek homeland.[81]

[81] See G. P. Henderson, *op. cit.*, pp. 159 ff. The Ἑλληνικὴ Νομαρχία has a connection with another short work published in 1819 under the title Στοχασμοὶ τοῦ Κρίτωνος (*The Thoughts of Crito*). The author is unknown, but apparently lived in Adrianople. See D. Ghinis, Στοχασμοὶ τοῦ Κρίτωνος in *Ἔρανος εἰς Ἀδαμάντιον Κοραῆν* (*Contributions to the Study of A. Koraïs*), Athens, 1954, pp. 140–56.

IX

Some General Principles in the National and Political Life of Modern Greece

In the long course of Greek history there have been three major periods during which the Greek nation has ceased to form one or more independent or autonomous states—the periods of Roman, Latin and Turkish rule. This is true only as a broad generalization based on their chief characteristics with no account of variations of time and place. The period of Roman rule, which begins in 168 and 146 B.C. for the Greeks of Macedonia and Greece and in 133 and 30 B.C. for the Greeks of Asia and Egypt, has only a vague lower limit since it melts into the emerging Byzantine Empire. Latin (Frankish) rule, which starts from the year 1204, has also its local variations in the date of its end. Its last vestiges did not disappear until the Treaty of Campo Formio in 1797. The Turkish period, as the reader already knows, we date from the fall of Constantinople to the outbreak of the Greek War of Independence (1453–1821), but both these are conventional dates since in fact some Greek territories were subjected to the Turks before 1453, while others fell to them after the taking of Constantinople.

We have then before us three historical periods which, while at a distance from each other in time and springing from different causes, finally broke up the power which they had supplanted and the forms of political life which had derived from it. The two which were closest to each other in time were the two later periods, the Latin and the Turkish, since both derived from the dismemberment of the Byzantine Empire and because the Turkish occupation often directly succeeded the Latin. And yet the two, when examined from a number of points of view, exhibit great differences both in their origins and in their development. On the other hand the drawing of parallels between the two dominations furthest apart in time, the Roman and the Turkish, can lead us to some extremely thought-provoking historical conclusions. As early as 1846 Constantine Paparrhegopoulos drew attention to the connection between the two periods. Looking for survivals of the self-governing institutions of Roman times, he concluded that the origin of the communes of Turkish times went back to the autonomy of the Greek cities under the Romans. The tracing of this connection led him to formulate certain general views on the problem.[1]

The immense amount of material which research has brought to light since that time confirms, if not Paparrhegopoulos's conclusions about the origin of communal institutions, at least his general view. The Roman and Turkish periods are indeed from many points of view counterparts.[2] Both arose out of the conquest of former major powers (the successors of Alexander the Great in one case, the Byzantine Empire in the other) which had reached an advanced stage of decay. In both cases the conquerors recognized or tolerated existing cultural and religious institutions and, sometimes at once, at other times later on, some of the existing institutions of self-government. Thus both under the Romans and under the Turks, Greek civilization formed a solid unit within the foreign state.

Under both conquests the Greeks, although they lost their political independence, not only kept their identity but succeeded in achieving something which they had never done in more favourable circumstances, namely the formation, while

---

[1] C. Paparrhegopoulos, 'Ρωμαίων πολίτευμα πρὸς τὴν 'Ελλάδα ('The Roman form of Government in Greece'), in the periodical Θέμις, 1846. Reprinted in 'Ιστορικαὶ Πραγματεῖαι (Historical Essays), pt. I, Athens, 1858, pp. 188–225.

[2] See Chap. IV above, passim.

under subjection to a foreign power, of a broad national and moral community of all Greeks. This community found its realization, under the Romans, within the miniature unit of the city, and under the Turks, within the widespread network of the Church's organization. The city, with all its religious, institutional, economic, educational and emotional riches, became outstandingly the power-house generating the forces which preserved the Greek nation and directed its activity. Attention has already been drawn above to the significance of the Turkish recognition of the Church.[3] The re-establishment of its huge network contributed greatly to the re-establishment of the Greek community which had been rent apart by the events of the fatal year 1204. As time went on, other institutions would come into existence as centres of national self-preservation and national action—the communes and similar bodies.

The Greeks abandoned the country and turned to the towns. At the time of the Roman, as of the Ottoman, conquest they had been widely dispersed about the countryside. In the "agglomeration of cities (*civitates*, πόλεις), self-governing communities . . ."[4], which was the Roman Empire, they were the *mens agitans molem*. Recent excavations, more eloquently than any other testimony, throw light on what took place in Asia, Africa, Italy, in the Balkan Peninsula and at the mouths of the Danube. The cities of the Roman Empire were the starting points for other advances.

From the time when Horace wrote the line *Graecia capta ferum victorem cepit* . . . the problem of the relationship between the two great peoples of Antiquity has been a subject of constant research. A. H. M. Jones has recently given a concise and penetrating review of the questions which it raises. He exaggerates perhaps when he says: "The most surprising feature of Roman rule in the Greek East is that despite its long duration

[3] See Chap. III above, pp. 43–52
[4] A. H. M. Jones, *The Later Roman Empire, 284–602. A Social, Economic and Administrative Survey*, II, p. 712, Oxford, 1964.

it had so little effect on the civilization of the area." But it remains true that "the influence was in the other direction".[5] The Romans and the Greeks were not rival peoples. In a way, without any express constitutional sanction or any basis of jointly approved principle, but as it were tacitly and unconsciously, the Greeks became linked as fellow-workers with the Romans in the universal monarchy of Rome. To this strange condominium each of them made their own contribution and extended their own influence. The Romans provided the Greeks with the opportunity of expansion by establishing new cities and reviving old ones. "So far from encouraging Romanization," Jones observes, "the Government favoured Hellenization in the surviving backward areas of barbarism. The main evidence for this is its activity in founding Greek cities."[6]

The advances made in the spread of the Greek language under Roman rule are one aspect of the great task of Hellenization which was also a task of civilization. The unacknowledged condominium with the Romans also implied a division of spheres of influence. Ever since the third century B.C. Greek had been infiltrating the upper ranks of the Roman community, and an early form of bilingualism—what André Aymard calls *précocité du bilinguisme*—had grown up.[7] After the conquest of the eastern provinces Rome favoured the expansion of Greek in the belief that any progress in the Hellenizing of backward civilizations was to her advantage. Greek was therefore able to continue the advance begun in the Hellenistic era. Before long Greek was to prevail as the language of administration, so that

[5] A. H. M. Jones, 'The Greeks under the Roman Empire', in *Dumbarton Oaks Papers*, No. 17 (1963), p. 3. On the Greek-Roman Symbiosis see also the recent works of A. N. Sherwin-White, *Racial Prejudice in Imperial Rome*, Cambridge, 1967, and J. S. Touloumakos, Συμβολή στὴν ἔρευνα τῆς ἱστορικῆς συνειδήσεως τῶν Ἑλλήνων στήν ἐποχὴ τῆς Ῥωμαϊκῆς κυριαρχίας (*Contribution to the Research into the historical consciousness of the Greeks during the Period of Roman Domination*), Athens, 1972.

[6] *Ibid*, p. 5.

[7] André Aymard, 'Rome et son Empire', in *Histoire Générale des Civilisations*, vol. II, Paris, 1954, p. 213 ff.

Greece, though deprived of its cramped political boundaries, would acquire far-flung linguistic frontiers. "A linguistic frontier divided the Empire into two almost equal halves, the Greek East and the Latin West."[8]

There is no need to dwell on the outcome of this division of spheres of influence nor on the way in which the Roman Empire was led by Christianity to take on its Greek Byzantine form. This subject does not fall within our present enquiry. It is enough to say here that the 'Hellenism' of Alexander's successors and the kingdoms continued under Roman rule, and the term 'Hellenism' or 'Hellenization' retains its original significance. By the second century B.C. it had come to signify imitation of the Greeks, and the use of the Greek language among those peoples of non-Greek origin who had become familiar with Greek culture, more particularly the 'Hellenizing' Jews.[9] But as a historical phenomenon and as a cultural and artistic process, Hellenization is not confined to this period. It has been capable of repetition in other periods and recurs more than once in the history of the Greek race. The present writer has therefore not hesitated to use the term in other contexts to denote similar moments in the history of civilization.[10]

Continuing the comparison, the parallels drawn between the Roman and Turkish periods of Greek history present some instructive features. The Ottoman conquest, with its tragic passages and its worldwide repercussions, cut short the development of a new Hellenization which, during the fourteenth and fifteenth centuries, was beginning to produce in the Balkan Peninsula a marvellous blending of cultures, intellectual, spiritual and artistic. This Greek culture of the conquered city was now to direct its energy towards western Europe where it would be absorbed into the great currents of Renaissance

[8] *Ibid.* pp. 403 ff.

[9] Marcel Simon and André Benoît, *Le Judaïsme et le Christianisme Antique d'Antiochus Epiphane à Constantin*, Paris, 1968, pp. 69 ff., 243 ff.

[10] D. A. Zakythinos, 'États-Sociétés-Cultures. En guise d'introduction', *Art et Société à Byzance sous les Paléologues*, Venice, 1971, p. 12.

thought. But even under the Sultans Greek culture and the Greek language would remain dynamic forces.

The reader will already have found in the preceding chapter some information about the successive phases of Greek culture during the Turkish period. Here it is only necessary to bring out certain salient points in the relations between the Greeks and their conquerors on the one hand and peoples who shared their subjection on the other. As under the Romans, the Greeks now occupied a special position in the Empire. We have already seen how, acting on principles derived from his own Law and also with wider political aims in view, the Conqueror granted the Greek Patriarchs ecclesiastical authority over all Orthodox populations. This in time developed into what amounted to a devolution of religious, legal and administrative authority. This crucial step opened the way to the progressive creation of a distinctive religious, social, economic and intellectual way of life.

The position of the Greeks was also a special one from another angle. Like the Romans, the Turkish conqueror fully realized the points in which the conquered were superior to himself. In many ways, therefore, he felt the attraction and the influence of their system of government and their intellectual life. The subject of Byzantine influence on the organization of the Ottoman Empire has long been a matter of debate, recently revived by Speros Vryonis jr., in the light of fresh research. His contribution is of especial value for the early period and in relation to the institutions of government and to social and economic life.[11] From the point of view of the present study it may be said that Byzantine influence was felt by the Ottomans before the fall of Constantinople and during the first century after it. One proof of this is the widespread use of Greek as an official language in the conduct of international relations.[12] The turning away of the Turks towards Asia Minor and their

[11] Sp. Vryonis jr., 'The Byzantine Legacy and Ottoman Forms', in *Dumbarton Oaks Papers*, nos. 23/24 (1969–70), pp. 251–308.

[12] Sp. Lambros, Ἡ Ἑλληνική ὡς ἐπίσημος γλῶσσα τῶν Σουλτάνων ('Greek as an Official Language of the Sultans'), in *Νέος Ἑλληνομνήμων*, vol. V (1908),

conquest of Syria (1516), Egypt (1517), the Persian territories on the Euphrates (1534) and Southern Arabia (1568) moved the Empire away from the orbit of Greek influence and stressed the Islamic element in its culture.[13] Later on, in the seventeenth century and particularly after the second siege of Vienna in 1683, the Sultans would once again look to the Greeks, when they abandoned their plans of conquest and concentrated on European politics.[14]

Religious and political factors, deeply based on the different mentalities of the two peoples, limited the degree of influence which the Greeks could exert on the Conqueror. That influence related mainly to the operation of institutions, to methods of government and taxation, to diplomacy and to points of popular custom or culture (what Vryonis terms *Volkskultur*). Very widespread, by contrast, was the cultural effect of the Greeks on the Christian peoples of the Balkan Peninsula and eastern Europe and, secondarily, on the Christian minorities of the Levant.[15] Its achievements here were more lasting. The reader has already had presented to him some aspects of the supranational character of post-Byzantine and modern Greek

pp. 40–78, and Ἑλληνικὰ δημόσια γράμματα τοῦ σουλτάνου Βαγιαζίτ Βʹ ('Greek Public Documents of Sultan Bayezid II'), *ibid.*, pp. 155–89. F. Babinger and Fr. Dölger, Mehmed II. Frühester Staatsvertrag (1446), in Fr. Dölger, *Byzantinische Diplomatik*, Ettal, 1956, pp. 262–91. A. Bombaci, 'Due clausole del trattato in greco fra Maometto II e Venezia, del 1446', in *Byzantinische Zeitschrift*, Vol. 43 (1950), pp. 267–71, and 'Nuovi firmani greci di Maometto II', *ibid.*, vol. 47 (1954), pp. 298–319. Hélène Ahrweiler, 'Une lettre en grec du Sultan Bayezid II (1481–1512)', in *Turcica. Revue d'études turques*, vol. I (1969), pp. 150–60. Elisabeth A. Zachariadou, 'Early Ottoman Documents of the Prodromos Monastery (Serres)', in *Südost-Forschungen*, vol. 28 (1969), pp. 1–12.

[13] Sp. Vryonis jr., *op. cit.*, p. 307.

[14] Philip K. Hitti, *History of the Arabs*, London, 1961, pp. 716 ff.

[15] Scholars have directed their attention more particularly to cultural relations within the Balkan Peninsula and have relegated to second place the affairs of Levantine Christianity in later times. Yet here too there is an immense field for fruitful research. A recent publication has revealed hitherto unknown aspects of the problem in the field of post-Byzantine art: *Icones Melkites. Exposition organisée par le Musée Nicolas Sursock du 16 mai au 15 juin, 1969*, Beirut, 1969.

culture, the bearer of which, we may recall, was the Church of Constantinople. The Church's growing influence throughout the East enabled it, under and through the Sultans, to continue the imperial policy of the Byzantine rulers and to create a unified civilization in this non-political community.[16] Post-Byzantine art is the expression *par excellence* of this common culture; the imperishable achievement of post-Byzantine Greece. The last stage, still later, of a Greek supranational culture was that of the humanism described in the previous chapter.[17] This belongs properly to the sphere of 'higher culture (*Hoch-* as opposed to *Volkskultur*) and was the fruit of life in urban communities and of the mingling of the values of the Greek tradition with those of western European thought.

This analysis of two parallel periods of Greek history is no pointless enquiry nor is it lacking in practical significance. On the contrary it helps us to grasp the nature of Greek reactions to two foreign conquests and thus leads us on to an interpretation of certain fundamental views which have underlain the later political life of Greece. We may not go all the way with the Hegelian concept of the indwelling spirit of a people (*Volksgeist*) through which the World Spirit (*Weltgeist*) manifests itself; but we can still recognize, running through Greek history, the thread of Greek national self-consciousness.

Modern sociologists have perceived this distinguishing mark of the Greek people.[18] In contrast to other non-historically-minded racial groups, the Greeks are a 'historical' nation, not merely because they have preserved unbroken their consciousness of their historical continuity but also because they have transmitted their conception of this to others. An isolated race, without kindred, unassociated by race with any of the major European racial groupings—the Latins, the Germans, the Slavs—established at a vital but also much-disputed point of

[16] See recent observations by Eugen Stanescu, 'Byzance et les Pays Roumains aux IXe–XVe siècles', *XIVth Congrès International des études byzantines*, Bucharest, 6–12 September, 1971, Rapports IV, p. 44 ff.

[17] See above, pp. 143–4.

[18] Hans Kohn, *The Idea of Nationalism*, pp. 534 ff.

the Eurasian continent, they based their independent existence not on their mass or on their compactness but on the clarity of their historical self-consciousness. The periods during which the nation ceased to exist as a power in its own right (the chief mark of a State)—the Roman and Turkish periods, for example—are particularly instructive in this regard. When the political activity of the Greeks is split up between small community groups, their historical sense emerges with greater force than ever. The historian who is studying the origins of the political life of modern Greece will find in these periods the first beginnings of future developments.

If this historian, rising above individual events, were to try to seize and define the train of thought underlying modern Greek history, he might maintain that the way to do this lay in considering and sifting three basic concepts—the concept of Race (Γένος), the concept of Nation ("Έθνος) and the concept of the 'Great Idea'. These three concepts represent between them the triple aspect of modern Greek political life, and individually they are the expression of three different periods and of three different ideological attitudes. This theme has already been treated in the preceding chapter; summing up the observations made there we are led to some final conclusions.

To express their feeling of themselves as a national and moral community, the Greeks, from the first years of foreign sub-jection, used the term Race (Γένος), which they took over ready-made from the last centuries of Byzantium. Expressions like 'the Romaic race', 'our race', 'the thrice-wretched race' are common phrases in the literature of the fourteenth and fifteenth centuries. The term came into general use at the moment when the Byzantine Empire was being torn apart and was closely connected with that event.[19]

---

[19] N. B. Tomadakis, Ὁ Ἰωσὴφ Βρυέννιος καί ἡ Κρήτη κατὰ τό 1400 (*Joseph Bryennius and Crete in 1400*), Athens, 1947, pp. 72 ff. See also, by the same author, Οἱ Ἕλληνες ὡς γένος καὶ ἔθνος κατὰ τὴν ἱστορικὴν ἡμῶν διαδρομὴν καί ὁ ἱερὸς Αγών τοῦ 1821 (*The Greeks as Race and Nation in the Course of our History, and the Holy War of 1821*), Athens, 1970.

At a very early stage the concept of Race became bound up with the reactions of the Greek ecclesiastical and intellectual leadership to foreign rule. The great problem to be faced and the chief goal to be attained by the policy of Race was national preservation. Orthodoxy, which symbolized the union of Faith and Nation, took an unyielding stand both against the foreign overlord and against the opposing Western Christian world. It guarded with unbending, if at times barren, consistency its doctrine, its administrative independence, its traditional education. It extended its organizational network, restored its structural unity, codified its Canon Law, on all of which the survival of the nation and the Church's own activity were in future to depend for support. But it was not only in the sphere of Church government that the Orthodox Church prepared the way for a huge expansion of Greek influence. As has already been pointed out in Chapter VI above, the Patriarchate at Constantinople was the nursery of the new administrative aristocracy which rose to positions of great responsibility and influence both within the Court bureaucracy and in the Danubian Principalities.

The concept of the Nation (Ἔθνος) is also a pre-eminently Greek one[20]. Although during the Middle Ages it had long denoted, in Greek, a class of people quite outside its original meaning,[21] the word returned to its older usage and became a familiar term in the traditional thinking of the Turkish period. At first the concept of Nation was frequently confounded with that of Race; but in time a distinction came to be made between them, and the term Nation came to be associated with the new

---

[20] D. A. Zakythinos, Εἰσαγωγή εἰς τήν Ἱστορίαν τοῦ Πολιτισμοῦ (*Introduction to the History of Civilisation*), Athens, 1955, pp. 38 ff.

[21] To the Greeks of early Christian and medieval times the ἔθνη and ἐθνικοί were the heathen or Gentiles, the dwellers in the country districts and foreigners generally. The same word ἔθνη was also used to denote the bodies of foreign soldiery serving in Byzantium, their leader being termed ἐθνάρχης. There is also a mention of a regiment of foreigners (ὁμοεθνῶν). The Emperor Theophilus (829–42) was called φιλοεθνής on account of his partiality for foreign troops.

ideas and became the bearer of them.[22] These ideas were by no means strangers to the Greek tradition, whether classical or Byzantine, but they have this special feature, that while in a sense they represent a return to the ideas of the past, they add to these a particular flavour of their own derived from the contact of contemporary Greek thought with the currents of progressive European thinking. And so, while the term Race was used above all to denote the mass of Greeks who were living under Ottoman rule and came under the administration of the Orthodox Church, the term Nation was associated with the nationalism now beginning to develop. Over against the conservative notion of Race stood the revolutionary world of the Nation. Modern Greek nationalism, itself with its roots in history, was the dynamic expression of a patriotism which had remained unabated ever since the latest centuries of the Byzantine Empire.[23]

As has already been remarked, there were deep divisions and violent clashes of opinion on the very eve of the Greek Revolution. As if they felt some foreboding of the coming change, the Greeks stood hesitant before two totally divergent paths. One led towards imperial rule and a multi-racial state, the other towards independent national life and a national state. Arnold Toynbee seized this deeper significance of the Greek dilemma. Between the outbreak of the French Revolution, he says, and the Greek War of Independence, "the Greeks were under the spell of two incompatible aspirations. They had not given up the Phanariot ambition of entering into the whole heritage of the 'Osmanlis' and keeping the Ottoman Empire intact as a 'going concern'; and at the same time they had conceived the ambition of establishing a sovereign independent national state of their own—a Greece which should be as Greek as France was French. The incompatibility of these two aspirations

[22] N. Tomadakis, Οἱ Ἕλληνες ὡς γένος καὶ ἔθνος, pp. 6 ff.

[23] Xydis, 'Mediaeval Origins of Modern Greek Nationalism', in *Balkan Studies*, vol. IX (1968), pp. 1–20, and 'Modern Greek Nationalism', in P. Sugar and I. Lederer, *Nationalism in Eastern Europe*, Univ. of Washington Press, 1969, pp. 207–58.

was demonstrated conclusively in 1821 when the Greeks attempted to realize them both simultaneously."[24]

In the end the national ideal eclipsed the universal. The last attempt of the Greeks to reconcile the two and to give a more universal aspect to the national war was made in the Danubian Principalities. If one disregards the inadequacy of his preparations and the ultimate failure of his project, the decision of Alexander Hypsilanti to proclaim the rebellion of 1821 in Wallachia and Moldavia was a stroke of genius;[25] but the collapse of the rising in the Principalities marked the end of the universalist dream founded on Race.[26] As C. M. Woodhouse has observed, casting the responsibility on the leader of the rebellion,

[24] Toynbee, *A Study of History*, (abr. version of chaps. I–VI by D. C. Somervell), Oxford, 1946, p. 132.

[25] See the opinion of Paparrhegopoulos in Ἱστορία τοῦ Ἑλληνικοῦ Ἔθνους (*History of the Greek Nation*), vol. VI, 1, (1932 ed.), pp. 13 ff. Also see E. Kyriakides, Ἱστορία τοῦ Συγχρόνου Ἑλληνισμοῦ (*History of Contemporary Greece*), vol. I, Athens, 1892, pp. 65 ff. See also D. A. Zakythinos, Ἡ ἐπανάστασις τῶν Παραδουναβίων Ἡγεμονιῶν καὶ ἡ ἔναρξις τοῦ Ἀγῶνος τῆς Ἀνεξαρτησίας ('The Rising in the Danubian Principalities and the Beginning of the War of Independence'), in Πρακτικὰ Ἀκαδημίας Ἀθηνῶν (*Proc. of the Academy of Athens*), vol. 46 (1971), pp. 42* ff.

[26] It is worth noting that the Greek nation in arms was once again faced with the problem of Greek universalist plans when Nesselrode, the Russian Foreign Minister, submitted his *Memorandum of the Russian Privy Council on the Pacification of Greece*, dated 9 January 1824, in which he proposed the creation of three independent principalities tributary to the Sultan. The first was to include Thessaly, Boeotia, Attica and Eastern Greece; the second that part of the former Venetian sea-coast which was not assigned to Austria, together with Epirus, Acarnania and western Greece; and the third was to be formed out of the Peloponnese and southern Greece, to which Crete might also be added. The Aegean islands were to be placed under a form of orgainzation based on local communities like that which had been in force among them for centuries. But this scheme was rejected by the Greek Provisional Government. On this plan for three principalities, see Anton von Prokesch-Osten, *Geschichte des Abfalls der Griechen*, vol. IV, Vienna, 1867, pp. 62 ff. É. Driault and M. Lhéritier, *Histoire Diplomatique de la Grèce*, vol. I, Paris, 1925–6, pp. 223 ff.; P. Argyropoulos, 'Le Projet des Trois Tronçons', in *Les Balkans*, vol. X (1938), pp. 121 ff.; D. A. Zakythinos, Ἡ Ἑλλὰς τῶν τριῶν ἡγεμονιῶν. Πολιτική, οὐτοπία καὶ πραγματικότης ('The Greece of the Three Principalities. Policy, Utopia and Reality'), in Παρνασσός, vol. VIII (1966), pp. 17–27.

"Hypsilantis had destroyed whatever hope existed that the Greeks would succeed in inheriting intact the administration of the Empire from the Ottoman Turks."[27] Thus the centre of gravity shifted to the Peloponnese, where the ground was better suited to the development of a purely Greek regionalism. For the feeble state founded on a purely national basis the first and supreme duty was to carry through the struggle for liberty. The 'Great Idea' was thus thrust into the foreground of Greek history.

The ideal behind the 'Great Idea', and the political programme which evolved from it, was intended to offer a compromise between the two opposed schools of universalism and nascent nationalism and to reconcile the contradictory doctrines behind the political, ideological and intellectual leanings of the modern Greeks.

The elements which went to make up the 'Great Idea' had been forming since at least the first centuries of Turkish rule. It has even been asserted that the first embryonic traces of them are to be met with earlier still, at the time of the Greek reconquest of Constantinople by Michael VIII Palaeologus.[28] I have observed elsewhere that one of the first texts containing a forerunner of the 'Great Idea' is the *Silentium* (Σιλέντιον) written by Nicetas Choniates and read in 1206 by the Emperor Theodore I Lascaris.[29] But neither the expression 'the Great Idea' nor the completed theory is older than the War of Independence. First came the term 'the Idea', which the organizers of the Greek Revolution used to denote the ideal of liberation. It was followed

[27] C. M. Woodhouse, *The Greek War of Independence. Its Historical Setting*, London, 1952, p. 54.

[28] J. Boyatzidis, ῾H ᾽Αρχὴ καί ἡ ἐξέλιξις τῆς Μεγάλης ᾽Ιδέας ('The Origin and Development of the Great Idea'), in ῾Ημερολόγιον τῆς Μεγάλης ῾Ελλάδος (*Yearbook of Greater Greece*), 1923, pp. 161 ff. D. A. Zakythinos, ῾H Βυζαντινὴ ᾽Ιδέα καί ἡ ῾Ελληνικὴ ᾽Επανάστασις (*The Byzantine Idea and the Greek Revolution*), Athens, 1946.

[29] D. A. Zakythinos, Βυζάντιον. Κράτος καί Κοινωνία. ῾Ιστορικὴ ᾽Επισκόπησις (*Byzantium. State and Society. A Historical Survey*), Athens, 1951, pp. 129 ff. See also Johannes Irmscher, 'Nikäa als Zentrum des griechischen Patriotismus', in *Revue des Études Sud-Est Européennes*, vol. VIII (1970), pp. 33–47.

later by the expression 'the Great Idea'. We find this as a technical term and as a fully formed political programme in the speech by John Kolettis in the National Assembly, on 14 January 1844, when discussion turned on Article 3 of the Constitution which dealt with the definition of a Greek citizen and passionately divided the Assembly on the distinction between 'Native Greeks' (Αὐτόχθονες) and 'Aliens' ('Ετερό-χθονες).³⁰ Later the line of the 'Great Idea' repeatedly engaged the minds of the Greek leadership and of the nation's representatives. A document of special interest is the memorandum drafted in 1848 by Alexander Mavrocordato which combines patriotic feeling with sobriety and sense.³¹

Neither the thinking nor the history of the 'Great Idea' has as yet been adequately analysed. A fuller treatment of its rise and development will require a concentration and comparative study of the immense mass of material at present scattered in political and historical articles, in speeches, proceedings of the Chambers, newspapers, pamphlets, collections of poetry and other sources. According to Paul Karolides the Idea "had the broadest but at the same time the simplest thought behind it; the raising up of the fallen and the fall of that which now

---

³⁰ Ἡ τῆς τρίτης Σεπτεμβρίου ἐν Ἀθήναις Ἐθνικὴ Συνέλευσις. Πρακτικά, Ἔκτακτον Παράρτημα τοῦ ἀρ. 40 τῆς Ἐφημ. τῆς Κυβερνήσεως τοῦ 1843 (Proc. of the National Assembly of Sept. 3 in Athens. Extraordinary Suppl. to no. 40 of the Government Gazette of 1843), pp. 190 ff. E. Kyriakides, Ἱστορία τοῦ Συγχρόνου Ἑλληνισμοῦ (History of Contemporary Greece), vol. I, pp. 487 ff. P. Karolides, Σύγχρονος Ἱστορία τῶν Ἑλλήνων καὶ τῶν λοιπῶν λαῶν τῆς Ἀνατολῆς (Contemporary History of the Greeks and of the Other People of the East), vol. III, Athens, 1923, pp. 338 ff., 342 ff. On the occasion of the death of Kolettis the newspaper Aion, assessing his policy, pub. three articles under the title of The Great Idea (10, 13 and 17 September 1847). On the term 'Great Idea' see Th. Dimaras, "Τῆς Μεγάλης ταύτης Ἰδέας Σχεδίασμα φιλολογικό" (This 'Great Idea'. A Literary Essay), Athens, 1970. See also É. Driault, La Grande Idée. La Renaissance de l'Hellénisme, Paris, 1920. É. Driault and M. Lhéritier, Histoire Diplomatique de la Grèce, vol. II, pp. 267 ff., 373 ff. Th. Astrinos, Ἡ Μεγάλη Ἰδέα τοῦ Ἑλληνισμοῦ (The Great Idea of the Greeks), Athens, 1945. S. Xydis, Modern Greek Nationalism, op. cit., pp. 255 ff.

³¹ Nicholas Dragoumis, "Ἱστορικαὶ Ἀναμνήσεις (Historical Reminiscences), vol. II. Athens, 1925, pp. 137 ff.

stands", the thought of "the liberation of all that is Greek, the recovery of Byzantium and Santa Sophia and the re-establishment of the throne of the Constantines".[32] The Greek 'Idea' "looked first of all for a rebirth, or rather a restoration, of this kind which would be chiefly of a religious nature, but later on, as it assumed a more positive and historical character, it came to signify a programme which was not merely defined in terms of national-historical tradition but was dictated by the vital needs of our national life".[33]

The national and political conception of the 'Great Idea' contained contradictory elements within itself. In consequence, as the political theory of it developed and under the influence of international events, splits and differences arose to such an extent that, while the 'Great Idea' remained a united whole in its basic aims, it was torn in other respects between a number of competing versions. The chief differences arose out of the very principles on which the national ideology had been based. In the Provisional Constitution of Epidaurus (1822) the nation, then still at war, proclaimed, in the section laying down the "procedure of the Judiciary when dealing with political offences", the renewal of the ties between modern Greece and traditions of 'our ever-memorable Christian Emperors". This decision was fully in accord with popular feeling. It is also typical that in the $\Delta\iota\acute{\alpha}\tau\alpha\xi\iota\varsigma$ $\delta\iota o\iota\kappa\acute{\eta}\sigma\epsilon\omega\varsigma$ $\tau\hat{\eta}\varsigma$ $E\lambda\lambda\eta\nu\iota\kappa\hat{\eta}\varsigma$ $E\pi\iota\kappa\rho\alpha\tau\epsilon\acute{\iota}\alpha\varsigma$ (Administrative Provisions of the Greek State) arrangements are made for the division of the country into Themes ($\Theta\acute{\epsilon}\mu\alpha\tau\alpha$), the designation by which the provincial and military districts were known in Byzantine times. Later on, at the session of the Panhellenion[34] on 6 April 1828, the word Theme was replaced

[32] P. Karolides, '*Ιστορία τοῦ ΙΘ' αἰῶνος* (*History of the Nineteenth Century*), vol. II, Athens, 1892–3, p. 164.

[33] P. Karolides, '*Αναμνήσεις Σκανδιναυικαί* (*Scandinavian Recollections*), Athens, 1890, p. 177.

[34] Andreas Mamoukas, *Τά κατὰ τὴν 'Αναγέννησιν τῆς 'Ελλάδος* (*The Rebirth of Greece*), vol. VIII, Piraeus, 1839–52, pp. 121 ff. The Panhellenion was the nominated body of twenty-seven members set up by Capodistria to replace the Senate established by the Constitution of 1827.

by the less historically evocative word Section ($T\mu\hat{\eta}\mu\alpha$)[35]. This reference to the Byzantine past contrasts with the classical principles and ideals to which the educational system was firmly directed. Thus the mind of the nation was split between two illustrious centres of Greek tradition, the Parthenon and Santa Sophia. Side by side with the Byzantine Great Idea there grew up a new and unique Greek Great Idea, sprung from the old Hellas, looking back to classical times and tracing its origins back to the unity of Ancient Greece. The champions of these classical ideas failed to grasp the essence of Byzantine history and underestimated the world mission of Byzantine Greece.

From this point of view one of the most typical documents is the speech made on 20 May 1853 by Stephen Koumanoudes, Associate Professor of Latin Literature, on the anniversary of the founding of the University of Athens.[36] The 'more historical' and 'more political' approach which the speaker attempted on this official occasion dealt with Greek nationality "considered from a political viewpoint, that of unity" and was a search for unity over the whole of Greek history. The "tiny seed of Greek unity in classical times" seems to have made its first appearance at the time of Roman rule. A Greek nation existed "throughout the Middle Ages", Koumanoudes says later on, but "declining into a pitiful ignorance, it yielded to the autocratic doctrines of [Byzantine] Caesarism which, having an alien [i.e. Roman] past, never expressly renounced it. The sense of a political individuality died out among the people or fell into a deep sleep" and "it is highly doubtful whether, if the life of the

---

[35] See an interesting text of the lawyer and historian Paul Kalligas, ῾Η ἐξάντλησις τῶν κομμάτων ἤτοι ἠθικὰ γεγονότα τῆς κοινωνίας μας (*The Exhaustion of the Parties, or Moral Events of our Society*), publ. first in 1842 and reprinted in his Μελέται νομικαί, πολιτικαί, οἰκονομολογικαί, ἱστορικαί, φιλολογικαί κλπ. (*Legal Political, Economic, Historical and Philological Studies*), vol. I, Athens, 1899, pp. 483–505. The author uses the suggestive term 'The Trisecting of the Nation' (῾Η τριχοτομία τοῦ ῎Εθνους).

[36] Stephen Koumanoudes, Λόγος ἐκφωνηθεὶς τῇ 20 Μαΐου 1853 κατὰ τὴν ἐπέτειον ἑορτὴν τῆς ἱδρύσεως τοῦ Πανεπιστημίου ῎Οθωνος (*Speech delivered on 20 May 1853, at the Annual Celebration of the Founding of the Otho University*), Athens, 1853.

Byzantine Empire had been prolonged further, the Greeks could ever have come to realize their true identity". The Greek element was only remembered "when, following the major disaster of the Turkish capture of Constantinople, Greek letters were reborn in the West". Now, after sixteen centuries of subjection during which the Greek nation has been autocratically governed "both by native and by foreign rulers", "a Greek state has been set up embracing, not indeed all the Greek lands, but at any rate more than have ever been brought together under that name and, in 1833, a King of Greece was truly and sovereignly installed, recorded and proclaimed for the first time. Freedom was established in Greece under law, without burdensome privilege and without the curse of subjection, likewise for the first time". The ideas of Koumanoudes were in accord with the convictions of at least a part of the intellectual leaders of liberated Greece.[37]

About the time when Stephen Koumanoudes was making his speech the *Folksongs* of Spyridon Zampelios were in circulation. This book and another published by the same author some years later, Βυζαντιναὶ Μελέται (*Byzantine Studies*), published at Athens in 1857, were, in spite of their shortcomings, works which helped the modern Greek nation to come to a knowledge of itself. Zampelios examined the history of medieval and modern Greece in the light of the philosophy of history "with a view to a more Greek interpretation" (ἐπὶ τὸ ἑλληνικώτερον), as he phrased it.[38] Out of his cloudy, wordy enquiry there nevertheless emerge some suggestive conclusions. "Equality of rights", he says, "is the mainspring behind Greek activity, an instinctive force by which the race moves and acts. . . . There are two chief impulses behind this motive, on the one hand religion or, in the

---

[37] Equally anti-Byzantine was the spirit of the address given by another professor at the University, Michael Potlis, in his Εἰσαγωγικὸν Μάθημα εἰς τὸ Ἐκκλησιαστικὸν Δίκαιον τῆς Ἀνατολικῆς Ὀρθοδόξου Ἐκκλησίας (*Introductory Lecture to the Ecclesiastical Law of the Eastern Orthodox Church*), Athens, 1859.

[38] Sp. Zampelios, Ἄσματα δημοτικὰ τῆς Ἑλλάδος, ἐκδοθέντα μετὰ μελέτης περὶ Μεσαιωνικοῦ Ἑλληνισμοῦ (*Folksongs of Greece, published with a Study on Medieval Greece*), Corfu, 1852, p. 19.

absence of religion, philosophy . . . and on the other hand politics, which is the field of the race's practical action."[39] The immediate and decisive effect of Zampelios's historical speculations, opening up a new line of thought, was to rehabilitate Byzantium and to renew the connection in mens' minds between Byzantium and modern Greece. "The Byzantine Middle Age", the historian says, "appears once more in its true colours as a system resting firmly on three dominant elements, the ancient Greek, the Christian and the Roman. . . . Instead of the fatalism which hastens the decline and fall of Rome, the operative force in the Byzantine state is the law of Greek intellectual and spiritual revival. This law prevails, to a greater or lesser degree, according to the extent to which each of the three traditions holds its proper place; the ancient Greek tradition uppermost, the Christian tradition in the middle and the Roman lowest."[40] In this medieval Greece, Zampelios looks for the roots of modern Greece. "The springs of modern Greece", he writes, ". . . break the surface in the time of Constantine and Theodosius; they seek a more direct and unimpeded channel from the time of Leo the Thracian (457–74) to that of Leo the Isaurian (717–41), and they become an irresistible current in the days of Basil the Macedonian (867–86) and his successors, and from that time onwards they flow straight forward to the revival or our own time."[41] We shall see later how Zampelios envisages the future of Greece.

It is clear then that the 'Great Idea' presented itself in a variety of forms in the middle of last century: as time went on, still further varieties appeared. One of the most typical was that which took shape in the very heart of the enslaved country. In the reign of Abdul Aziz (1861–76) "the newspaper which *par excellence* represented Greek public opinion in Turkey, the *Neologos*, proclaimed as the Great Idea of the Greek race the

[39] *Ibid.*, p. 582.

[40] Sp. Zampelios, Βυζαντιναὶ Μελέται. Περὶ πηγῶν Νεοελληνικῆς Ἐθνότητος ἀπὸ Η' ἄχρι Ι' ἑκατονταετηρίδος (*Byzantine Studies. On the Origins of Modern Greek Nationality from the 8th to the 10th Century*), Athens, 1857, pp. 33 ff.

[41] *Ibid.*, pp. 62 ff.

spread of Greek education and of Greek life and civilization in the Ottoman Empire and throughout the East under the protection of the Ottoman power." Economically, Turkey "is a Greek state, since all economic activity and many public services are carried on by Greeks and with the aid of Greek capital". Impartial judges, both Greek and foreign, who saw this condemned the aggressively anti-Turkish policy which had been pursued hitherto, since they considered the Hellenization of the Ottoman Empire to be merely a question of time.[42] As things turned out, however, the revival of Greek economic supremacy was checked by German penetration into the East. The *Drang nach Osten* stifled Greek enterprise outside Greece.[43]

The policy and doctrine of the 'Great Idea' reached their highest point in the Treaty of Sèvres (10 August 1920), under which almost all the Greek-populated territories on the mainland of Europe (though not Constantinople), almost all the Aegean islands and, provisionally, a large slice of western Asia Minor, including Smyrna, passed into Greek hands from a defeated and collapsing Turkey. But three years later these last gains were buried under the ruins of the military catastrophe in Asia Minor and the ensuing Treaty of Lausanne (23 July 1923) which, while confirming, with certain minor exceptions, all Greece's territorial acquisitions in Europe, drove her from the mainland of Asia.

Conclusions

The three great motifs of Greek policy, the universalist, the national and the 'Great Idea', each achieved its purpose. Through them the truth was confirmed which had been uttered by a Greek historian over seventy years ago when speaking of

[42] P. Karolides, Συμπλήρωμα εἰς Κ. Παπαρρηγόπουλον Ἱστορία τοῦ Ἑλληνικοῦ Ἔθνους (*Supplement to C. Paparrhegopoulos's, History of the Greek Nation*), vol. VI, 2, p. 393.

[43] É. Driault and M. Lhéritier, *Histoire Diplomatique de la Grèce*, vol. IV, pp. 151ff.

the third of them, namely that "this [Great] Idea, judged from a purely and strictly practical point of view, is now, and will be for a long time to come, a real necessity which Greece cannot abandon without denying her own history and without destroying the very springs of her historical existence".[44]

In the course of this book an attempt has been made to explain, in historical and sociological terms, the origins of the diverse and often contradictory currents of thought during the period of Turkish rule. Particular stress has been laid on the great and real diversity of the trends within the Greek intellectual tradition and the tensions, the differences and the consequent many-sidedness displayed by Greek society. All this is clearly illustrated by the variety of strains of thought and culture, that 'polyphony' which is to be heard throughout Greece itself and in every country where Greeks are living—most of all when the polyphony achieves harmony. In the last analysis, the explanation of the developments we have been considering lies in the very texture of Greek history and is to be interpreted in the light of that. The scholar who studies Greek history as a whole from the point of view of historical theory, has to admit that it displays typically and constantly certain kinds of situation, certain trends and tendencies which proceed from the spirit informing the nation itself. Generally speaking, the forces which govern its world mission are mutually contradictory. The people which first evolved the concepts of nation and state, which framed ideals of government and was brought up within the narrow limits of the 'ideal' but self-centred city-state was in fact the most un-national of all nations. Through having to struggle against external forces it came at last to an unbreakable unity, but in spite of its expansion and its rise to power it kept its aristocratic, exclusive character, it created supra-national standards which spread beyond its mountains, the seas, beyond its own native air. It was always impatient of its own confined territory and moved out beyond

[44] P. Karolides, 'Αναμνήσεις Σκανδιναυικαί (Scandinavian Recollections), pp. 177 ff.

its frontiers. Within its own territory it was rent and divided, yet, divided as it was, it swept along with it the unthinking masses of mankind and the long centuries of its tempestuous career formed deeply-rooted habits of thought within itself.

From this point of view the idea of Race was for the Greeks the creed most conducive to their survival. Mid-nineteenth-century writers, following in the steps of Rhigas, conceived a daring vision of the universal Greek empire of the East. Spyridon Zampelios, attempting in the light of past history to foretell the shape of "the fourth age of Greece", wrote the following remarkable words: "If ever a New Greece is fated to arise from the ruins of Ancient Greece and Byzantium, two principles will be fused in the nation that will return to life—first, that of the old Greek tradition, bearing also the imprint of the earlier medieval period,[45] and secondly, the principle of the later medieval doctrine of the Nation according to which all the various peoples which made up the Byzantine Orthodox world when the later Middle Ages began in the ninth century at the time of Basil the Macedonian will amalgamate to form a single political unit having the same religion." Within this "great confederation of equal peoples" we may arrive at "the complete fusion of racial elements".[46]

[45] The terms 'earlier' and 'later' Middle Ages (flexible in any case) necessarily refer to different periods when considering Byzantine history from those applied in considering the history of western Europe, since the 'Middle Ages' of the two have differed in their starting point and in their duration. In the passage quoted the reference is, of course, to the sub-divisions of Byzantine history.

[46] Sp. Zampelios, Ἄσματα δημοτικά, pp. 584 ff., and Βυζαντιναὶ Μελέται, pp. 31 ff. Other observations from the same point of view which deserve attention are to be found in the anonymous pamphlet entitled Ἑλληνισμὸς ἢ Ῥωσσισμός; ἤτοι ἡ μεταξὺ Ἀγγλίας καὶ Ῥωσσίας ἀπόρρητος καὶ ἐμπιστευτικὴ πραγματεία περὶ τοῦ Ἀνατολικοῦ Ζητήματος ('Hellenism or Russification? Or the Secret and Confidential Negotiations between England and Russia on the Eastern Question'). This document appeared in Athens in 1854. Its publication was prompted by the British but the comments made on the secret papers reflect Greek views (É. Driault and M. Lhéritier, Histoire Diplomatique de la Grèce, vol. II, pp. 384 ff.). It is believed that the writers were Constantine Dosios and Aristides Palaiologos: see D. Ghinis and V. Mexas, Ἑλληνικὴ Βιβλιογραφία (Greek Bibliography), vol. II, p. 410 (no. 6217).

But the doctrine of Race was incompatible with the various nationalisms then reviving in Europe, which the Greeks with their political sensitivity and their own national tradition had understood and had helped to encourage. The Greeks therefore were obliged to carry out their transformation of their national life within their own country and to incorporate within it what they had created beyond the frontiers of Greece. Within those stiflingly narrow frontiers these same divisive and disruptive forces continued to thrive, fostered by the rivalry of the Great Powers. In these conditions the struggles for the completion of a unified Greece, waged with indomitable persistence for a century, produced clashes and rivalries, disasters and collapses, as well as great successes, but they also did incalculable harm to the Greek people. This long conflict forms the central theme of the whole later history of modern Greece.

Appendix A: Chronological Tables

1. Sultans of Turkey from 1451 to 1839

Mehmed II	1451–1481
Bayezid II	1481–1512
Selim I	1512–1520
Süleyman I	1520–1566
Selim II	1566–1574
Murad III	1574–1595
Mehmed III	1595–1603
Ahmed I	1603–1617
Mustafa I	1617–1618
Osman II	1618–1622
Mustafa I	1622–1623
Murad IV	1623–1640
Ibrahim I	1640–1648
Mehmed IV	1648–1687
Süleyman II	1687–1691
Ahmed II	1691–1695
Mustafa II	1695–1703
Ahmed III	1703–1730
Mahmud I	1730–1754
Osman III	1754–1757
Mustafa III	1757–1773
Abdülhamid I	1774–1789
Selim III	1789–1807
Mustafa IV	1807–1808
Mahmud II	1808–1839

2. *Patriarchs of Constantinople from 1454 to 1821*

Gennadius II Scholarius	1454–1456
	1463
	1464–1465
Isidore II Xanthopoulos	1456–1462
Joasaph I Kokkas	1462–1463
Sophronius I Syropoulos	1463–1464
Mark II Xylokaravis	1466
Symeon of Trebizond	1465
	1471–1475
	1482–1486
Dionysius I	1466–1471
	1488–1490
Raphael I	1475–1476
Maximus III	1476–1482
Niphon II	1486–1488
	1497–1498
	1502
Maximus IV	1491–1497
Joachim I	1498–1502
	1504
Pachomius I	1503–1504
	1504–1513
Theoleptus I	1513–1522
Jeremias I	1522–1546
Joannikios I	1524–1525
Dionysius II	1546–1556
Joasaph II	1556–1565
Mitrophanes III	1565–1572
	1579–1580
Jeremias II	1572–1579
	1580–1584
	1587–1595
Pachomius II Patestos	1584–1585
Theoleptus II	1585–1586

Matthew II	1596
	1598–1601/2
	1603
Gabriel I	1596
Theophanes I Karykes	1597
Meletios Pigas (Locumtenens)	1597–1598
Neophytus II	1602–1603
	1607–1612
Raphael II	1603–1607
Timothy II	1612–1620
Cyril I Loukaris (Locumtenens)	1612
(Patriarch)	1620–1623
	1623–1633
	1633–1634
	1634–1635
	1637–1638
Gregory IV	1623
Anthimos II	1623
Cyril II Kontares	1633
	1635–1636
	1638–1639
Athanasius III Patellarios	1634
	1652
Neophytus III	1636–1637
Parthenius I	1639–1644
Parthenius II	1644–1646
	1648–1651
Joannikios II	1646–1648
	1651–1652
	1653–1654
	1655–1656
Cyril III	1652
	1654
Païsios I	1652–1653
	1654–1655
Parthenius III	1656–1657

Gabriel II	1657
Parthenius IV	1657–1662
	1665–1667
	1671
	1675–1676
	1684–1685
Dionysius III Vardales	1662–1665
Clement	1667–1668
Methodius III	1668–1671
Dionysius IV Mouselimes	1671–1673
	1676–1679
	1682–1684
	1686–1687
	1693–1694
Gerasimus II	1673–1674
Athanasius IV	1679
Iakovos (James)	1679–1682
	1685–1686
	1687–1688
Callinicus II	1688
	1689–1693
	1694–1702
Neophytus IV	1688–1689
Gabriel III	1702–1707
Neophytus V	1707
Cyprian	1707–1709
	1713–1714
Athanasius V	1709–1711
Cyril IV	1711–1713
Cosmas III	1714–1716
Jeremias III	1716–1726
	1732–1733
Païsios II	1726–1732
	1740–1743
	1744–1748
	1751–1752

Seraphim I	1733–1734
Neophytus VI	1734–1740
	1743–1744
Cyril V	1748–1751
	1752–1757
Callinicus III	1757
Seraphim II	1757–1761
Joannikios III	1761–1763
Samuel Hantzeris	1763–1768
	1773–1774
Meletios II	1768–1769
Theodosius II	1769–1773
Sophronius II	1774–1780
Gabriel IV	1780–1785
Procopius	1785–1789
Neophytus VII	1789–1794
	1798–1801
Gerasimus III	1794–1797
Gregory V	1797–1798
	1806–1808
	1818–1821
Callinicus IV	1801–1806
	1808–1809
Jeremias IV	1809–1813
Cyril VI	1813–1818

3. The Greek Grand Dragomans[1]

Panayiotis Nikousios	1661–1673
Alexander Mavrocordato	1673–1709
Nicholas Mavrocordato (son of A.)	1709–1710
John Mavrocordato (brother of A)	1710–1717
Gregory Ghica	1717–1727

[1] Cf. M. Guboglu Paleografie şi diplomatică turco-română, Bucharest 1958, p. 108.

Alexander Ghica (brother of Gregory)	1727–1740
John Callimachi (1st term)	1741–1750
Matthew Ghica (son of Gregory)	1750–1752
John Callimachi (2nd term)	1752–1758
Gregory Ghica (son of Alexander)	1758–1764
George Karatzas (Caradja)	1764–1765
Scarlatos Karatzas (1st term)	1765–1768
Nicholas Soutsos	1768–1769
Scarlatos Karatzas (2nd term)	1770–1774
Alexander Hypsilanti	1774
Constantine Mourouzis	1774–1777
Nicholas Karatzas	1777–1782
Michael Soutsos (brother of Nicholas)	1782–1783
Alexander John Mavrocordato	1783–1785
Alexander Callimachi (1st term)	1785–1788
Constantine Rhallis	1788
Manuel Karatzas	1788–1790
Alexander Mourouzis	1790–1792
George Mourouzis (1st term)	1792–1794
Alexander Callimachi (2nd term)	1794
George Mourouzis (2nd term)	1795–1796
Constantine Hypsilanti	1796–1799
Alexander Soutsos (son of Nicholas)	1799–1801
Alexander Soutsos (son of Michael)	1802–1807
John Nicholas Karatzas	1808
Demetrius Mourouzis	1808–1812
John George Karatzas	1812
James (Iakovos) Argyropoulos	1812–1817
Michael Soutsos	1817–1818
John Kallimachis	1818–1821
Constantine Mourouzis	1821
Stavrakis Aristarches	1821

4. The Princes of Wallachia and Moldavia in the Phanariote Period[1]

WALLACHIA	MOLDAVIA
	Nicholas Mavrocordato Nov. 1709–Nov. 1710
	Demetrius Cantemir Nov. 1710–July 1711
Stephen Cantacuzene March 1714–Dec. 1715	Nicholas Mavrocordato Sept. 1711–Dec. 1715
Nicholas Mavrocordato Dec. 1715–Nov. 1716	Michael Racovitsa Dec. 1715–Sept. 1726
John Mavrocordato Nov. 1716–Febr. 1719	
Nicholas Mavrocordato March 1719–Sept. 1730	Gregory II Ghica Sept. 1726–April 1733
Constantine Mavrocordato Sept.–Oct. 1730	Constantine Mavrocordato April 1733–Nov. 1735
Michael Racovitsa Oct. 1730–Oct. 1731	Gregory II Ghica Nov. 1735–Sept. 1739
Constantine Mavrocordato Oct. 1731–April 1733	RUSSIAN OCCUPATION OF
Gregory II Ghica April 1733–Nov. 1735	MOLDAVIA Sept–Oct. 1739
Constantine Mavrocordato Nov. 1735–Sept. 1741	Gregory II Ghica Oct. 1739–Sept. 1741
Michael Racovitsa Sept. 1741–July 1744	Constantine Mavrocordato Sept. 1741–July 1743
Constantine Mavrocordato July 1744–April 1748	John Mavrocordato July 1743–May 1747
Gregory II Ghica April 1748–Aug. 1752	Gregory II Ghica May 1747–April 1748
Matthew Ghica Aug. 1752–June 1753	Constantine Mavrocordato April 1748–Aug. 1749

[1] Cf. Documente privind Istoria României. Introducere (Documents relating to the history of Romania, Introduction), vol. I, Bucharest 1956, p. 493–495.

Constantine Racovitsa June 1753–Feb. 1756

Constantine Mavrocordato Feb. 1756–Aug. 1758

Scarlatos Ghica Aug. 1758–June 1761

Constantine Mavrocordato June 1761–March 1763

Constantine Racovitsa March 1763–Jan. 1764

Stephen Racovitsa Jan. 1764–Aug. 1765

Scarlatos Ghica Aug. 1765–Dec. 1766

Alexander Ghica Dec. 1766–Oct. 1768

Gregory III Ghica Oct. 1768–Nov. 1769

RUSSIAN OCCUPATION OF WALLACHIA Nov. 1769–July 1774

Alexander Hypsilanti Sept. 1774–Jan. 1782

Nicholas Karatzas Jan. 1782–July 1783

Michael Soutsos July 1783–March 1786

Nicholas Mavroyenis March 1786–June 1790

AUSTRIAN OCCUPATION OF WALLACHIA Nov. 1789–July 1791

Constantine Racovitsa Aug. 1749–June 1753

Matthew Ghica June 1753–Feb. 1756

Constantine Racovitsa Feb. 1756–March 1757

Scarlatos Ghica Feb. 1757–Aug. 1758

John Th. Kallimachi Aug. 1758–May 1761

Gregory Kallimachi May 1761–March 1764

Gregory III Ghica March 1764–Jan. 1767

Gregory Kallimachi Jan. 1767–June 1769

Constantine Mavrocordato June 1769–Dec. 1769

RUSSIAN OCCUPATION OF MOLDAVIA Sept. 1769–Sept. 1774

Gregory III Ghica Sept. 1774–Oct. 1777

Constantine Mourouzis Sept. 1777–May 1782

Alexander Mavrocordato May 1782–Jan. 1785

Alexander Mavrocordato Jan. 1785–Dec. 1786

Alexander Hypsilanti Dec. 1786–Apr. 1788

AUSTRIAN OCCUPATION OF MOLDAVIA 1787–1791

Appendix B: The Turkish Period in Greek Folk-Poetry

(Out of the immensely rich ballad literature of the Turkish period in Greece the few examples below are given only as illustrating two of the themes in this book—the child-levy and the relations between Klephts, Armatoles and Turks. Most ballads are known in a great many versions. The text from which the present translation has been made is named, also the date, where known or conjectured.)

1. The Child-Levy

(a) A curse upon you, Sultan, and a threefold curse upon you for the evil you have done and the evil that you do. You send and summon the elders, the headmen, the priests, so that you may muster your child-levy, that you may make Janissaries. Mothers weep for their children and sisters for their brothers. And I too weep and am consumed and while I live I shall weep. Last year they took my son, this year my brother.

(Epirus, 1580. Ἠπειρωτικὰ Δημοτικὰ Τραγούδια, ed. A. Yiankas.)

(b) A Pasha came down from the midst of the City. He did not dismount at the inn nor at the council-house of the elders, but went on and dismounted at the widow's mansion.

"Quickly bring bread, quickly wine, quickly good fare. We have no children to be made Janissaries."

"Bring me the widow's child, the one that knows his letters."
And they took and brought him from the midst of the Holy
Sanctuary, with his hair unbraided and his paper in his hand.
His mother too came close at hand and from close at hand she
pleaded: "Why has this evil come upon me, wretched that I
am? The first time they took my brother to be a Janissary, the
second time my husband, and now my son."

('Ελληνικὰ Δημοτικὰ Τραγούδια (Εκλογή). Vol I, p. 133. pub.
Academy of Athens, 1962).

2. Klephts, Armatoles and Turks

(a) CAPTAIN DELAS

White papers came to us, black letters, from the midst of the
City, from the Sultan.
"All you who are Klephts and have been in the high moun-
tains, all of you come and make your submission to Khalil Aga
and become Armatoles in the Greek villages."
All the Klephts who heard this made their submission. Captain
Delas did not but took the nearest way up the mountain, over
two ranges, to the lairs of the Klephts and the cold waters.
As he went on his way, there where he went, he found an old
man, a hundred years old.
"Come with me, my old man. Let us go where the Klephts
are, so as not to pay poll-tax to the rascally Turk."
"I can't, my lad, for I am old; but take my elder son who
knows the paths and all the mountains. For forty years he has
not made his submission or paid poll-tax to the rascally Turk."

(Legrand, c.1725, *Chansons Populaires Grecques*. No. LV, Paris,
1874.)

(b) CAPTAIN MALAMOS

Malamos was coming down the mountain to make his
submission. The elders went in front and Malamos behind. As

they went along the way, the way they went, Malamos stopped short and called out to the elders: "Halt, you elders. There is something I want to ask you. Last night I saw in my sleep, in my sleep as I lay, my sword of Damascus snapped in the middle and my long gun would not fire. My dream, you old men, was a bad omen. That is why I halted you. So go on and God be with you; but I am going to the mountains and the old retreats, to live by the cold waters and camp under the trees. The Turks are faithless, they do not keep their word and they have taken the heads of all the Klephts who submitted."

(1585. Legrand, *op. cit.*, No. LII.)

(c) OLYMPUS

Olympus and Kissavos, those two mountains, are quarrelling. Then Olympus turns and says to Kissavos: "Don't wrangle with me, Kissavos, you who are trampled by the Turks from Konya. I am old Olympus, famous all the world over. I have forty-two peaks and sixty-two springs: every spring has its standard and every bough its Klepht, and on my topmost peak there sits an eagle holding in his claws a hero's head."

"O head of mine, what have you done that this judgement has come upon you?"

"Feed on my youth, bird, and feed on my courage, to make your wing two feet longer and your talons a span long. I was once an Armatole at Louros and at Xeropotamos and twelve years a Klepht at Khasia and on Olympus. Sixty Agas I killed and burnt their villages; and all those I have killed on the field, Turks and Albanians, they are many, bird, and beyond counting. But my turn came to fall in battle."

(Fauriel. *Chansons Populaires de la Grèce Moderne.* I.7. Paris, 1824.)

Appendix C: Index of Bibliographical References

(This Index lists the books, articles and other publications quoted in the footnotes to each chapter, where bibliographical details, with translations of Greek titles, will be found. Roman numerals refer to the number of the chapter concerned, Arabic numerals to the relevant footnotes in that chapter.)

Ahrweiler, H.   Une lettre en grec du Sultan Bayezid II ...
                                        V, 14; LX, 12.
Alexandris, C. A.   Ἡ ἀναβίωσις τῆς θαλασσίας μας δυνάμεως ...
                                        VII, 48, 50, 51, 52.
Alivisatos, B. B.   La Réforme agraire en Grèce ...   VI, 55.
Amantos, K.   Οἱ προνομιακοὶ ὁρισμοὶ τοῦ Μουσουλμανισμοῦ
              ʿυπὲρ τῶν Χριστιανῶν.   II, 36; III, 22.
              Α. Μαυροκορδᾶτος ὁ ἐξ ἀπορρήτων.   VI, 17.
Anastasiou, J.   Σχεδίασμα περὶ τῶν Νεομαρτύρων.   II, 7.
Angelus, C.   Εγχειρίδιον περὶ τῆς καταστάσεως τῶν σήμερον
              εὑρισκομένων ʿΕλλήνων.   II, 18.
Anghelou, A.   Comment la pensée hellénique a fait la con-
              naissance de l'Essai de John Locke. VIII, 39.
Anheggar, R.   Martoloslar Hakkında.   V, 1.
Antoniadis, S.   Τὰ Δημοτικά ...   IV, 29.
Aravantinos, P.   Χρονογραφία τῆς ʿΗπείρου.   II, 19.

Argyropoulos, P.   Δημοτικὴ Διοίκησις ἐν ʽΕλλάδι.   IV, 29.
Une correspondance diplomatique, 1816–18.
VI, 37.
Le Projet des Trois Tronçons.   IX, 26.
Argyros, Sp.   ʽΗ πειρατεία ἀπὸ τοῦ 1500 ἕως τὸ 1860 . . .
II, 29.
Arnakis, G.G.   The   Ottoman   Empire   and   the   Balkan
States . . .   I, 1.
Astrinos, T.   ʽΗ Μεγάλη Ιδέα τοῦ ʽΕλληνισμοῦ.   IX, 30.
Aymard, A.   Rome et son Empire.   IX, 7, 8.
Babinger, F.   Beiträge zur Frühgeschichte der Türkenherr-
schaft in Rumelien.   I, 3.
Documenta Islamica inedita.   II, 4.
Ein Freibrief Mehmeds II . . .   II, 42.
Johannes Darius . . .   V, 13.
Barkan, Ö. L.   Les Déportations comme méthode de dépeuple-
ment . . .   VI, 2.
Essai sur les données statistiques des registres
de recensement . . .   VI, 3.
Barker, J. W.   Manuel II Palaeologus . . .   I, 4.
Beaujour, F.   Tableau du Commerce de la Grèce . . .
IV, 14; VII, 41.
Beck, H.-G.   Geschichte   der   byzantinischen   Volksliteratur.
IV, 8; V, 2, 26.
Bees, N. A.   Χαρτία τοῦ Κλαβάζου.   IV, 10; VI, 53.
Beldiceanu, I.   La Conquête d'Andrinople par les Turcs . . .
I, 3.
Les Actes des premiers Sultans . . .
III, 8; IV, 20.
Belon du Mans, P.   Les observations de plusieurs singulari-
tez . . .   IV, 21.
Blancard, T.   Les Mavroyeni . . .   VI, 41.
Blanken, G. H.   Introduction à une Étude du Dialecte de
Cargèse (Corse).   VII, 20.
Les Grecs de Cargèse (Corse) . . .
VII, 20.

Bombaci, A.   Due clausole del trattato in greco di Maometto
              II e Venezia.   IX, 12.
Botzaris, N.   Visions Balcaniques . . .   VIII, 24.
Boyatzidis, J.   ʿΗ ᾿Αρχὴ καί ἡ ᾿Εξάλιξις τῆς Μεγάλης ᾿Ιδέας.
                                                              IX, 28.
Bradford, E.   The Sultan's Admiral.   II, 30.
Bratianu, G.   Privilèges et Franchises dans l'Empire byzantin.
                                                              IV, 33.
Bryer, A.   The Tourkokratia in the Pontos . . .   II, 10.
Cahen, C.   Pre-Ottoman Turkey.   I, 2.
Camariano, N.   Alexandre Mavrocordato . . .   VI, 17.
Camariano-Cioran, A.   Academiile Domneşti din Bucureşti şi
              Iaşi.   VI, 32.
              Iosip Moisiodax . . .   VIII, 39.
Cambridge Medieval History.   I, 2.
Cândea, V.   Les Bibles grecque et roumaine de 1687–8 . . .
                                                              VI, 30.
              Les Intellectuels du Sud-Est Européen au XVIIIe
              Siècle.   VI, 42; VIII, 13, 16.
Capodistria, Count J.   Correspondance (ed. Bétant).   II, 46.
Caratzes, S. C.   L'Origine des Dialectes néo-grecs de l'Italie
              méridionale.   VII, 3.
Chronicle of Morea.   IV, 8.
Clogg, R.   The 'Dhidhaskalia Patriki' . . .   VIII, 71.
Constantinescu, N.   La Résidence d'Argeş des Voïvodes
              roumains.   VI, 28.
Coumarianou, C.   Cosmopolitisme et Hellénisme dans le
              Mercure Savant.   VII, 28.
              ᾿Ενέργειες τοῦ Κ. Σταμάτη γιὰ τὴν ἀπελευθέ-
              ρωση τῆς ῾Ελλάδος.   VIII, 70.
Crusius, M.   Turcograeciae Libri Octo.   II, 17.
Cvetkova, B.   Quelques problèmes du Féodalisme ottoman . . .
                                                              I, 6.
Daskalakis, A. B.   Rhigas Velestinlis . . .   VIII, 48.
              Μελέται περὶ ῾Ρ. Βελεστινλῆ.   VIII, 48.

Scholarios, G.   See under Petit, L. above.

Schreiner, P.   Zur   Geschichte   Philadelpheias   im   14
    Jahrhundert.   I, 4.

Sherrard, P.   The Greek East and the Latin West . . .
                                                 VIII, 15.

Sherwin-White, A. N.   Racial Prejudice in Imperial Rome.
                                                    IX, 5.

Sigalas, A.   Ἡ πατέντα τῶν Κοτζαμπάσηδων.   IV, 4.

    Ἀνέκδοτα ἔγγραφα ἀφορῶντα εἰς τὴν ἐκλογὴν τῶν
    Κοτζαμπάσηδων.   IV, 4.

    Ἐπιστολαὶ τῶν ἐν Κωνσταντινουπόλει Καπουκεχα-
    γιάδων τῆς Σύρου.   IV, 5.

Simon, R. and Benoît, A.   Le Judaïsme et le Christianisme
    Antique . . .   IX, 9.

Skendi, S.   Crypto-Christianity in the Balkan area under the
    Ottomans.   II, 10.

Skopeteas, S.   Ἔγγραφα ἰδιωτικά ἐκ δυτικῆς Μάνης . . .   VI, 48.

Skouvaras, V.   Ἰωάννης Πρίγκος . . .   VII, 37.

Spano, B.   La grecità bizantina e i suoi riflessi geografici
    nell'Italia meridionale e insulare.   VII, 3.

Sphyroeras, B. B.   Τὰ Ἑλληνικὰ πληρώματα τοῦ Τουρκικοῦ
    στόλου.   II, 27.

    Οἱ Δραγομάνοι τοῦ Στόλου . . .   VI, 22.

Stamatiades, E.   Βιογραφίαι τῶν Ἑλλήνων μεγάλων διερμήνεων. . .
                                          VI, 41.

    Ἐπιστολιμαία διατριβὴ περὶ Ι.Γεωργειρήνου . . .
                                          VII, 35.

Stanescu, E.   Les Stratiotes . . .   V, 25.

    Byzance et les Pays roumains . . .   IX, 16.

Stavrianos, L. S.   The Balkans since 1453.   I, 1.

Stefani, G.   I Greci a Trieste nel Settecento.   VIII, 29.

Stephanos, K.   Ἀνέκδοτα ἔγγραφα ἀποσταλέντα πρὸς τοὺς
    κατοίκους τῶν Κυκλάδων . . .   V. 32.

Sterghellis, A. P.   Τὰ δημοσιεύματα τῶν Ἑλλήνων σπουδαστῶν
    τοῦ Πανεπιστημίου τῆς Πάδοβας . . .
                                          VII, 12.

Index

234